9.40

LOGIC AND THE NATURE OF GOD

LOGIC AND THE NATURE OF GOD

Stephen T. Davis

Department of Philosophy
Claremont McKenna College
Claremont, California

William B. Eerdmans Publishing Company
Grand Rapids, Michigan

First published 1983 by
THE MACMILLAN PRESS LTD
London and Basingstoke
Companies and representatives
throughout the world

First American edition published 1983
through special arrangement with Macmillan by
WM. B. EERDMANS PUBLISHING CO.,
255 Jefferson S.E.,
Grand Rapids, MI 49503

ISBN 0–8028–3321–7

Printed in Hong Kong

Contents

Introduction

This is a book about the nature of God. But which God? Since the book is written by a Christian philosopher, it is not surprising that it is concerned with the Christian view of God. It is a discussion of the attributes or properties of God from a Christian perspective.

My approach in this book will be both theological and philosophical. It will be theological in two ways. The first is that it will explore claims that have been made about God by Christian theologians. The second is that the book can be looked at as a theological effort: my main aim is to produce a concept of God that is or at least ought to be satisfying to Christians. The book will be philosophical in both method and content - in method because I write as a philosopher trained in logic and philosophical anaysis, and in content because much of the material of the book is provided by arguments of past and present philosophers who have discussed the attributes of God.

A word about the book's title is needed. Despite the title, there is very little formal logic in the book. I have deliberately avoided formalized arguments. This is mainly because I believe there are many people who won't attempt to read a book which contains lots of symbols and formalized arguments. I call the book <u>Logic and the Nature of God</u> to signal two facts - first, that I intend to subject the notion of God to rigorous philosophical analysis; and second, that my method in the book will primarily be that of analytic philosophy of religion rather than, say, biblical or dogmatic theology.

The book can be looked at as a defence of main aspects of the view of God that is to be found in the Christian tradition. On some points, of course, Christian tradition is divided - whether God is timeless, simple and impassible, for example, are questions about which theologians have disagreed. But this should not obscure the fact that the term 'God' has meant for virtually all Christians an omnipotent, omniscient, loving spirit who created the world and who works for the salvation of human beings. Here, and on other points, there exists what can be called a traditionally Christian view of God.

My intention is to take this tradition seriously and to abandon aspects of it only if absolutely necessary. Though I will usually agree with the traditional view of God, I will also feel free to disagree with it where I feel I must. This tradition is said to be based on what Christians believe is revealed to them about God in the Bible. And although the Bible is not a book of systematic theology, I believe this claim is largely true - the tradition <u>is</u> largely based on the Bible. There are of course various views of the Bible among

1

Christians - all the way from the view that the Bible is inspired and inerrant in every detail to the view that the Bible is an interesting and religiously helpful but entirely human book [1]. Perhaps it can be said that most Christians take the Bible at least to be an authoritative record of God's acts of self-disclosure at various points in human history. Thus, obviously, the Bible has been crucial in shaping the traditionally Christian view of God.

In the chapters that follow I will therefore occasionally refer to biblical texts that seem to touch on the attributes of God. I do not propose to do serious exegesis or biblical theology in this book. Typically, I will merely cite a few biblical texts at the outset of each chapter to show why Christians have held the belief about God under discussion. All I will claim is that the plain sense of each passage I cite seems to support the conclusions usually drawn from it. As a fairly theologically conservative Christian, I will not feel the same freedom to disagree with the Bible as I will occasionally feel free to disagree with aspects of the Christian tradition.

It may seem to some readers of this book that I have unnecessarily jettisoned some of the things that have been traditionally said about God. For example, as will be seen in Chapters 1 and 3, I abandon the notion of God's timelessness and radically reinterpret the notion of God's immutability. However, I feel it necessary here to say a word about jettisoning doctrines, because I too believe that this is done all too often.

In the past century or so there has been, in my opinion, something of a theological loss of nerve among Christians. One of my dominant impressions of nineteenth and twentieth century theology is that of theologians trying desperately to please real or imagined critics of religion. It is almost as if they have said: If doctrines V, W, X, Y and Z are unacceptable to you, we will amend V, abandon W, popularize X, bring Y up to date, and interpret Z symbolically. Then they have presented the new package to the critic as if on a platter, hoping for approval.

Of course this is grossly oversimplified. Nor should it be taken as an argument for wooden theological obscurantism. Theology is and ought to be a flowing enterprise. Theology is the work of fallible human beings not God. So Christians for various reasons must occasionally change their theological formulations. Still, I believe there has been too much surgery on the Christian view of God in recent years. As I said, my main aim is to come up with a concept of God that is philosophically defensible and theologically satisfying. I am not particularly interested in trying to present something critics will like or approve of: only in presenting what seems to me true, consistent with the Bible and, in its main outlines, consistent with Christian tradition.

In philosophy just about every argument or topic is somehow logically connected to every other argument or topic. It is probably true that a person cannot solve one serious philosophical problem without solving them all. But since no one can solve all philosophical problems, what philosophers typically do is conveniently mark off given areas of inquiry, hoping to say relevant, helpful and true things on those topics, ignoring many questions that are surely relevant to them. This is what I propose to do in this book.

Let me first introduce the topics I intend to cover and then mention several I will not discuss. Since much of what one says about God is affected by opinions one holds on the question of God's relation to time, I propose to consider the notion of God's eternality in Chapter 1. The main question is whether God is timelessly eternal or temporally eternal. I will discuss both options and will conclude in favour of the latter. One of the issues that is strongly affected by God's eternality is the thorny and multifaceted problem of divine omniscience. Arriving at an acceptable notion of omniscience will be the main aim of Chapter 2. In Chapter 3 I will discuss the traditional notion that God is immutable or changeless. I will argue that, as he must be for Christians, God is immutable in a certain sense - but not in the traditional sense. In Chapter 4 I will raise the difficult question of whether divine omniscience, and especially that aspect of omniscience called foreknowledge, is compatible with human freedom. I will argue that it is.

Undoubtedly the divine attribute that has attracted the most interest of contemporary philosophers is omnipotence. This too is an extremely difficult area. In Chapter 5 I will discuss two paradoxes connected with omnipotence and attempt to arrive at an acceptable definition of the word 'omnipotent'. In Chapter 6 I will consider the notion that God is loving or benevolent. The main question on the agenda will be whether it is possible for God to do evil. Contrary to the intuition and arguments of many other Christian philosophers, I will say that it is possible for God to do evil, though in fact he does not do evil. In Chapter 7 I will discuss the problem of evil, that is, the problem of reconciling belief in a wholly good, omnipotent God with belief that evil exists. I believe the two can be reconciled, and I will use the so-called 'free will defence' to try to do so.

In Chapters 8 and 9 I will consider two theological claims that are crucial to Christians - the notion that Jesus Christ was God in human form and the notion that God is a Trinity. Both are said to be deep mysteries or paradoxes. I will not try to resolve the paradoxes; I will simply make as good a case as I can for the conclusion that both doctrines are coherent. While I cannot hope to show that they are true, I hope at least to show that Christians have good reason to accept them.

Finally, in the conclusion I will discuss two related questions. First I will ask whether the conception of God presented in this book can be considered (using Pascal's famous distinction) 'the God of Abraham, Isaac and Jacob', that is whether the God defended here is the God of the religious believer instead of the cold, distant 'God of the philosophers and the learned'. Second, I will ask whether the God presented in this book is worthy of worship. My answer will be yes on both counts.

These are the topics I will cover. However, there are several topics which are surely relevant to my concerns that I will not discuss. For example, there are several traditional attributes of God that I will not consider, either because I have nothing helpful to say about them -e.g. omnipresence, holiness - or because I either do not understand them or do not believe them in any case - e.g. simplicity, impassibility, infinity. Second, I do not wish to become involved in disputes over theological predication. I hope some day to say something on this topic, but for now I will accept the convenient fiction that we all know what it is to assign properties to God, that we all know what is meant by such sentences as 'God is   ', where the blank is filled in by some attribute such as 'loving', 'omniscient' or the like. Thirdly, I will largely avoid the question of what grammatical or logical status the term 'God' has - whether it is a proper name, a definite description, a title, or whatever. This question too is relevant to my concerns, and occasionally I will have to mention it, but I will not address myself to it in any systematic way.

Also, as much as possible, I will avoid talk of 'essential properties' of God. There is, of course, a legitimate distinction that can be made, both for God and other beings, between properties they possess contingently and those they possess essentially [2]. Let us say that an essential property of x is a property x has and cannot fail to have and be x (three-sidedness, for example, for a triangle). And let us say that a contingent property of x is a property x has and can fail to have and still be x (right-handedness, for example, for me).

I will be forced occasionally to talk about essential properties of God, but will avoid the topic as much as possible. I will concentrate on developing a proper understanding of the properties God in fact has, ignoring for the most part the question whether these properties are contingent or essential to him. I do this in part because this is an area where, in my opinion, it is easy to do bad philosophy. Some philosophers and theologians, for example, have argued that all God's properties are essential properties. But this cannot be true: I believe, for example, that God has the property of knowing at what age Pele first kicked a soccer ball, but this is surely a contingent property of God. Pele might never have existed, or might have been born a life-long cripple, or the game of soccer might never have been invented. Again, some philosophers and theologians say that omniscience is an essential property of god, but is this so obvious? Suppose God knows the answer to any question that can be asked except this: What colour shoes did Martha Washington wear on the day of her wedding to George? Suppose God has somehow forgotten this fact and has forgotten how to deduce it from other facts he knows. Is it so clear he would then no longer be God? Now I believe that God is in fact omniscient - he does know the answer to this question. But I am not prepared to grant that if he didn't he would no longer be divine.

Some philosophers have argued that God must have all his properties essentially in order to be 'religiously adequate'[3]. If he were contingently wise, good, powerful, etc., that is, if he just happened to have these properties it would follow, they say, that somebody or something made him this way. But this doesn't follow. Of course I agree that God, like any other being, must have some essential properties. Perhaps it is true that God wouldn't be the being that he is or wouldn't be divine if he were no longer wise, good and powerful. But is it so clear that he would no longer be the being that he is or divine if he weren't <u>perfectly</u> wise, good and powerful, e.g. if there were something he couldn't do no matter how hard he tried, for example, crush Mt Baldy flat or make Clark Kucheman love horses and hate dogs?

The reader will notice that some of the topics discussed in this book are entered into more deeply than others. In the case of many of them I am quite conscious of the fact that more could have been said. Unanswered questions abound. But my major aim in the book is to develop and defend a given view of God, and in some cases that did not seem to require as much detailed discussion as might otherwise have been desirable. I also happily admit that many of the arguments and conclusions of the book are not original with me - in fact, I owe much to the work of many classical and contemporary philosophers and theologians who have probed these issues.

Developing a view of God is of course a theological task, and some may wonder about the appropriateness of analytic philosophy as a method of doing theology. I have no hidden agenda on this score: I won't argue, for example, that the results of philosophical theology in the past two millennia have been any better or worse than those of dogmatic theology or biblical theology. My only defence is that as a philosopher I simply find myself thinking philosophically and (I hope) logically whenever I confront a theological question.

But I must also confess to a strong feeling that philosophy, or at least the firm emphasis on reason that philosophers strive for, is sorely needed in today's world. Ours is often called an age of irrationality. And although those who make this statement do not perhaps have in mind the point I am about to make, I must agree. Let me ask this question: Are there really people who believe any of the following propositions?

Ancient astronauts once visited the earth and helped people build pyramids.
Apricot pits can cure cancer.
Huge ape-like creatures roam the wilds of Western Canada and the United States.
The positions of the stars significantly influence our lives.

The answer, as we well know, is that there are such people. And this creates in me the melancholy feeling that these are sad days for reason. Why do people believe such things? Think also of the Bermuda Triangle, UFOs and the many bizarre conspiracy theories connected with the assassinations of the 1960s. One even wonders whether the strange attractiveness for certain people of weird, esoteric and preposterous theories ought to be a fit subject of inquiry for some social psychologist.

I will not bother here or elsewhere to argue against these propositions or theories. One suspects those who believe them would not listen anyway. Of course, such people may well respond that they find some of my beliefs preposterous - for example, that a good and omnipotent God exists, or that Jesus Christ is 'truly God and truly man'. Perhaps so. My point is just this: from my perspective at least these are sad days for reason, and thus philosophy - good philosophy - is badly needed. I hope what I provide in this book is good philosophy.

No Christian can write a book about God without being acutely conscious of the relativity of statements we make about God. Although I am prepared to defend what I say about God in this book, I would like to record here my acute feeling that all our thoughts about God are halting, inadequate and partial. God is much too superior to us for us to be able to understand him well. What we know about him we know because he has chosen to reveal it to us, so theology is in a sense the science of God's revelation of himself to us rather than of God as he is in himself. Whether I have adequately described God as he has revealed himself to us, let alone God as he is in himself, I do not know. I will only say I have done my best. If I have made any harmful errors, I hope he will forgive me. Perhaps God chuckles at our fumbling attempts to do theology. Perhaps one day we will see how laughably worthless our attempts have been. But this does not mean we should not do theology to the best of our ability here and now.

Sincere thanks are due to several friends and colleagues who made suggestions about all or parts of this book. I should mention especially Alvin Plantinga, Joseph Runzo and Del Ratzsch, who read and commented helpfully on the entire manuscript. John Hick, the editor of the series in which the book appears, also provided significant assistance and encouragement. Several others helped me improve various chapters of the book, including Rebecca Pentz, Nicholas Lash, Brian Hebblethwaite, Dick France and David Griffin.

Much of the first draft of the book was written in 1978 while my family and I were residence at St Edmund's House, Cambridge. I would like to thank the Master, Fellows and students of that college for their warmth, hospitality and helpfulness during our very pleasant stay there.

My own college, Claremont McKenna College, also provided important help in completing the project. The manuscript was typed by Pat Padilla, Polly Baker and Mary Anderson, the loyal and helpful philosophy department secretaries at the college. And I was also

awarded two different Claremont McKenna College summer
fellowships, in 1977 and 1980, which helped support the work.

Scripture quotations are from the Revised Standard Version of the
Holy Bible, Old Testament Section, copyright 1952; New Testament
Section, first edition, copyright 1946; New Testament Section, second
edition, copyright 1972 by the Division of Christian Education of the
National Council of Churches of Christ in the USA. Used by
permission.

I would like to thank the following for permission to reprint
copyright material: Religious Studies, vol. 15, no. 3 (Sept. 1979) for
permission to use much of 'Divine Omniscience and Human Freedom'
by Stephen T. Davis; Christian Scholar's Review, vol. IX, no. 3 (1980)
for permission to use much of 'Is "Truly God and Truly Man"
Coherent?' by Stephen T. Davis. Chapter 7 is taken substantially
from my contributions to a book I edited entitled Encountering Evil:
Live Options in Theodicy (John Knox Press, 1981).

Square brackets are used throughout the book to denote references
to notes, which can be found in the Notes and References section at
the back of the book.

1 Time

One divine property that we will deal with early in the book is God's eternality. It will be best if we discuss it here because one's opinion on this subject is likely to affect opinions one has about several other divine properties, especially omnipotence, omniscience and immutability. Thus we must now raise the thorny question of God's relation to time.

It is part of the Christian tradition that God is eternal.

Lord, thou has been our dwelling place in all generations.

Before the mountains were brought forth, or ever thou hadst formed the earth and the world, from everlasting to everlasting thou art God.

Thou turnest man back to the dust, and sayeth, 'Turn back, O children of man!'

For a thousand years in thy sight are but as yesterday when it is past, or as a watch in the night. (Ps. 90:1-4)

Of old thou didst lay the foundation of the earth, and the heavens are the work of thy hands.

They will perish, but thou dost endure; they will all wear out like a garment.

Thou changest them like raiment, and they pass away; but thou art the same and thy years have no end. (Ps. 102:25-7)

I am the Alpha and the Omega, the first and the last, the beginning and the end. (Rev. 22:13)

But what does it mean to say that God is eternal? Christians agree that God's eternality entails that he has always existed and always will exist, that he has no beginning and no end. But from this central point there are two routes that might be taken. One is to say that God is <u>timelessly eternal</u> and the other is to say that he is <u>temporally eternal</u>.

Let us first consider the view that God is timelessly eternal or 'outside of time'. There are a variety of reasons a Christian might be tempted by this thesis. One might be to emphasize God's transcendence over his creation as much as possible. Another might be to reconcile divine foreknowledge and human freedom. (Boethius and others have argued that human beings can be free despite God's knowledge of what they will do in their future because God's

8

knowledge is timeless.) Another might be to retain consistency with other things one says about God, for example that he is immutable. (And it certainly does seem true that a timeless being - to be defined below - must be immutable.)

Whatever the reasons, a variety of Christian theologians and philosophers have claimed that God is timeless. For example, Anselm graphically depicts God's relation to time as follows:

> Thou wast not, then, yesterday, nor wilt thou be tomorrow; but yesterday and today and tomorrow thou art; or, rather, neither yesterday, nor today nor tomorrow thou art; but, simply, thou art, outside all time. For yesterday and today and tomorrow have no existence, except in time; but thou, although nothing exists without thee, nevertheless dost not exist in space or time, but all things exist in thee[1].

That God is timeless was also claimed by Augustine and Boethius before Anselm, and was also held after him, notably by Aquinas and Schleiermacher. In a famous definition, Boethius called eternity 'the complete possession all at once of illimitable life'; it is a kind of 'now that stands still'. (Notice that Boethius is using 'eternal' as a synonym for 'timeless', which I am not.) Since God is eternal, he lives in what might be called an 'everlasting present'; he has an infinity of movable time - past, present and future - all at once everlastingly present to him. Boethius is perhaps most clear on this point when he speaks of divine foreknowledge:

> Wherefore since . . . God hath always an everlasting and present state, his knowledge also surpassing all motions of time, remaineth in the simplicity of his presence, and comprehending the infinite spaces of that which is past and to come, considereth all things in his simple knowledge, as though they were now in doing. So that, if thou wilt weigh his foreknowledge with which he discerneth all things, thou wilt more rightly esteem it to be the knowledge of a never fading instant than a foreknowledge as of a thing to come[2].

Following Boethius, Aquinas stressed that for God there is no past, present and future, and no before and after, that all is 'simultaneously whole' for him[3].

These statements are not easy to understand. What precisely is meant by the term 'timeless' or 'timeless being'? Following Nelson Pike, let us say that a given being is timeless if and only if it:

(1) lacks temporal location

and

(2) lacks temporal extension[4].

A being lacks temporal location if it does not make sense to say of it, for example, that it existed before the French Revolution or that it will exist on Jimmy Carter's seventieth birthday. Thus, if God is timeless, statements like these cannot meaningfully be made about him. A being lacks temporal extension if it has no duration, i.e. if it makes no sense to say of it, for example, that it has lived for eighty years or that it was alive during the entire period of the Truman administration.

It is not easy to feel that one has fully grasped the notion of a timeless being. Perhaps this is in part because it is difficult to see precisely what criteria (1) and (2) imply. Very possibly they imply another characteristic of a timeless being, one which is also difficult to state and explicate precisely:

(3) Temporal terms have no significant application to him.

What is a 'temporal term'? Without wishing to suggest that my list is exhaustive, let me stipulate that a temporal term is one like those included in the following list: 'past', 'present', 'future', 'before', 'after', and other similar terms like 'simultaneous', 'always', 'later', 'next year', 'forever', 'at 6:00 p.m.', etc. Now there appears to be a sense in which temporal terms cannot meaningfully be predicated of a being that lacks temporal location and temporal extension. Neither the timeless being itself, nor its properties, actions or relations with other beings can be significantly modified by temporal terms. Thus if God is a timeless being, the following sentences are either meaningless or necessarily false:

God existed before Moses.
God's power will soon triumph over evil.
Last week God wrought a miracle.
God will always be wiser than human beings.

Does this imply that time as we understand it is unreal, a kind of illusion? If the timeless being in question is God, the ultimate reality of the universe, the creator of the heavens and the earth, one might well push the argument in this way: if from God's point of view there is no past, present and future, and no before and after, then - it might well be argued - there is no ultimately real past, present and future, and no ultimately real relationship of before and after. Thus time as we experience it is unreal.

But the argument need not be pushed in this direction. Even if God is a timeless being, it can be argued that time is real and that our temporal distinctions are apt just because God created time (for us to live 'in'). Perhaps an analogy from space will help. Just because God is spaceless (he has no spatial location or extension) no one wants to say that space is unreal. It is just that God does not exist in space as we do. Similarly, he does not exist 'in' time, but time is still real, both for us and for God. Well then - one might want to ask at this point - if God is timeless is it or is it not meaningful to say that 'God existed before Moses' or that 'God will always be wiser than human beings'? The answer is that it depends on who you are: for us these statements are meaningful and true; for God they are meaningless or at least necessarily false.

Is the doctrine of divine timelessness coherent? I do not know. I suspect it is possible for a philosopher to lay out a concept of divine timelessness which I am unable to refute, i.e. prove incoherent. I will discuss one such attempt later in this chapter. However, throughout this book, for reasons I will presently explain, I do not propose to assume that God is timeless. In fact, I plan to make and argue for the assumption that God is temporally eternal. In my view, this is a far simpler procedure, with far fewer theological dangers, as I will explain. For the fact is that every notion of divine timelessness with which I am familiar is subject to difficulties which, at the very least, seem serious.

I will argue against the doctrine of divine timelessness on two counts: first, that a timeless being cannot be the Christian God; and second, that the notion of a timeless being is probably incoherent. The first point has been convincingly argued by both Nelson Pike and Richard Swinburne[5]. I will not mention all of the traditional attributes of God they claim timelessness rules out; I will instead concentrate on just two: the claim that God is the creator of the universe, and the claim that God is a personal being who acts in human history, speaking, punishing, warning, forgiving, etc. Both notions are obviously crucial to Christianity; if timelessness really does rule them out this will constitute a very good reason for a Christian to reject the doctrine.

Notice the following argument:

(5) God creates x.
(6) x first exists at T.
(7) Therefore, God creates x at T.

If this argument is valid, it seems to rule out the possibility of a timeless God creating anything at all, the universe or anything in it, for 'x' here is a variable ranging over anything at all about which it is logically possible that it be created. The reason the argument rules out the doctrine that God is creator is that (7) cannot be true if God lacks temporal location. For we saw earlier that no temporal term like 'at T' can meaningfully be applied to a being or to the actions of a being that lacks temporal location and temporal extension. God is not the creator Christians have traditionally believed in if he is not the creator of things like me and the eucalyptus tree outside my office. But no timeless being can the creator of such things since they came into existence at various points in time. Thus timelessness is inconsistent with the Christian view of God as creator.

But cannot God, so to speak, timelessly create something temporal? Aquinas, at least, argued that he can. God may create something at a certain point in time (say, create me in the year 1940), but it does not follow from this, Aquinas would say, that God's act of creating occurred at that point in time (or indeed at any point in time); his creating may well be based on changeless and eternal aspects of his will. Thus Aquinas says:

> God's act of understanding and willing is, necessarily, His act of making. Now, an effect follows from the intellect and the will according to the determination of the intellect and the command of the will. Moreover, just as the intellect determines every other condition of the thing made, so does it prescribe the time of its making; for art determines not only that this thing is to be such and such, but that it is to be at this particular time, even as a physician determines that a dose of medicine is to be drunk at such a particular time. So that, if his act of will were of itself sufficient to produce the effect, the effect would follow anew from his previous decision, without any new action on his part. Nothing, therefore, prevents our saying that God's action existed from all eternity, whereas its effect was not present from eternity, but existed at that time when, from all eternity, He ordained it[6].

Thus - so Aquinas would say - (5) and (6) in the above argument do not entail (7) after all.

Is Aquinas correct? It depends on what he means by 'eternity' in the above lines. If he means temporal eternity I believe he is correct. It may well be true that God can, so to speak, 'from all eternity create x at T'. I have no wish to deny this, at any rate. A temporally eternal being apparently can eternally (that is, at all points in time) will that a given temporal being come to exist at a certain point in time. Of course, this case is not precisely parallel to the case of Aquinas's physician at a given point in time willing that a dosage be taken at a later point in time. But nevertheless, as concerns temporal eternality, Aquinas appears to be correct: as it stands, the (5)-(7) argument is invalid.

But Aquinas's argument, which in my opinion successfully applies to temporally eternal things, does not apply to timeless things. (Notice that the physician in his example is not timeless.) Even if it is true that I was created in 1940 not because of a choice God made in 1940 (or at some other time) but because of a temporally eternal divine choice, this does not make the choice <u>timeless</u> in the sense of lacking temporal location and extension. Temporally eternal things certainly do have temporal extension. It would still make sense and quite possibly be true to say, 'God willed in 1940 that Davis exist' (although it would also be meaningful and perhaps equally true to make the same statement with 3469 B.C. or A.D. 2610 or any other date substituted for 1940). Equally, if all God's decisions and actions are temporally eternal they are <u>simultaneous</u> with each other; and statements like 'x's desire to create a and x's decision to do b are simultaneous' cannot, as we saw, meaningfully be made about a timeless being[7]. This too is to apply a temporal term - 'simultaneous' - to it.

Of course, nothing prevents a defender of timelessness from simply insisting that an action (e.g. the causing of something to exist) can be timeless and the effect (e.g. its coming into existence) temporal. Such a person can ask why the temporality of the effect requires that the cause be temporal. But to anticipate a point I will make in more detail later, the answer to this is that we have on hand no acceptable concept of atemporal causation, i.e. of what it is for a timeless cause to produce a temporal effect. Surely, as Nelson Pike argues, in all the cases of causation with which we are familiar, a temporal relationship obtains between an action and its effect. We are in no position to deny that this need always be the case unless we are armed with a usable concept of atemporal causation, which we are not.

Let us return to the argument mentioned above:

(5) God creates x.
(6) x first exists at T.
(7) Therefore, God creates x at T.

What we need to notice is that (7) is ambiguous between (7a) and (7b):

(7a) God, at T, creates x.
(7b) God creates x, and x first exists at T.

Now (7a) clearly cannot be true of God if God is timeless - a being that performs some action at a certain point in time is temporal. So (7b) is the interpretation of (7) that will be preferred by the defender of divine timelessness. Notice that (7b) is simply the conjunction of (5) and (6), and accordingly is indeed entailed by (5) and (6). But can (7b) be true of God if God is timeless? Only if we have available a usable concept of atemporal causation, which, as I say, we do not have. Therefore, we are within our rights in concluding that (5) and (6) entail that God is temporal, i.e. that a timeless being cannot be the creator of the universe.

Accordingly, it is not clear how a timelessly eternal being can be the creator of this temporal universe. If God creates a given temporal thing, then God's act of creation is itself temporal (though it may be temporally eternal). If God is timelessly eternal in the sense defined earlier, he cannot create temporal things.

Second, a timeless being cannot be the personal, caring, involved God we read about in the Bible. The God of the Bible is, above all, a God who cares deeply about what happens in history and who acts to bring about his will. He makes plans. He responds to what human beings, do, e.g. their evil deeds or their acts of repentance. He seems to have temporal location and extension. The Bible does not hesitate to speak of God's years and days (see Psalm 102:24, 27; Hebrews 1:12). And God seems to act in temporal sequences - first he rescues the children of Israel from Egypt and later he gives them the Law; first he sends his son to be born of a virgin and later he raises him from the dead. These are generalizations meant to be understood as covering the whole Bible rather than specific passages; nevertheless here are two texts where such points seem to be made:

> If you obey the commandments of the Lord your God . . . by loving the Lord your God, by walking in his ways, and by keeping his commandments and his statutues and his ordinances, then you shall live and multiply, and the Lord your God will bless you . . . But if your heart turns away, and you will not hear, but are drawn away to worship other gods and serve them, I declare to you this day, that you shall perish. (Deut. 30:16-18)

> In many and various ways God spoke of old to our fathers by the prophets; but in these last days he has spoken to us by a Son. (Heb. 1:1-2)

But the obvious problem here is to understand how a timeless being can plan or anticipate or remember or respond or punish or warn or forgive. All such acts seem undeniably temporal[8]. To make plans is to formulate intentions about the future. To anticipate is to look forward to what is future. To remember is to have beliefs or knowledge about what is past. To respond is to be affected by events that have occurred in the past. To punish is to cause someone to suffer because of something done in the past. To warn is to caution someone about dangers that might lie in the future. To forgive someone is to restore a past relationship that was damaged by an offense.

On both counts, then, it is difficult to see how a timeless being can be the God in which Christians have traditionally believed. It does not seem that there is any clear sense in which a timeless being can be the creator of the universe or a being who acts in time.

The other and perhaps more important argument against divine timelessness is that both the notion of a timeless being per se and the notion of a timeless being who is also omniscient are probably incoherent. The incoherence of the notion per se can be seen by considering carefully the Boethius-Anselm-Aquinas claim that for

God all times are simultaneously present. Events occurring at 3021 B.C., at 1982, and at A.D. 7643, they want to say, are all 'simultaneously present' to God. If this just means that at any point in time God knows in full and complete detail what happens at any other point in time, I can (and do) accept it. But it clearly means something different and much stronger than this, and in this stronger sense (whatever precisely it comes to) the claim does not seem possibly true[9].

That is, if the doctrine of timelessness requires us to say that the years 3021 B.C. and A.D. 7643 are simultaneous, then the doctrine is false, for the two are not simultaneous. They may of course be simultaneous in some sense if time is illusory. But since I see no good reason to affirm that time is illusory and every reason to deny that it is illusory, I am within my rights in insisting that the two indicated years are not simultaneous and that the doctrine of divine timelessness is accordingly probably false.

Suppose an event that occurred yesterday is the cause of an event that will occur tomorrow, e.g. suppose your having thrown a banana peel on the pavement yesterday will cause me to trip and break a bone tomorrow. How can the throwing of the banana peel and the breaking of the bone be simultaneous? Surely if the first caused the second the first must be temporally prior to the second; and if so, they are not simultaneous. (Perhaps some causes are simultaneous with their effects, but not causes of events of this sort.)

But the following objection might be raised: 'Any argument for the conclusion that timeless beings cannot exist must be mistaken for the simple reason that timeless beings do exist'. It has been seriously suggested, for example, that numbers are timeless beings. Thus William Kneale says:

An assertion such as 'There is a prime number between five and ten' can never be countered sensibly by the remark 'You are out of date: things have altered recently.' And this is the reason why the entities discussed in mathematics can properly be said to have a timeless existence. To say only that they have a sempiternal or omnitemporal existence (i.e., an existence at all times) would be unsatisfactory because this way of talking might suggest that it is at least conceivable that they should at some time cease to exist, and that is an absurdity we want to exclude[10].

Is the number seven, for example, timeless? I do not think so. (I agree that it is eternal and that it would be absurd to suggest that it might not exist; it is, in short, a sort of 'necessary being'.) But if the number seven is not just eternal but timeless, then on our earlier definition of 'timeless', the following statements cannot meaningfully be made:

The number seven existed on 27 July 1883.
The number seven was greater than the number six

during the whole of the Punic wars.
The number seven existed yesterday and will
   exist tomorrow.

But the number seven is not a timeless being; all three of these sentences, in my opinion, are not only meaningful but true. (The fact that the first might be taken by someone to suggest that the number seven might not exist at some time other than 27 July 1883 is only an interesting psychological fact about the person who misreads it in this way. The statement implies nothing of the sort.)

But defenders of divine timelessness can raise an objection to this argument that their notion is incoherent. They can say something like this:

> Of course talk about 'eternal present', 'simultaneously whole', etc. seems incoherent to us. This is because such talk is at best a stumbling way of understanding a mystery - the mystery of God's transcendence over time - that we cannot really understand. Statements like 'my nineteenth birthday occurred before my twentieth' only seem indubitable to us because, unlike God, our minds are limited. If we had God's intellectual prowess, if we understood temporal reality as he does, we would see that this statement is false or inadequate or misleading. We would then see time correctly.

There may be some sense in which the claims being made here are true. I will not deny them, at any rate. (We will encounter an analogous move when we consider in Chapter 5 whether divine omnipotence entails that God can violate the laws of logic.) God's consciousness of time may indeed so far transcend ours that the best way we have of expressing it is by making apparently incoherent statements. But whether or not these claims are true, I am quite sure that we have no good reason to believe them. Like it or not, we are stuck with these limited minds of ours; if we want to be rational we have no choice but to reject what we judge to be incoherent. It may be true, in some sense, that some statements we presently consider true (like 'my nineteenth birthday occurred before my twentieth') are really false or inadequate or misleading when understood in some way which we cannot now understand. But it is irrational for us now to affirm that this is true.

Recently Eleonore Stump and Norman Kretzmann have impressively defended the Boethian concept of divine timeless eternity[11]. Their term is simply 'eternity', a concept which, as they explain it, is broader than timelessness, but essentially involves it. Their argument is dense and opaque in places. What they first try to do is explain and defend the notion of eternity classically expressed by Boethius - 'The complete possession all at once of illimitable life'. They then raise several theological issues such as whether an eternal being can act in time, answer prayers, become incarnate, or be both omniscient and immutable. I will only quarrel with their answers to the first two.

According to Stump and Kretzmann (interpreting Boethius) anything that is eternal has life. A number may be timeless, they say, but not eternal. Besides life, eternal things possess the following properties:

(8) illimitability;
(9) duration;
and
(10) atemporality.

Let me explain each point in turn. First, a being is illimitable just in case it has infinite duration, i.e. has no beginning or end, is unlimited in either temporal direction. Second, no being can have life without having duration, so eternal things have duration (although, as we will see, it is a special sort of duration). Third, Boethius insists that an eternal being is 'fully realized, all present at once'. That is, it possesses all its life all at once; for it there is no past or future, and no earlier than or later than. (If a being is, say, earlier than some event, or past in relation to some event, then it is part of a temporal series and thus is not eternal.) Combine this "all at once" condition with duration (property (2)), and you have an atemporal being. Finally, an atemporal being is simultaneous with all temporal events.

Criteria (8) and (10) together create what Stump and Kretzmann rightly consider the crucial notion in their argument, viz. the notion of 'atemporal duration'. They say:

Atemporal duration is duration none of which is not--none of which is absent (and hence future) or flowed away (and hence past). Eternity, not time, is the mode of existence that admits of fully realized duration [12].

We immediately notice that what is being talked about here is a special sort of duration, because criterion (10) entails that the events in the life of an eternal being cannot be ordered sequentially. What we are talking about, then, is a type of duration in which all events are in some sense simultaneously present (as Boethius specificially said). The notion of 'eternal present', Stump and Kretzmann say, is of 'an infinitely extended, pastless, futureless duration.'

The notion that an eternal being is simultaneous with all temporal events is possibly meant by Stump and Kretzmann to be entailed by (8) and (10). 'From the standpoint of eternity,' they say, 'every time is present'. Since we naturally wonder how an atemporal event can be simultaneous with a temporal event (surely simultaneity is a temporal concept), Stump and Kretzmann explain with their concept of 'Eternal-Temporal Simultaneity' (they call it ET-simultaneity). Two events, x and y, are ET-simultaneous if and only if:

(4) either x is eternal and y is temporal, or vice versa; and
(5) for some observer, A, in the unique eternal reference frame, x and y are both present--i.e., either x is eternally present and y is observed as temporally present, or vice versa; and
(6) for some observer, B, in one of the infinitely many temporal reference frames, x and y are both present--i.e. either x is observed as eternally present and y as temporally present, or vice versa[13].

It follows that if x and y are ET-simultaneous, then x is neither earlier than nor later than, and neither past nor present with respect to, y. Furthermore, x and y are not temporally simultaneous either, since one or the other must be eternal.

One way of seeing the implications of the notion of ET-simultaneity is to note that the following three statements can form a consistent triad:

(11) Richard Nixon is alive in the temporal present.
(12) Richard Nixon is alive in the eternal present.
(13) Richard Nixon is dead in the eternal present.

What this means is not that Nixon exists in eternity where he is simultaneously both alive and dead but rather than 'one and the same eternal present is ET-simultaneous with Nixon's being alive and is also ET-simultaneous with Nixon dying; so Nixon's life is ET-simultaneous with and hence present to an eternal entity, and Nixon's death is ET-simultaneous with and hence present to an eternal entity, although Nixon's life and Nixon's death are themselves neither eternal nor simultaneous'[14].

Stump and Kretzmann admit that the notion of eternity, thus described, may seem incoherent. But they claim this is primarily because we erroneously think of duration as duration through time. Temporal duration, they claim, is only apparent duration. This is because of one of the classical paradoxes of temporal passage - the past is not because it is over and done with, the future is not because it is not yet, and the present is a mere durationless instant, a dimensionless boundary between the past and the future. 'Such radically evanescent existence', Stump and Kretzmann say, 'cannot be the foundation of existence'. Permanence and persistence are only possible in eternity, not time. Thus (summarizing approvingly certain Greek views that gave rise to the concept of eternity) they say: 'Genuine duration is fully realized duration - not only extended existence (even that is theoretically impossible in time) but also existence none of which is already gone and none of which is yet to

come--and such fully realized duration must be atemporal
duration' [15]

Now Stump and Kretzmann are not arguing, as did Parmenides and
F. H. Bradley, that time is unreal. They are arguing that there are
two separate modes of real existence, time and eternity. But they do
appear to need the Greek argument noted above in order to convince
us that the notion of atemporal duration is coherent and not readily
dismissable.

But is Stump and Kretzmann's notion of eternity coherent? I do not
believe so, although I am not able to prove that it is incoherent. Let
me focus on the notion of atemporal duration. Though the word
'duration' is used here, it is hard to see how what Stump and
Kretzmann are talking about really amounts to duration. Surely the
notion of duration just is the notion of existing through a series of
sequentially related moments, i.e. surely duration essentially involves
succession. So we must ask precisely how a being can sensibly be said
to have duration without sequentiality in the moments of its
existence. That is, how can a being both be atemporal and have
infinite duration?

The reply of Stump and Kretzmann to this would be that what I say
is true of temporal duration but that what they are talking about is
atemporal duration. But is this reply sufficient? Despite their
argument that atemporal duration is the only genuine duration, what
they say smacks of being a merely verbal solution to the problem.
Even if Stump and Kretzmann are correct (following the Greeks) that
the basic idea of duration is extended existence and that extended
existence in time is an illusion or at least a distortion, it does not
follow that extended existence is possible in eternity. (Maybe
extended existence is impossible in either mode of existence.)
Naturally, just saying that duration is possible in eternity does not
make it so.

Take the person who tries to reconcile divine predestination of all
events with human freedom by saying, 'Well, I'm talking about a kind
of predestination that allows for human freedom'. Until it is
explained precisely what this species of predestination is, we will be
suspicious that the proposed reconciliation is spurious. Similarly, we
would be suspicious of a person who tries to explain how an
incorporeal being can be spatially located somewhere by the use of
what this person calls 'an aspatial concept of "inside of".' Again, until
it is explained precisely what this species of 'inside of' is, we will
reject the proposed reconciliation.

Likewise, since the notion of duration seems essentially a temporal
notion, we find ourselves wondering what 'atemporal duration'
amounts to, or whether the notion even makes sense. Stump and
Kretzmann emphasize that their notion of atemporal duration rules
out temporal relations like 'earlier than' or 'past in relation to' but
not the relation of simultaneity, though they stress that they have in
mind a nontemporal type of simultaneity. But if the problem is to

explain or make coherent the notion of 'duration without succession', we can wonder why we can't equally well do so by positing some 'nontemporal species of "earlier than" or "past in relation to".'

Is the notion of ET-simultaneity coherent? Again, I can't tell for certain, but I have my doubts. For one thing, it is at least puzzling how a temporal being can 'observe' an entity or event as eternally present. Suppose I am the temporal observer and that there exists an eternal entity x of which I am aware. What then is it for me to 'observe x as eternal'? I might perhaps believe or become convinced or argue or even argue cogently that x is eternal, but how can I observe that x is eternal? I find it equally puzzling to imagine an eternal being observing something as temporally present. Temporally present to whom? Presumably not to it (that would make the being temporal); presumably, then, to other beings that are temporal. The problem here is typically disguised by the fact that the eternal being theologians have in mind is God, who is assumed to be omniscient. But what is needed is an explanation of precisely how an eternal observer can observe something as temporally present.

Stump and Kretzmann quote disapprovingly the following criticism of the notion of eternality by Anthony Kenny:

> But, on St. Thomas' view, my typing of this paper is simultaneous with the whole of eternity. Again, on his view, the great fire of Rome is simultaneous with the whole of eternity. Therefore, while I type these very words, Nero fiddles heartlessly on[16].

Stump and Kretzmann argue that criticisms like this one are based on a misunderstanding of the concept of eternity. Once we understand ET-simultaneity, they say, we see that Kenny's alleged entailment does not follow. But my response to this is that if the solution proposed by Stump and Kretzmann (i.e. the notions of atemporal duration and ET-simultaneity) is merely verbal, as I believe it is, Kenny's criticism still stands. Nor do we know for sure (if the proposed solution is merely verbal) whether propositions (11), (12), and (13) are, as argued, consistent. There is no way for us to decide whether this is true until we are clear on the notion of ET-simultaneity. And given Stump and Kretzmann's account, we are not.

Futhermore, though I will not dwell on the matter here, the venerable paradox of temporal passage mentioned earlier (the present as only an infinitely thin boundary rather than a substantial reality) seems a frail reed on which to hang the argument that the only genuine duration is atemporal . duration. Surely philosophers have discussed this paradox for centuries, and various solutions have been suggested to it[17]. It does not seem true (and certainly not obviously true) to say that 'extended existence' is 'theoretically impossible in time'. So it won't do just to display the paradox as Stump and Kretzmann do, as if that alone settled the fact that temporal duration is not real duration.

Let us move on to two of the theological issues Stump and Kretzmann raise. First, can an eternal being act in time? Stump and Kretzmann criticize Nelson Pike's negative answer to this question, claiming that he relies on the assumption that a temporal relationship must hold between an action an its effect. They say:

> But if we do adopt co-occurrence as a theoretically justifiable condition of causal connection between an action and its effect, we can point out that any and every action of an eternal entity is ET-simultaneous with any temporal effect ascribed to it. And since it would simply beg the question to insist that only temporal simultaneity between an action and its effect can satisfy this necessary condition of causal connection, we see no reason for denying of an eternal, omnipotent entity that its atemporal act of willing could bring it about that a mountain came into existence on yesterday's date [18].

I agree with the claim that Pike makes the above assumption; indeed, I believe his assumption is correct - a temporal relationship must obtain between an action and its effect. However, while Stump and Kretzmann (naturally enough given their commitment to ET-simultaneity) focus on the claim that causes and effects must be simultaneous, I would rather argue as Hume did that causes must be prior to their effects. Again, perhaps some effects are simultaneous with their causes, but in the vast majority of cases where we are paradigmatically willing to say that A causes B, A occurs before B.

If so, an obvious problem is created: How can a temporal effect (e.g. the coming into existence of a mountain) of an eternal being's action be temporally later than the (eternal) action of the eternal being? Stump and Kretzmann argue that it begs the question for the critic simply to insist that temporal priority is what is required. Perhaps so. But even if so we need a clear explanation of how we can be justified in holding that A causes B where there is no temporal relationship of any sort between A and B. And that is what Stump and Kretzmann do not provide. In other words, what we need, in order to see if Stump and Kretzmann's claims are true, is a usable, coherent notion of atemporal causation, i.e. causation in which an eternal cause produces a temporal effect. Now I do not wish to be taken as dogmatically insisting that temporal priority is required in causation. Perhaps it is not. I only say it seems to be required, and that therefore those like Stump and Kretzmann who argue that it is not owe the rest of us a clear explanation why it is not. In the absence of any such explanation, Stump and Kretzmann's argument is not convincing.

Second, can an eternal being answer prayer? Stump and Kretzmann agree that something constitutes an answer to a prayer if and only if it is done because of the prayer, but of course they do not agree that the occurrence must be later than the prayer. 'If at 3:00 a mother prepares a snack for her little boy because she believes that when he gets home at 3:30 he will ask her for one, it does not seem unreasonable to describe her as preparing the food because of the child's request, even though in this case the response is earlier than the request'[19]. But is this correct? Is this the proper analysis of the situation? Wouldn't it be more accurate to say that the mother prepares the snack not because of her son's future request but because of her present anticipation of his future request? (There may not in the event even be a request - perhaps for some reason this time the boy will not be hungry.)

But, more importantly, Stump and Kretzmann go on to argue as follows: suppose Hannah prays at T1 to have a child and that at T2, several days later, she conceives. Notice, they say, that

> The day of her prayer and the day of her conceiving are ET-simultaneous with the life of an eternal entity. If such an entity atemporally wills that Hannah conceive on a certain day after the day of her prayer, then such an entity's bringing it about that Hannah conceives on that day is clearly a response to her prayer, even though the willing is ET-simultaneous with the prayer rather than later than it[20].

But this does not necessarily follow. Her prayer might not have had anything to do with her conceiving. I am not disputing that Hannah's prayer had to do with her conceiving in the story in I Samuel. I am disputing Stump and Kretzmann's contention that this conclusion is entailed by the considerations they cite in the above quotation. But the major problem here is again the absence of any clear explanation of eternal causation, i.e. of what it is for an eternal being to cause something temporal to occur in response to a prayer. In the absense of any such explanation, the argument of Stump and Kretzmann is again unconvincing.

We have been discussing the notion of timelessness as an attempt to understand the Christian tradition that God is eternal. It can now be seen why I find the notion inadequate and why I much prefer the other alternative, which is to say that God is temporally eternal. Let us say that a temporally eternal being is (1) eternal in the sense that there never was or will be a moment when it does not exist, (2) temporal in the sense that it has both temporal location and temporal extension, and (3) temporal in the sense that the distinctions among past, present and future, and between before and after, can meaningfully be applied to it. If God is such a temporally eternal being, there are still several ways of understanding his relation to time.

Perhaps the simplest way is to say that time has always existed alongside God. This is difficult to state coherently - 'Time has always existed' reduces to the tautology 'There is no moment of time in which time does not exist'. Perhaps it is better to state this view as the simple claim that time is not a contingent, created thing like the universe.

A second possibility is espoused by Augustine[21]. He says that time was created by God, exists, and then will cease to exist. Before the creation of the universe and after the universe ceases to exist there exists not time but timeless eternity. Thus God has control over time - he created it and can presumably destroy it whenever he wants. While this view has some attractions - time or at least our consciousness of it does seem in some sense dependent on the existence of mutable things - a possible problem is that the notion of timeless eternity before the creation of the universe and after it ceases to exist may be just as difficult to understand as the doctrine of timeless eternity itself. This problem may well be solvable, however. In timeless eternity there will presumably be no appearance of temporal succession, i.e. of events occurring before or after each other, which is at least one of the fundamental problems connected with regarding God as timeless at the same time that we live in a world of apparent temporal succession.

A third possibility was suggested by the eighth-century church father John of Damascus[22]. Time has always existed, John appears to say, yet is only measurable when things like the sun and moon exist. Thus before the creation there existed non-measurable time, and after the end of the heavens and the earth non-measurable time will again exist. Measurable time is what exists from the point of creation of the world to the point of its destruction.

Since it is probably the simplest, and since I see no danger in it for Christianity (as I will argue below), I will adopt the first alternative: time was not created; it necessarily exists (like numbers); it depends for its existence on nothing else. Time, perhaps, is an eternal aspect of God's nature rather than a reality independent of God. But the point is that God, on this view, is a temporal being. Past, present and future are real to him; he has simultaneity and succession in his states, acts and knowledge. He knows statements like 'Today is 24 April' and 'My nineteenth birthday occurred before my twentieth'. He has temporal location. It makes good sense to say: 'God exists today' and 'God was omniscient on Napoleon's birthday'. And he has temporal extension. It makes good sense to say 'God existed during the entire period of the Punic wars' and to ask, 'How long has God existed?' The answer to the latter is: forever.

The three main motives for the theory of timeless eternity, I suggested, were to reconcile human freedom and divine foreknowledge, to retain consistency with other things one says about God, and to exalt God's transcendence as much as possible. As to the first, I believe foreknowledge and freedom can be reconciled without appealing to any doctrine of timelessness, and I will try to do so in Chapter 4. As to the second, I do not believe that anything I say about God in this book (or indeed anything said about God in the Bible) logically requires that he be timeless. And as to the third, I feel no need to exalt God's transcendence in every possible way. What Christians must do, I believe, is emphasize God's transcendence over his creation in the ways that scripture does and in ways that seem essential to Christian theism. And I do not believe that the Bible teaches, implies or presupposes that God is timeless. Nor do I feel any theological or philosophical need to embrace timelessness.

Nor is there any reason to doubt that a temporal God who is 'in' time just as we are is everything the Judeo-Christian God is traditionally supposed to be. He can still be an eternal being, i.e. a being without beginning or end. He can still be the creator of the universe. He can still be immutable in the sense of remaining ever true to his promises and purposes and eternally retaining his essential nature. (But he cannot be immutable in other stronger senses – see Chapter 3 where this is discussed.) He can still have complete knowledge of all past, present and future events. (If he 'transcends time', it is only in the sense that he has this power – a power no other being has.) He can still be the loving, omnipotent redeemer Christians worship.

Some might still wish to object to this as follows: 'Surely God must be free of all temporal limitations if he is truly God. But a temporal God is not so free. Thus God must be timeless'. The answer to this is that a temporally eternally God such as I have described is free of certain temporal limitations, e.g. he is free of our inability to remember things that happened hundreds of years ago. Furthermore, not even a timelessly eternal God is free of all temporal limitations, for he is actually unable to experience 'before' or 'after'. His nature limits him; he is unable to experience such things, for if he did experience them he would be temporal. There is temporal limitation whichever view we take. It appears that however we look at it, the doctrine of divine temporal eternity is greatly preferable to timeless eternity. So it is the former that I will embrace.

2 Omniscience

Christians typically say that God is all-knowing. Clearly this is because the Bible seems to describe God in this way:

> O Lord, thou hast searched me and known me! thou knowest when I sit down and when I rise up; thou discernest my thoughts from afar.
> Thou searchest out my path and my lying down, and art acquainted with all my ways.
> Even before a word is on my tongue, lo, O Lord, thou knowest it altogether.
> Thou dost beset me behind and before, and layest thy hand upon me.
> Such knowledge is too wonderful for me; it is high, I cannot attain it. (Ps. 139:1-6)

> And before him no creature is hidden, but all are open and laid bare to the eyes of him with whom we have to do. (Heb. 4:13)

> God is greater than our hearts, and he knows everything. (1 John 3:20)

The conviction that God is all-knowing is often expressed by saying that he is omniscient. But what does this term mean? Sometimes omniscience is defined in terms of facts, that is, it is sometimes said that 'God is omniscient' means 'God knows all facts'. But since I wish to talk about truth and falsity in this chapter, I will instead speak of divine omniscience as primarily related to propositions or statements rather than facts. Only lawyers talk about 'true facts' - as if there were a separate set of facts called 'false facts'. (Facts and propositions are closely related, however. Perhaps a fact is merely the state of affairs described by a true proposition. Accordingly, we will occasionally discuss facts as well as propositions.) But precisely how can we then define omniscience in terms of propositions? This is not easy to do, as will soon be seen.

Let us say that there are three criteria that a definition of 'omniscient' must satisfy in order to be acceptable. First, it must be coherent. Second, it must roughly agree with our intuitions about what knowledge is. And, third, for the Christian philosopher at least, an adequate definition of 'omniscient' must agree with what has been revealed in the Scriptures and expressed in Christian tradition about God's knowledge.

The second condition presents considerable problems in itself even before we get to omniscience. Philosophers have debated for centuries about the proper definition of knowledge, and this debate continues to rage. Fortunately, there is no need for me to become involved. For purposes of this book, I will accept what might be called the 'traditional analysis' of knowledge, that is, I will say that knowledge is justified true belief. This means that I know a proposition p if and only if I believe p, p is true, and my belief is based on good reasons or adequate evidence. It is notorious that difficulties can be raised about each of the conditions in this traditional scheme, especially the third,[1] but none of them seem relevant to our concerns here. So I will accept the convenient fiction that the traditional analysis is adequate.

Keeping in mind that I wish to define omniscience in terms of propositions, the most obvious candidate is this: a being B is omniscient if and only if <u>for any proposition p, B knows p</u>. But this won't do: B obviously can't know propositions like <u>2+2=5</u> or <u>A tadpole wrote the B Minor Mass</u>. Obviously, these propositions are false. No one can know them; the second condition of knowledge is not satisfied in such cases.

An obvious remedy appears: a being B is omniscient if and only if <u>for any true proposition p, B knows p</u>. Now it seems quite correct and helpful to say that an omniscient being knows a proposition p if and only if p is true. But unfortunately this definition is problematical too: it does not exclude the possibility of B believing lots of false propositions along with all the true ones. B might believe both the true proposition <u>Balitzer is a bachelor</u> and the false proposition <u>Balitzer is married</u>. Of course the two are logically inconsistent, but B still might (inconsistently) believe both. And clearly we will not want to allow that a being is omniscient who believes some false propositions, even if that being also believes all the true ones.

So we will want to propose a further refinement. Let us now say that a being B is omniscient if and only if <u>for every true proposition p, B knows p; and for every false proposition q, B does not believe q</u>. Further refinements would be necessary if we were to accept the view, held by some philosophers, that there are more than two truth values, i.e. that some propositions are (neither true nor false but) indeterminate. But I do not hold this view, nor do I find the arguments that these philosophers present convincing, and so will suggest no such covering refinements.

There is a difficulty with this last definition, however - a difficulty raised pre-eminently by considerations of time. The problem is that the truth value of at least some propositions apparently changes with the passage of time. (Some philosophers dispute this; I will consider their views presently.) Take an event E that occurs (only) at time T. Now unless God is non-omniscient, he cannot know the proposition <u>E is occurring</u> at any other time than T. If he believes this proposition before or after T, he believes a false proposition and is therefore non-omniscient. Similar things can be said about the propositions <u>E will occur</u> and <u>E occurred</u>: an omniscient being can only know the first before T and the second after T. E is a temporal event; it occurs in time; and it appears that the temporality of E affects at least some of the things that can be known about it, by God or anyone else.

It follows from this, I believe, that God can only be omniscient if he knows both (1) when events occur in temporal relation to each other (before, at the same time, after, etc.), and (2) when events occur in the temporal flow of past, present and future (i.e. whether they occurred, are occurring, or will occur). Now some sentences can be timelessly known because they forever retain the same truth value.   That is, they can be known both by timeless beings and by temporal beings no matter what their temporal location. For example, I take it that the sentences

2 + 2 = 4
In A.D. 1864 Lincoln is president of the United States
World War I occurs before World War II

can be timelessly known. The truth value of these sentences remains the same through the passage of time. But certain other sentences, as we have seen, cannot be timelessly known because their truth value changes with the passage of time. For example, the sentence

Davis is wearing shoes

is true as I write this paragraph at 10:17 a.m. on 16 June, 1982, but it was false at many times before this date and doubtless will again soon be false.

Now some philosophers find this argument unimpressive. They believe that all propositions are such that their truth value never changes and that sentences whose truth value does apparently change can be analysed into, or can be shown to mean the same thing as, or at least can be shown to report the same facts as sentences whose truth values never change. For example, take this sentence (also written on 16 June, 1982):

(1) Ronald Reagan is now president.

This is an example of the sort of sentence whose truth value apparently changes in time: it was not true one hundred years ago nor will it be true one hundred years from now - but it is quite true today.

But the proper analysis of (1), what it really means, so these philosophers say, is something like:

(2) Ronald Reagan is president on 16 June, 1982.

(The 'is' here is a timeless is, and could be read as 'is, was, or will be'.) And this statement, they will say, is eternally true; its truth value never changes. Now let us here leave aside the strong claims that (1) means the same thing as (2) or could be analysed into (2); let us focus instead on the weaker and more careful claim that (1) and (2) report the same fact (in different words). Is this true?

Well, in general how do we go about deciding whether two different sentences report the same fact or facts? I think everyone will agree that the two sentences

(3) Jones is taller than Smith

and

(4) Smith is shorter than Jones

report the same fact. Likewise, everyone will agree that the two sentences

(5) Sontag seldom stutters

and

(6) Kucheman's smallest dog bites

report different facts. But what about (1) and (2) - do they report the same fact, or not?

Let me suggest two closely related criteria which two sentences, S1 and S2, must fulfil before we can correctly conclude that they report the same fact or facts:

(C1): S1 and S2 always have the same truth value, i.e. there is no conceivable state of affairs where one is true and the other is false;

(C2): A person cannot know S1, i.e. the fact or facts it reports, without knowing S2, i.e. the fact or facts it reports.

I am not going to argue for the adequacy of these criteria. They seem acceptable to me - primarily because they seem to work well in cases where we are quite sure ahead of time either that two sentences do (e.g. (3) and (4)) or do not (e.g. (5) and (6)) report the same fact or facts. In fact, (C1) and (C2) seem utterly plausible to me. But I will not try to defend them further.

One point about them should be especially noted, however, namely my emphasis on reporting the same facts (plural). Here I mean to be understood as claiming that if (C1) and (C2) are satisfied for two sentences S1 and S2, then of the facts reported by S1, all those same facts and no others are reported by S2. Without this emphasis, (C1) and (C2) are obviously poor criteria. We can see this as follows: suppose that S1 is '2 + 2 = 4' and that S2 is '2 + 2 = 4 and Nixon lived in Whittier'. It can be fairly claimed that S1 and S2 report at least one identical fact (namely that 2 + 2 = 4) despite the fact that they clearly fail by both criteria (C1) and (C2). We can imagine states of affairs in which S1 is true and S2 is false; and there are probably millions of people who know S1 but not S2. But the point to note is that the failure of these two sentences to satisfy (C1) and (C2) entails that they do not report the same facts, i.e. all and only the same facts. And, obviously, it is the question whether S1 and S2 report the same facts that is important here. For part of what is at issue is whether a timelessly eternal being can be omniscient. If such a being can know some but not all of the facts reported by true statements in which temporal terms appear, he is not omniscient.

Armed with criteria (C1) and (C2), we can ask whether

(1)   Ronald Reagan is now president

(written on 16 June, 1982), and

(2)   Ronald Reagan is president on 16 June, 1982

report the same facts or facts. It does not appear that they do; in fact, they appear to fail by both criteria. Consider (1) and (2) in the light of (C1), for example. We can easily conceive of states of affairs in which (1) is false and (2) is true. This will doubtless be the case in the twenty-first century, for example. Ronald Reagan will not then be president (i.e. it will be false for a twenty-first century philosopher to say, 'Ronald Reagan is now president'), but it will still be true (because it will always be true) that 'Ronald Reagan is president on 16 June, 1982'. We can see this same result via (C2). It is perfectly possible for a twenty-first century philosopher to know (2), i.e. the fact it reports, without knowing (1), i.e. the fact it reports. Doubtless many people will then know (2), but nobody will then know (1) because (1) will then be false. Another way of making the point: the people who know (1) (on 16 June, 1982) necessarily know something -namely, who is president at the time they are speaking - which it is possible for the people who know (2) not to know.

In Chapter 1 I argued that the Christian God is best not thought of as timeless. Here we have support for that conclusion. Since a timeless being can never know at what temporal stage the world is (all time is 'simultaneously present' to such a being), a timeless being cannot be omniscient. If it can truly be said of a given being X that 'X exists on 16 June, 1982' then X has temporal position and is not timeless. And if a being cannot be omniscient unless it knows on 16 June, 1982 that it is 16 June, 1982, and if this fact can only be know by a being about whom it can truly be said that 'It exists on 16 June, 1982', then no omniscient being can be timeless. Thus, again, if God is omniscient, God is temporal; past, present and future are real to him.

Several arguments can be raised against the line (following Prior, Kretzmann and others) I have been taking here. First, Nelson Pike[2] uses a facinating and clever spatial analogy which he calls 'the ten man game'. His aim is to show that a timeless being can know the fact or facts reported by propositions like (1) by means of propositions like (2). Suppose, he says, that Jones, Smith and eight other men are together in a room containing two large painted circles. Suppose further that Smith and Jones are standing together inside one of the two circles and that this fact is observed by Brown, an eleventh man, who is outside both circles. The question is then asked: Where is Jones? Now Smith reports Jones's location by saying

(7)   Jones is here,

and Brown reports it by saying

(8)   Jones and Smith are in the same circle.

Perhaps the sentences spoken by Smith and Brown do not mean the same thing, Pike admits, but they do report the same fact (in different words) and if challenged would be justified in similar ways.

Now I will grant the part about justification - presumably Smith and Brown would indeed engage in similar procedures if asked to verify their statements. But Pike's main point does not follow from this, nor does it appear to be true. (7) and (8) do not report the same facts, for they fail by (C2). Anyone like Smith who knows (7) knows something - namely what circle Jones is in - which a person like Brown who knows (8), need not know. This would in fact be the case for a person who does not know which precise circle Smith is in but only that whichever circle Smith is in, Jones is in it too. That is, (7) and (8) differ in this way: Smith in (7) is necessarily reporting what circle Jones is in; Brown in (8) is not[3].

We can imagine ways of amending Pike's argument slightly to take care of this point,[4] but then it will no longer carry the weight he wants it to carry. For one thing, suppose Pike had claimed that (7) reports the same fact (not as (8) but) as

(8a)   Jones and Smith are in <u>that</u> circle

(said by Brown). If so, this claim might well be correct. But of course (8a) does not provide suport for the temporal point Pike is trying to make with his ten man game, namely, that a timeless being can know the fact or facts reported by propositions like (1) by means of propositions like (2). The sentence 'Ronald Reagan is president at <u>that</u> time' (said by someone who by ostentation indicates 16 June, 1982) does report the same fact as (2). But the sentence runs into precisely the same difficulties I pointed out earlier that (2) does - for the reasons given, it does not report the same fact or facts as (1).

Another possible amendment: Pike might answer the charge that the person who knows (7) knows something that need not be known by the person who knows (8) by changing the game slightly. Suppose that there are now many circles, that Smith finds himself in the same circle as Jones, but that Smith does not know what precise circle he, Smith, is in. Then Smith can say

(7)   Jones is here

without knowing what circle either of them is in. This much is true. But, again, there is no help here for Pike's main claim. For it is surely the case that most of us temporal human beings do indeed know what time it is (what circle we are in). Unlike a timeless being, we can typically state with some precision what time and date it is. When asked what time it is, we can say much more than 'I don't know what time it is, but whatever time it is, it is the same time that it is for Jones'. Thus, however we manipulate the ten man game, it does not appear to establish Pike's point.

The second objection that might be raised against the line I have been taking in this chapter is based on the distinction, made by many philosophers, between sentences and propositions. Paul Helm states the objection as follows:

> But if the expressing of the same proposition by various sentences is allowed, then there seems to be no reason why indexicals should not be replaced by dates and places. Any emotional attachment there may be to expressing a given proposition in one way rather than another is surely irrelevant. What Prior was pleased about in August 1960 is the fact that the final examinations were in June 1960.[5]

Now I have not felt it necessary in this book to make systematic use of the distinction between sentences and propositions, though I have no objection to it and agree that it is a useful distinction in some contexts.

It is quite clear, for example, that we can express what amounts to the same thought or concept or judgment in more than one way. Notice the following:

It is raining.
It is raining here now.
It is true that it is raining.
It is false that it is not raining.

Es regnet.
Il pleut.

If it is true, as it surely seems, that all six of these sentences express in different words the same judgment, then there must be some one thing (the meaning of these sentences?) that is expressed equally by all of them. And if we want we can certainly call that thing a proposition. (Furthermore, the same sentence - e.g. 'I feel poorly' - can in different contexts mean quite different things, i.e. express different propositions.) All this amounts to a relatively innocuous linguistic claim. The important question is whether the substantive epistemological claim Helm thinks follows from it does indeed follow from it. I think not. Take, for example, the statement (made on 16 June):

(9)   It is 16 June.

Given the distinction between sentences and propositions, it is probably true that there are different ways of expressing what (9) says. But does it follow that

(10)   Yesterday was June 16

(said on June 17) is one such way? The substantive epistemological claim that sentences like (10) express the same proposition as sentences like (9) does not follow, as Helm claims it does, from the simple admission that the same proposition can be expressed by various sentences. Of course, some users of the distinction between sentences and propositions accept it as an article of faith that all propositions timelessly retain the same truth value. But why must this be the case? I see no reason to say it is.

But perhaps the problem here is that we have been looking at the wrong statement. Perhaps what reports the same fact as (9) is something like:

(11)   The day on which I utter the words 'It is 16 June' is the one
       day of this year when these words present a true statement.

On the basis of sentences like this, Brian Davies says: 'Thus, A can say "Today is [16 June]" and on [17 June] B can know what A knew, and we can express his knowledge by saying "B knew on [17 June] what A knew on [16 June] when he said "Today is [16 June]"'[6]. But surely this claim is false, for reasons similar to those mentioned earlier. On 17 June (9) is false and (11) true.

The third objection to the line I have been taking is raised by Castaneda[7] and Swinburne[8]. They appeal to a principle they call

(P):
    (P)   If a sentence of the form 'X knows that a person Y knows
              that . . . ' formulates a true statement, then the person X
              knows the statement formulated by the clause filling in the
              blank ' . . . '

Their argument (to be explained below) is that (P) entails that
propositions like (1) and (2) report the same fact. Now Castaneda
calls (P) 'perfectly trivial', and it does seem innocuous and quite
acceptable. By it we can infer that if the statement 'Davis knows
that Kucheman knows that Robbie is paranoid' is true, then the
statement 'Davis knows that Robbie is paranoid' is also true.

    The problem is that it is difficult to see the precise relevance of
(P) to the matter at hand since the sorts of sentences we are
concerned about (e.g. (1) and (2)) do not fit the schema precisely.
Even if we grant the truth of (P), how does it show that (1) and (2)
report the same fact? By itself (P) says nothing about the translation
of sentences containing indexical or quasi-indexical terms into
sentences not containing them or vice versa. (These are terms like
'you', 'I', 'here', 'there', 'now', 'tomorrow', 'this', 'that' - terms that pick
out places, persons, times, events and things by listing their
temporal, spatial or personal relations to the speakers of sentences in
which they are mentioned.) Swinburne argues, however, that (P) can
help us in such cases as long as we are prepared to change the
relevant indexical or quasi-indexical terms in the ways that are
obviously called for. Thus the sentence, 'John knows that Mary knows
that her own house has four bedrooms' does not via (P) entail 'John
knows that her own house has four bedrooms' (which does not even
make sense) but rather 'John knows that Mary's house has four
bedrooms'.

    (P) might help us in the temporal cases we are concerned about if
it warranted a move from

(12)   Timeless being T knows that Davis knows that it is 16 June,
       1982

to

(13)   Timeless being T knows that it is 16 June, 1982.

If this were the point being made, I would agree that (P) allows one
correctly to infer (13) from (12). But I would strongly deny that (12)
can be true: I don't see how a being that has no temporal location or
extension can know what (12) says T knows.

    Swinburne thinks that (P) entails that the same fact is reported by:

(14)   I know that it is now 16 June[9]

(known by A on 16 June), and either:

(15)   I know that A knew yesterday that it was then 16 June

(known by B on 17 June), or:

(16)   B knew on 17 June that on the previous day A knew that it was then 16 June

(known by us on any day later than 17 June). Is this true? Well, for simplicity's sake let's ignore (16). Let's instead ask whether (P), as Swinburne claims, entails that despite their verbal differences (14) and (15) report the same fact, namely <u>that a certain day</u> (which can be picked out in many ways, according to the temporal location of the person who does the picking out) <u>is 16 June</u>.

Does (P) show this? Certainly not by itself. (If it did, (P) would not nearly be so innocent a principle as it seems - in fact, I for one would reject it.) Perhaps (P) can show what Swinburne says it shows with the addition of some new principle about the translation of sentences containing indexical or quasi-indexical terms, but then this new principle would be for me the culprit. Changing the relevant terms in the way Swinburne wants to be free to do changes the item known in many cases (in my opinion). (14) and (15) simply report different facts, as I argued earlier. B does not report the same fact on 17 June when B says 'Yesterday it was 16 June', as A does on 16 June when A says 'Today is 16 June'. The difference I am concerned about has nothing to do with the fact that there are two fact-reporters here, namely A and B. The point holds even if we omit B from the picture. A does not report the same fact on 16 June when A says 'Today is 16 June' as A does when A says on 17 June 'Yesterday was 16 June'. But surely -Swinburne might insist - other people on other days can report what (14) says A knew on 16 June. Not so, I reply. The fact reported by A in (14) can only be known on 16 June; when that day is past this precise fact can no longer be known by anyone.

To adapt an example used by Prior (alluded to earlier in the quotation from Helm), [10] one which I believe has never been refuted, the claim that 'Today is 16 June' (said by A on 16 June) and 'Yesterday was 16 June' (said by A on 17 June) report the same fact does not account for the common human experience of being relieved that a given episode is over. 'Thank goodness that's over', A may say on 17 June if on 16 June A had a particularly distasteful experience - say, a visit to the dentist. The claim that the two statements mentioned above (in the context noted) report the same fact does not square with the sense of relief A feels on 17 June but not on 16 June. On 16 June A may be utterly depressed that the statement 'It is 16 June' is true and on 17 June be overjoyed that the statement 'Yesterday was 16 June' is true.

This is far from denying, of course, that <u>some</u> of the things A knows on 16 June when A says 'Today is 16 June' can be known by A or even by some other person B on 17 June. It can be known by both people on both days, for example, that 16 June is the day that follows 15 June. But there does not seem to me to be any timeless way of capturing what A knows on 16 June that makes A relieved. It is, of course, timelessly true that the day (17 June) on which A says 'Thank goodness that's over' is subsequent to the day of the visit to the dentist. But, again, this truth is surely not what A is relieved about. The fact that the date of the dreaded event is timelessly prior to A saying 'Thank goodness that's over' is always a fact, even before the visit to the dentist. But the statement, 'The dreaded event is over' is only true subsequent to it. That is, what A is pleased about is surely not the fact that the visit to the dentist is prior to his saying 'Thank goodness that's over', for he could know that fact prior to the visit to the dentist and yet not be pleased.

Anthony Kenny[11] adds an acute point: the knowledge on 16 June that 'Today is 16 June' gives A certain powers - e.g. the power to keep appointments made for 16 June, meet deadlines that expire on 16 June, celebrate birthdays that occur on 16 June - that are quite different from the much lessened powers given A by knowledge on 17 June that 'Yesterday was 16 June' (especially if on 16 June A did not realize that it was 16 June).

Castaneda's argument is more complex. He asks us to attend to the following sentences:

(4b) At T1 X knows [tenselessly] that it is [tenselessly] then T1 but not T2, and at T2, later than T1, X knows that it is then T2, but not T1.

(4d) Time T2 is later than T1, and at T1 X knows both (1) that it is then [t1] T1, but not T2, and (2) that someone knows (or would know) at T2 that it is (would be) then [t2] T2 but not T1.

(The bracketed [t1] and [t2] - subscripts in the original - after the two occurrences of 'then' in (4d) are meant by Castaneda to show that 'then' is there what he calls a quasi-indicator having the time referred to in the subscript as antecedent.) He then claims: 'By (P), (4d) entails that at T1 X knew not only the two propositions that according to (4d) he knew at T1, but also the two other propositions that by (4b) he knew at T2'[12].

In other words, Castaneda's claim is that (P) and (4d) together entail that at T1 X knows four facts. At T1 X knows:

(17) that at T1 it is [tenselessly] then T1
(18) that at T1 it is [tenselessly] then not T2

(19)   that at T2 it is [tenselessly] then T2
(20)   that at T2 it is [tenselessly] then not T1.

Is this correct? Well, (17) and (18) present no problem; I agree that at
T1 X knows them. The difficulties arise with (19) and (20). I certainly
agree that at T1 X knows that at T2 it will then be T2 and not T1. No
one will doubt this. But the question is whether (19) and (20) report
the same facts as

(19') It is now T2

and

(20') It is not now T1.

I believe the answer is: obviously not. A person can know (19) and (20)
at any time. But a person can only know (19') at T2 and a person can
only know (20') at some time other than T1.

But perhaps there is more to Castaneda's argument than at first
meets the eye. Let us again consider (P):

(P)   If a sentence of the form 'X knows that a person Y knows
       that . . . ' formulates a true statement, then the person X
       knows the statement formulated by the clause filling in the
       blank ' . . . '

Possibly the point he wishes to stress here is the notion of
tenselessness. Perhaps (P) more plausibly supports the conclusion
Castaneda draws from it if we understand the occurrences of the
word 'knows' in (P) as meaning 'knew, knows, or will know'. What (P) is
saying, then, is something like:

(P')   If at T2 X knew, knows, or will know that Y at T1 knew,
       knows, or will know that it is, was, or will be then [t1] T1,
       then at T2 X knew, knows, or will know that it is, was or will
       be then [t1] T1.

Perhaps Castaneda thinks that (P') is not a different principle from
(P) but a simple substitution-instance of it.

Is (P') acceptable? It depends on what precisely it means. Again,
there is an innocuous interpretation of it and an interpretation that
entails a substantive epistemological claim. If (P') entails only that on
Tuesday I can know 'On Monday it was Monday' or 'On Monday Jones
knew it was Monday', there is no problem. Anyone can accept (P').
But interpreted in this way it does not bear the weight that
Castaneda wants it to bear. However, if (P') entails the much
stronger claim that on Tuesday I can know the fact or facts reported
by 'It is Monday' or can know the same facts reported by Jones when

on Monday Jones said 'It is Monday', (P') is unacceptable for the same
reasons I have been giving all along.

I still wish to hold, then, that God can only be omniscient if he has
full knowledge of temporal reality, i.e. if he knows both when events
occur in temporal relation to each other (before, after, etc.) and
when events occur in the temporal flow of past, present and future.
That is, he must always know what time it is now and in the case of
every event that has ever occurred, is occurring, or will occur, he
must know whether it is past, present or future.

Let us backtrack a bit. We entered this complex topic of
omniscience and time by trying to find an adequate definition of the
word 'omniscient'. The definition we were considering is as follows: a
being B is omniscient if and only if for every true proposition p, B
knows p; and for every false proposition q, B does not believe q. But
now we must take into consideration the fact that the truth-value of
certain propositions (e.g. 'It is now 16 June, 1982') changes with the
passage of time and accordingly that the facts an omniscient being
knows will change from time to time.

There are perhaps several ways of adjusting the above definition to
meet these considerations. I will adopt the simplest, namely, that of
placing temporal indicators in the definition. Accordingly, I will now
define 'omniscient' as follows: a being B is omniscient at time T if
and only if for every proposition p that is true at T, B knows p at T;
and for every proposition q that is false at T, B does not believe q at
T[13].

This, then, is omniscience. But now we must face another question: Is
it logically possible for an omniscient being to exist? Let me now
discuss three fascinating arguments that have been raised against the
possibility of omniscience.

Roland Puccetti argues as follows: let X be an omniscient being,
and let Y be the totality of facts (which X must know fully in order
to be omniscient). Now, says Puccetti, in order for X not just to be
omniscient but to know that X is omniscient (which, if it is fact that
X is omniscient, X must know), X must also know 'something besides
Y', i.e. Z, which is the truth of the statement 'There are no facts
unknown to me'. But it turns out that X logically cannot know Z and
thus cannot be omniscient. In limited factual situations we can know
the truth of certain negative existential statements, e.g. 'There are
no elephants in this room'. But, says Puccetti, Z 'makes an existential
claim which is completely uncircumscribed, spatially and temporally.
Knowing Z, then, would be like knowing it is true no centaurs exist
anywhere, at any time'[14]. Furthermore, X

has to ascertain that the limit of the known, so to speak, is also the
limit of the factual. Yet he can only arrive at the limit of the
known. It makes no sense to imagine X arriving at this limit,

peering beyond it (at what?), and satisfying himself that no further
facts exist[15].

Since X cannot know that X is omniscient, X cannot be omniscient.
That is, there can be no omniscient being.

But surely in reponse to Puccetti we are entitled to wonder why Z
can't be known. Perhaps the world is a 'limited factual situation' to
God just as the room I am in is to me. More importantly, why does
Puccetti claim that Z is 'something besides' Y? It does not seem so.
Notice that if X knows Y, then Z cannot be false when said by X, for
if it is not a fact that 'there are no facts unknown to X', i.e. if there
are facts unknown to X, then X does not know Y (the totality of
facts) after all. Now it might be objected here that the issue is not
whether X knows Y but rather whether X knows that X knows Y. But
surely this is no serious problem: if the statement 'X knows Y' is true,
then it is a fact that 'X knows Y'. And if X knows all the facts (i.e.
Y), it follows that X knows that X knows Y. So Z must be true when
said by X. Accordingly, Z is not 'something besides' Y, as Puccetti
claims, but rather is included in Y - which is what we should have
expected anyway. For if X knows all the facts (i.e. is omniscient)
there are no facts unknown to X - which itself will be one of the
facts X knows. That is, if X knows Y then X knows both Z and the
fact that X knows Z.

But perhaps I have misinterpreted Puccetti. Perhaps he wants to be
interpreted as admitting that Z is not something besides Y but rather
is part of Y (his argument is ambiguous at this point). His claim, then,
would not be that X can know Y but not Z but rather that no
omnipotent being can exist because X cannot even know Y. This is
because:

> In order for X to know he is omniscient, if an X exists, he has to
> set a limit to the knowable . . . . So long as he, like us, can
> conceive there being facts still unknown it will never be
> contradictory to deny he knows Z.[16]

For this is surely incorrect. In order to know Z, X need not set a limit
to the knowable - just the known. It may be conceivable to X that
there are facts unknown to X - but this is no problem as long as it is
in fact false that there are facts unknown to X. It looks as if
Puccetti's elaborate argument fails. It is logically possible for an
omniscient being to exist.

  The other two arguments against the possibility of omniscience are
presented by John Lachs. First, he correctly points out that
omniscience is often defined in terms of knowing true propositions,
i.e. knowing that something is the case. But no being that knows
(only) all the true propositions is omniscient, for much human
knowledge is of the 'knows what it is to . . . ' rather than the 'knows
that . . . ' type. We human beings know what it is to love, experience

sorrow, and be happy, Lachs points out. But, he says, 'I am not acquainted with any way in which it may be shown that the object of knowledge in any of them is a state of affairs or a (true) proposition'[17].

Second, Lachs argues that even if omniscience can be defined in terms of propositions, the notion of omniscience is incoherent, for no beings can ever know all the true propositions. Surely there are certain things that can only be known if they've been experienced. If you've never tasted watermelon (this is not Lachs's example), you cannot know what watermelon tastes like no matter how hard the rest of us try to tell you how it tastes. Similarly, says Lachs, God cannot know (because he cannot understand) true statements about certain psychological states he has never experienced, e.g. doubt. If doubt is 'a consciousness of uncertainty or a sense of vacillation', Lachs says, God (the God of the Judeo-Christian tradition) cannot doubt, cannot fully understand the meaning of the word doubt, and so cannot know true statements like, 'Descartes doubted God's existence'. If God cannot experience doubt, Lachs concludes, 'He cannot fully understand propositions in which the term "doubt" (or any of its synonyms) occurs. If He cannot fully understand such propositions, He cannot in any important sense be said to know them'[18]. Statements about psychological and emotional states of affairs which God has never experienced are forever unintelligible to God.

To Lachs's first objection, it may merely be pointed out that 'knowing what it is to do φ' can indeed (in all cases I can think of, anyway) be understood in terms of combinations of 'knowing that' - type propositions. Even we non-omniscient beings can usually give pretty accurate propositional analyses of 'knowing what it is' to do or experience or be something. This is easy to see in certain cases, e.g. I know 'what it is to be a bachelor', even though I am not a bachelor, because I know the truth of the proposition, 'B is a bachelor if B is an unmarried adult male'. It is probably true that giving propositional analyses of 'knowing what it is to love', 'knowing what it is to experience sorrow', and 'knowing what it is to be happy' is more difficult than this. But I see no reason to deny that an omniscient being could succeed in achieving a correct and exhaustive analysis (perhaps it would take very many propositions) of such 'knowing whats' - analyses which would enable him successfully to recognize any occurrences of such states[19].

As to Lachs's second objection, even if it is true that certain things cannot be known unless experienced, there is nothing to prevent an omniscient being who is also omnipotent from taking whatever steps are necessary to experience them. If God wants to know what watermelon tastes like, why can't he take bodily form and find out? If God wants to know what it is to doubt, why can't he temporarily abandon some of his knowledge - e.g. his knowledge of when the world will end - and know doubt? Of course during that period he would not be omniscient, but unless omniscience is essential to God (using 'God' here as a proper name) I see no reason why he could not do so. And, as I will argue in Chapter 8, there is no good reason to affirm that omniscience is an essential property of God.

But is it true that certain things - e.g. doubt, sin - have to be experienced by people before they can know the true propositions in which they occur? Perhaps it is true for human beings (the watermelon case seems to suggest so, at any rate), but must it be true for God as well? Perhaps not. Just because we can't successfully express the experience of watermelon (or doubt) in propositions, doesn't mean it is impossible to do so. Why can't God, with his ability to read minds and formulate propositions, know precisely how we feel and what we know when we taste watermelon, experience doubt, or even commit sins?

So the above arguments are unsuccessful. It now appears entirely possible for there to exist an omniscient being. There are several further philosophical problems connected with omniscience, especially that aspect of omniscience called foreknowledge. In Chapter 4 I will consider some of them, e.g. whether God knows the result of choices free agents will make in the future (I will say he does); whether foreknowledge causes future events to occur (I will say it does not); and whether divine foreknowledge and human freedom are consistent (I will say they are). But first I must consider in Chapter 3 another problem that concerns omniscience: whether divine omniscience and divine immutability are logically compatible (I will say they are).

3 Immutability

It is part of the Christian tradition that God is immutable. Of course there are several ways in which the sentence 'God is immutable' can be understood, some of which we will explore later. But the notion that God is in some sense changeless is firmly imbedded both in Scripture and in Christian tradition. Here are two relevant biblical texts:

> For I the Lord do not change; therefore you,
> O sons of Jacob, are not consumed. (Mal. 3:6)

> Every good endowment and every perfect gift
> is from above, coming down from the Father
> of lights with whom there is no variation
> or shadow due to change. (Jas. 1:17)

The Bible's witness is that God is not a fickle, capricious god like the gods of the pagans - he can be relied on because he is ever and eternally the same. Not only is there scriptural support for the claim that God is immutable, there are several powerful philosophical arguments in its favour too. Let me now mention four such arguments; later in the chapter I will ask whether they are good arguments.

The first is a famous and simple argument from Plato[1]. Reduced to its essentials, it runs like this:

(1) God is eternally perfect
(2) Any change in a perfect being is a change for the worst
(3) Therefore, God does not change

Now the 'God' Plato speaks of in his writings is different in several respects from the Christian God; nevertheless, the above argument could easily be used by a Christian to argue that the God of Christianity is immutable. It is in this context that I will consider the argument.

The second is found in Aristotle:

(4) God's potentialities are completely actualized
(5) A being changes only if it has unactualized potentialities
(6) Therefore, God does not change.[2]

Again, Aristotle's God is not the same thing as the Christian God; but, again, a Christian could easily use this argument to try to prove that the God of Christianity is immutable. A word of explanation about Aristotle's terminology is required here. Premise (5) assumes that a being changes from one state to another only if before the change it was <u>potentially</u> in the second state - my hair, for example, can become grey only if my hair is now potentially grey. My hair cannot become loquacious or speedy or trangular because it is not now potentially in any of these states. If God has no unactualized potentialities, then on this scheme he cannot change.

The third argument, which has recently been offered by P. T. Geach, is that only an immutable being can coherently be considered the cause or creator of the world. He says:

> If God is changeless, then we may dismiss the question 'Who made God?' - the question of a cause for A does not arise if A is changeless. But if God is changed . . . then God will only be one more ingredient in that aggregate of changeable beings which we call the world, and will not be the Maker of the world. Even if we could consistently think of such a God as causing <u>all the rest</u> of the world (as I do not believe we could, not consistently), even then the causal questions that arise about other changeable beings could rightly be raised about such a changeable God; as Schopenhauer said, you cannot pick up an argument like a cab and pay it off when it has taken you as far as you want to go. So this God would not be God after all, since he, like his so-called creatures, would have to have a cause. So I dismiss any 'rethinking' of God's changelessness; it can lead only to an alien and incoherent view of the Divine.[3]

Keith Ward[4] similarly argues that only an immutable being can be the sustaining ground of change in the world; only if God is changeless do we have a guarantee of the stability, regularity and ordered continuity of temporal change. If God is mutable, he might cease to exist or cease to be the sustaining ground of the world.

Finally, Geach also argues that only if God is good, almightly and changeless can we have the absolute confidence in him and his promises that Christians typically have. If God is mutable, no such guarantee exists, and Christianity is destroyed[5].

But what precisely does it mean to say that something <u>changes</u>? We all have a usable pre-analytic grasp of the notion of change, but perhaps it would be helpful at this point to make some distinctions among different ways in which a given thing x can change[6].

First of all, x might change in its relations with another thing y. For example, x might at one time be taller than y and at a later time be shorter than y. Or x might be unknown to y at one time and known to y at a later time. When such a relationship changes, we know for sure that either x or y has changed (or both) in some non-relational way, but we do not know for sure that x has non-relationally changed. For example, x might have remained precisely the same in height but become shorter than y because y grew. In such a case, let us say that x has been subject to 'relational change'.

Second, x might change in position or location; this is what I will call 'positional change'. Now some positional changes are also relational: perhaps x was north of y and is now south of y despite having remained motionless; if so, y has obviously moved. But changes in location involving motion on the part of x are what I mainly have in mind here, e.g. when x was north of y and is now south of y because x rather than y has moved.

Third, a thing might change in age. I will call this 'pure temporal change' because I am speaking only about growing older (or younger if that were causally possible) and not about the process of decaying or ageing which the passage of time normally entails - e.g. getting grey, developing wrinkles, etc. Now all things (except timeless things, if there are any) are subject to pure temporal change; this is part of what we mean by the 'passage of time'.

The final category is what I will call 'alteration'. It includes all the sorts of change not included in any of the first three categories. It is change entailed by having a (certain type of) property at one point in time and not at another. I add the parenthetical proviso to signal that the property must not be one whose change would be relational, positional or pure temporal. Some such changes would be entailed by the following statements being true of x at one point and false at another:

x exists.
x is six feet tall.
x believes y is a liar.
x is wearing a brown sweater.
x is in pain.
x is frowning.
x is extinct.

I do not claim that this four-fold analysis of types of change is rigorous and satisfactory for all purposes. Perhaps my list is incomplete; perhaps the types of change overlap in ways that I have not seen; certainly it is not easy to produce a satisfactory criterion for what counts as a relational change (a problem I will return to later). All I wish to claim is that my analysis is at least initially plausible and satisfactory for the purposes of this chapter.

It should also be noted that I am not using the word 'alteration' honorifically, i.e. as a synonym for 'genuine change'. It is not part of my purpose to deny that relational, positional or pure temporal changes are genuine changes. We might be tempted to do so in the case of relational change - there is a sense in which we might want to say, for example, that a man can become hated or a woman shorter than her daughter without themselves being different than they were before. But the problem is that the reverse intuition is at least equally plausible: the man who becomes hated is (really) different just in that one more person than before detests him; the woman who becomes shorter than her daughter is different just in that she is now shorter rather than taller than her daughter. These are relational changes, to be sure, but I believe they are real changes none the less.

We certainly can ask, however, which of the above sorts of changes are relevant to the theological claim that God is immutable. And clearly the answer is that it is the fourth. As to the first, not even the classical defenders of immutability would deny that God changes relationally, e.g. at one point has the property of not being loved by Augustine and at another point has the property of being loved by him. As to the second, since according to the Christian tradition God is an immaterial being, God is not subject to positional change. And as to the third, what you say about it depends on your view of God's relation to time. Those who say that God is timelessly eternal will deny that he is subject to pure temporal change - he does not 'grow older'. Those like me who say that God is temporally eternal will affirm that God is subject to pure temporal change but will deny that this need imply that he changes in any other way. It looks, then, as if it is primarily the final category of change, alteration, that is importantly relevant to the theological claim that God is immutable. Accordingly, when I hereafter use the term 'immutable being' (and similar terms) I refer to a being that undergoes no <u>alteration</u> (whether or not it undergoes other sorts of change); and when I use the term 'change' it is <u>alteration</u> that I have in mind (unless otherwise indicated).

As just noted, there is a close connection between the doctrine of timelessness, discussed in Chapter 1, and immutability.   Often theologians have considered them together. Despite my rejection of timelessness as a property of God, it is well to point out here that any being that is timelessly eternal is also immutable (in the sense of undergoing no alteration). A being that has no temporal location or extension clearly cannot have a given property at one time and not have it at another. (It also cannot be subject to locational or pure temporal change either, although it might well be subject to relational change - a given timeless being z might be thought about by a given person at a certain point in time and not be thought about by that person at another point in time.) However, just because a being is temporally eternal does not mean that it must be changeless in <u>any</u> sense. I have argued that God is temporally eternal and I will soon argue that there are at least certain sorts of alterations that God must be subject to.

Norman Kretzmann[7] has argued that divine omniscience is logically inconsistent with divine immutability, i.e. that there cannot exist a being that is both omniscient and immutable. How does omniscience enter the picture? In this way: if the world itself is changeless or static (as some philosophers, e.g. Parmenides, have argued) there is no problem. God can be both omniscient and immutable. But if changes do occur in the world, as surely all rational persons will admit, there is a problem. For if God is omniscient he must know about all the changes that occur in the world (e.g. my hair being brown in 1982 and grey in, say, 1990). To know change is to be changed. Thus God cannot be both omniscient and immutable.

The sentence 'To know change is to be changed' requires explanation. Suppose that I live until 1990 and that my hair is then grey. God will then know the sentence 'Davis's hair is grey'. But this is a sentence God cannot know in 1982, since my hair is now (in 1982) brown and not grey. Thus God will change between 1982 and 1990. He will come to know something he didn't know (because he couldn't have know it) before. This can be shown by appealing just to the passage of time itself, i.e. apart from any changes that occur in physical objects (like my hair) with the passage of time. Today, I presume, God knows the sentence 'Today is 7 June, 1982'. (Don't object by raising Einsteinian notions about time; I can easily amend my sentence to account for such matters. For example, I might have said, 'At the time in Claremont that Davis writes this sentence it is 7 June, 1982 in Claremont', or some such locution.) Now since God didn't and couldn't have known this sentence yesterday (yesterday he knew the quite different sentence 'Today is 6 June, 1982'), he has changed, i.e. altered, from yesterday to today. He now knows something he didn't know before.

It might be objected here that we are talking about changes not in God but in created things like time or my hair. Geach, for example, takes this line. Suppose, he says, that in 1939 God knows the proposition 'Hitler is alive' and that in 1970 he knows the proposition 'Hitler is dead'. Then 'the description we give of God's knowledge concerning Hitler has to be different after Hitler's death; it is manifest that there has been a change on Hitler's side, and that this, in view of the logic of omniscience, makes a difference to what we can truly say about God's knowledge; it is not manifest that there must have been a real change of mind on God's side'[8].

Now the expression 'change of mind' is ambiguous. Geach is quite correct that we are not talking about a change of mind in God if this expression means, as it sometimes does, that at T1 God intended to perform a given action at T3 but at T2 decided instead not to perform that action at T3. But we surely are talking about a change of mind in God if that simply means that God had a certain belief at T1 which he did not have at T2. Geach admits that in the Hitler case there is a change in what we can truly say about God's knowledge. But surely it follows that if there is a change in what we can truly say about x there is a change in x; if there is a change in what we can truly say about God's knowledge there is a change in God's knowledge. And if this change looks not to be relational, positional or pure temporal, then we are within our rights in concluding that God is not immutable.

However, Geach will doubtless want to claim that the change we are talking about here is relational. Is this correct? I mentioned earlier that a relational change can occur if and only if a non-relational change occurs. If x is taller than y at T1 and shorter than y at T2, x has changed only relationally if x's height has remained the same from T1 to T2. But x can only have changed relationally in this case if some other, non-relational change has occurred, namely y's growing in height. Fortunately, this can help us decide, in the case of any change whatsoever, whether it is relational or non-relational. (Positional change, pure temporal change, and alteration, are all types of non-relational change, but it is the latter that is of major importance here.)

Let us say that a change c that occurs at T1 is relational just in case the following is true of it: it is logically impossible that c (together with every change that is part of c or is logically entailed by c) be the only change that occurs in the universe at T1 [9]. (Keep in mind that we are talking about logical impossibility, so it won't matter if as a matter of fact all changes are caused or occur simultaneously with other changes or even if - as was claimed in classical physics - every change has causal influences everywhere else in the universe.) We can now see that the sorts of changes we have been talking about - changes in a given being's beliefs - are non-relational. It certainly is logically possible, say, that someone's beliefs about Hitler change at a certain point in time without any other change occurring at that point in time.

The situation is complicated in the case of God by the doctrine of omniscience. Those who believe that God is <u>necessarily</u> omniscient will deny that God's beliefs can change without any other changes occurring, for that will entail that God can be in error. If <u>God's belief that Hitler is alive</u> changes at T3 without the quite separate change of <u>Hitler dying</u> at T3 occurring, God believes a falsehood and so is not omniscient. But as I argued in Chapter 2, while a Christian must believe that God is in fact omniscient, there are no good reasons to believe, and several good reasons to disbelieve (including the incarnation), the doctrine that God is necessarily omniscient. And if God is omniscient but not necessarily omniscient, it certainly is logically possible that at a certain point in time God ceases to believe 'Hitler is alive' and begins to believe 'Hitler is dead' without any other changes (not part of or entailed by that change) occurring. Although Geach is quite correct that there is an element of relationality in the change we are discussing (Hitler as well as God is involved), it is clearly a case of alteration. Thus Geach's objection to Kretzmann's line of argument fails.

This is a point where we might be tempted to go back on our

earlier rejection of divine timelessness. Aquinas, at least, develops the doctrine of timeless foreknowledge in a way that can be used to try to solve the present difficulty [10]. God, being timeless, he says, 'sees all things at a glance'. That is, he sees all history before him at a glance in his timeless present; he knows all things together; he sees all things 'in their presentality'. Thus, he does not change. But I do not believe this helps. The metaphor of seeing all things at a glance is interesting and succeeds in capturing our imagination - we think of a spectator on a high mountain surveying a vast spatial panorama. But when considered carefully, the metaphor does not help us solve the present difficulty.

Does a timeless God understand the (possibly mistaken or even illusory) distinctions we make among past, present and future? He must, on pain of being less than omniscient. Thus he must know how each event (according to human beings) occurs in temoral relation to every other event. He must know, for example, that human beings believe that Davis's hair is brown before it is grey and that they believe that Carter was president and that Reagan is now president. This much is clear. But what is quite unclear is how the metaphor of seeing all things at a glance helps us see how God can avoid having these very same beliefs. If he does not have them he is not omniscient because he does not know what events are occuring now (in human time). If he does have them, he changes. Thus we had best see if there is a way other than timelessness to solve the present problem.

I believe the route for the Christian philosopher to follow is happily to admit that there are senses in which God does indeed change, i.e. alter. I am quite prepared to say, for example, that he changes in his knowledge of propositions like Davis's hair is now brown, It is now 7 June, 1982, and the like. If anyone wants to insist that this undermines God's immutability I will admit that God is not immutable (in the sense of the term defined earlier). But was it immunity to changes like these that the doctrine of divine immutability (as suggested, for example, in the biblical passages quoted earlier) was designed to preserve? I doubt it. In fact, it is not easy to read the Bible without forming the strong impression that the God revealed there does indeed change in some senses. To pick an obvious case, very typically God is at one moment angry with someone (the person has sinned) and at a later moment forgives that person (the person has repented). Perhaps these sorts of episodes, which occur frequently in the Bible (see, for example, 2 Chronicles 32: 24-6) can somehow be reconciled with strong notions of divine immutability, but why try to do so? Why is it important that God be completely immune to genuine change?

What was the classical doctrine of divine immutability designed to protect? I believe the answer is this: as I noted earlier, it was designed to preserve the view that God is faithful in keeping his promises, that his basic benevolent nature remains the same; that he is not fickle and capricious and can be relied upon. A god who is mercurial and moody, a god who is benevolent one moment and malevolent the next, is not worthy of worship and is not the Christian God. But the conviction that God does not change in these ways is not at all threatened by the type of change involved in coming to know what date it is or what colour someone's hair is[11]. So we can admit that God changes in these ways without endangering what Christians want to protect.

Recently W. Norris Clarke has skilfully defended a basically Thomistic doctrine of divine immutability. Sensitive to the arguments of Process philosophers and to the concerns of religious people who want to feel that they make a real difference to God, Clarke argues that God, though immutable, can have truly personal relations with us. Clarke's case rests on a basic distinction between (1) the real or intrinsic being of a thing, and (2) its intentional being, i.e. the thing as known or loved. The two are not identical, Clarke says: 'The being of something as known and loved, as in the consciousness of the knower-lover, is not identical with its real natural being as it exists in its own right'[12]. This is a distinction that must be made, he says, lest we fall into the naive view in epistemology that when I know of a raging fire outside of me there is also a real raging fire in my mind.

Now God, Clarke says, is genuinely related to us and thus changes, but only on the intentional order of personal consciousness. Accordingly, we do make a difference to God. But although God as intentional being proceeds from and is grounded in his own real being, change in the order of intentional being does not entail change in the order of real being. God as he is in himself remains immutable. Thus Clarke says:

> But that the intentional content of His loving consciousness should be contingently other because of the unfolding expression of His unchanging personal love for us does not entail that His own intrinsic real being, the level of His own intrinsic perfection, in any way undergoes real change to acquire some new higher mode of perfection not possessed before.[13]

Clarke argues this point both at the level of causality and at the level of knowledge. Divine causality, he says, does not require divine mutability. If A causes B, A certainly changes in its intentional being but not necessarily in its real being. Following Aristotle and Aquinas, Clarke metaphysically 'locates' efficient causality (i.e. says it 'takes place') in the effect, not in the cause as such. 'Hence the affirmation of causal action e.g. in God , taken strictly and solely as such, gives no grounds for affirming any new intrinsic being in the agent'[14].

Nor does God's knowledge of change require change in him: ' . . . multiplicity, materiality, or motion, in the intentional objects of consciousness do not in any way of themselves divide up, materialize, or introduce change into the real being of the knower' [15]. Convinced that God is timeless, Clarke argues that the various 'moments' in God's cognitive consciousness of our temporal lives cannot be temporally distinguished. We cannot make true temporal statements about them - e.g. that they happen at different times, at the same time, that one occurs 'before' another, etc.

Clarke's conclusion is that since God is genuinely related to us at the level of intentional being, this is enough to satisfy the demands of both religious sensitivities and metaphysical argument. There is no need for, and compelling arguments against, saying that God changes in his intrinsic being.

There is much in Clarke's argument that is beyond reproach. I will not deny the appropriateness of his main distinction or his claims about what is required to satisfy religious people. It is also certainly true that a knower need not have a certain property just because an object of its knowledge has it. But serious questions can be raised about Clarke's arguments about both causality and knowledge (though it is only the second that I will stress). All agree that if A causes B, B changes. But need A change too? Well, perhaps not always. But there are at least some sorts of causality which imply change in the cause. If by my own muscular power I cause a heavy barbell to be raised, I too have changed.

But let's waive this point - perhaps, unlike us, God does everything he does effortlessly. For it is at the level of knowledge that the most strains appear in Clarke's argument. It appears that he simply sidesteps or even begs the question against Kretzmann's argument that when the content of God's knowledge changes God changes. Clarke's argument is dense and opaque at the point where he tries to reconcile omniscience and immutability, and even he admits that there are difficulties. He argues that we cannot distinguish temporally between the various 'moments' in God's cognitive consciousness, but surely we can do so at least to this extent - if x and y are two such 'moments' and if x is 'God knowing that it is 6:00 p.m. in Claremont' and y is 'God knowing that it is 6:05 p.m. in Claremont' we can truthfully say that there is a temporal space of five minutes between these two 'moments' in God's cognitive consciousness.

It is quite true that God can know a material being without being material. And I agree that he can know things in motion without being in motion. (I am not sure about God being able to know many different things without introducing multiplicity into his being, so I won't comment on that.) But if Kretzmann is correct - and Clarke has given us no reason to deny that he is - God cannot know a temporal process without being temporal. Acts of knowledge can be immutable and timeless only in so far as the objects known are immutable and timeless. If they are mutable and temporal, then mutability and temporality are introduced into the knower.

'Fine' - Clarke might say at this point - 'I admit that a God who knows temporal succession must himself be subject to temporal succession. But this is only at the level of intentional being, not real being. God as knower changes; God as he is in himself is immutable'. But while one must grant as valid the distinction between God as he is in himself and God as known, surely no such rigid distinction exists between God as he is in himself and God as knower. (There is an ambiguity in Clarke's article at this point - he seems to slip back and forth between these two quite different distincions.) Obviously, what God knows is an aspect of his real being. Again, this does not mean that if God knows material beings he is himself material; but it does mean, for example, that if God knows no material beings at T1 and knows a material being at T2, God has changed (in his real being). It appears, then, that Clarke's argument fails.

But what about the four philosophical and theological arguments for immutability I mentioned earlier? These, someone might say, and not the Bible or Christian tradition or religious sensitivities, are what push us toward the strongest senses of immutability. But I believe each argument, on investigation, turns out to be unconvincing.

As for the first argument, the one from Plato, why must we say that a perfect being cannot genuinely change at all? Some properties of perfect beings seem quite unrelated to their perfection. A circle, for example, can be perfectly circular whether its circumpherence is six inches or eight. A sentence can be grammatically perfect whether it is written in blue ink or green. It is true that there are some changes in God which if they occurred would destroy his perfection. But changes in his knowledge of what time it is or of the present colour of someone's hair, etc. are not such changes. As concerns these sorts of changes I see no reason to admit that 'any change in a perfect being is a change for the worse'.

As for the second argument, the one from Aristotle, I see no reason to say that God has no unactualized potential whatsoever. I would deny, of course, that God is potentially wiser or more benevolent than he is now. But why not admit he now has the unactualized potential to know that my hair is grey or that it is the year 1989? Are there any philosophical or theological dangers here? I certainly see none.

The third argument, from Geach, is condensed and complex. There are many things that could be said about it, but perhaps the most crucial is the fact that it seems to depend on certain dubious assumptions that are not argued for. Suppose we call the set of all created things 'the world'[16]. Now Geach's argument seems to presuppose the following two propositions:

(7) All changeable things are caused (and are thus part of the world)

(8) All unchangeable things are uncaused (and are thus not part of world).

Perhaps (8) is too strong; perhaps Geach only means that unchangeable things do not have to be caused, that causal questions about their origin do not require an answer. At any rate, he certainly is committed to (7), which allows him to argue that if God is changeable he is caused and thus is not God after all.

Now there is a difference that must not go unnoticed between two ways in which a thing can be 'caused'. A thing can be <u>caused to exist</u> and a thing can be <u>caused to change</u>. It may be true that every change in every mutable thing is caused. But it does not follow from this that every mutable thing must be caused to exist, i.e. must be contingent. Why cannot there be a mutable necessary being? I see no reason to deny that such a being can exist. Thus (7) is a dubious premise because it seems quite possible for there to be a changeable being that is uncaused in the sense of not having been caused to exist. And I see no reason why God cannot be such a being - an eternal necessary being who changes (in some ways). (Furthermore, (8) is dubious because it seems quite possible for there to exist an eternal, immutable being that is caused to exist, e.g. a changeless being which always has and always will exist and yet depends on God for its existence at every moment that it exists.)

The fourth argument, from Geach, has an element of truth in it. It certainly is true that God must be changeless in some sense if we are to have the absolute confidence in him that Christianity teaches that we are to have. But surely immutability in the sense of immunity to all genuine change is not required here. All that is needed is the type of changelessness I have argued for - that God's basic nature and faithfulness to his promises remains the same. Christianity is indeed destroyed if God is not changeless in this sense, but I see no reason to say that Christianity is destroyed if God is not immutable.

The conclusion I reach, then, is this: there are important senses in which God is immutable and there are also senses in which he changes. Once the distinction between these senses is grasped, the problem of omniscience and immutability can be solved, and a theologically and philosophically adequate notion of God's changelessness becomes available.

4 Foreknowledge

Christians typically believe the following two propositions:

(1) God is omniscient

and

(2) Human beings are free.

Are they consistent? In order to decide, we must first ask what they mean. We have discussed omniscience already. I concluded that a being B is omniscient at T if and only if for every proposition p that is true to T, B knows p at T; and for every proposition q that is false at T, B does not believe q at T. As noted in Chapter 2, I have no wish to deny that there are true and false propositions about future states of affairs (as some philosophers have done). Thus it follows that omniscience includes foreknowledge, which we can roughly say is knowledge of the truth-value of propositions about future states of affairs. For example, I believe the proposition 'Davis will wear shoes tomorrow' is true today, and if it is true today, i.e. if I will wear shoes tomorrow, an omniscient being knows today that it is true - and, if this being is eternally omniscient, he knew it millions of years ago.

Let us say that human beings are 'free' when two conditions are satisfied: first, when they are not coerced, i.e. when they are able to do what they want to do; and second, when they have genuine alternatives, i.e. when it is actually in their power, under the same antecedent conditions, to do something or not to do it. Another way of stating this second point is: beings are free when they do something if they could have failed to do it, i.e. could have done something else, given the same antecedent conditions. (Soft determinists typically restrict freedom to the first condition, and if they state something like the second it is with the quite different stipulation that persons are free if they could have done other than what they did given different antecedent conditions. But the sense of 'free' that raises the problem of compatibility with divine foreknowledge - and that I am interested in defending - includes my second condition.)

Now some philosophers have argued that (1) and (2) are inconsistent. Their argument is that God's foreknowledge, say, that I will mow my lawn tomorrow is inconsistent with my not mowing my lawn tomorrow. That is, God's foreknowledge that an event will occur is a sufficient condition for that event to occur. This is because if someone knows something, it must be true. 'I know that Feldmeth is in Claremont, but Feldmeth is not in Claremont', does not make sense. Given that knowledge is justified true belief, if I genuinely know that Feldmeth is in Claremont, then Feldmeth is in Claremont; if Feldmeth is not in Claremont then I do not know that Feldmeth is in Claremont (but perhaps merely believe it). This clearly entails that if God knew yesterday that I will mow my lawn tomorrow, I will mow my lawn tomorrow. And does this not rule out freedom (these philosophers would ask)? For if I will mow my lawn tomorrow it sounds as if I have no choice but to mow my lawn tomorrow, i.e. as if it is not in my power not to mow my lawn tomorrow. And this seems to rule out being free, in the above sense. Thus, so it seems, if God knew yesterday that I will mow my lawn tomorrow I am not free not to mow my lawn tomorrow; and if God is omniscient no one is ever free.

But let me try to reconcile divine omniscience and human freedom by means of the following statement. It is sometimes, I hold, a true statement:

(3)   What God knew yesterday is contingent upon what I will
       freely decide to do tomorrow.

The cases where (3) is true are those cases where I am free to decide what I shall do. (Obviously there are many cases where I am not so free, e.g. I am not free to decide whether or not to jump over Appleby Hall tomorrow morning.) What I mean is this: if it is true, say, that I am free to decide whether or not to mow my lawn tomorrow, then both mowing my lawn and not mowing my lawn are real options for me; it is up to me to decide which I shall do; and whichever I decide to do, God will have known yesterday and, indeed, from eternity that I will do it.

Is this claim coherent? I believe it is, and I will now try to defend it. First let me note that all I need to show is that (3) is possibly true. My aim in this chapter is to show that (1) and (2) are consistent. Let us say that two propositions are consistent just in case it is possible for them both to be true. One way of showing that (1) and (2) are consistent is to find some third proposition (in this case it will be (3)) which is consistent with (1) and which together with (1) entails (2)[1]. Now (1) and (3) certainly do entail (2) (assuming that I am a human being), and (3) at least to me seems consistent with (1) ((1) doesn't say what the truth of the proposition God knows is contingent upon). But are (1) and (3) consistent? Probably the most promising route for a critic who wants to argue that they are not is to try to impugn the consistency of (3) itself; naturally, if (3) is inconsistent it cannot be consistent with (1). So the question before us now is: Is (3) consistent? (Of course even if I could prove that both (1) and (3), taken separately, are consistent, that wouldn't guarantee that their conjunction is consistent. But since the critic can derail my strategy by arguing that (3) is inconsistent, I need to argue that (3) is consistent.)

Unfortunately I know of no obvious way of showing that (3) is possibly true. In fact, I know of no good way of showing that any proposition which is not known to be true is consistent. Of course all true propositions are possibly true (and so are all necessarily true propositions), and so, if 'Roth wears a crew cut' is true, then 'Roth wears a crew cut' is also consistent. But since (3) is not known to be true, I know of no way to prove it is consistent. What we normally do in such cases, as I suppose, is appeal to what might be called intuition, i.e. we simply ask ourselves whether the proposition in question seems consistent. Thus neither

(4)   There is life on Mars

nor

(5)   there are square circles on Mars

is known to be true, but (4) simply seems to us to be the sort of proposition that is possibly true, while (5) does not seem so to us.

Now (3) seems consistent to me: I can detect no contradiction in (3) or other reason to call it incoherent. But others apparently would claim that (3) is inconsistent. Perhaps the best I can do, then, in order to substantiate my belief that (3) is possibly true, is simply to reply to the arguments of those who claim that (3) is inconsistent. Of course, even if I succeed in doing so, (3) might still be inconsistent. Like any proposition whose truth-value is unknown, we may later discover an argument that demonstrates its incoherence. Nevertheless, if (3) seems consistent to me (as it does) and if I can successfully answer the arguments of those who claim that it is inconsistent, then I believe I am within my rights in holding (3) to be possibly true.

I know of only two arguments that (3) is inconsistent, but both are powerful. The first runs something like this: 'But if God knew yesterday that I will mow my lawn tomorrow, then it is true that I will mow my lawn tomorrow, and thus I am not free not to mow my lawn tomorrow.' The first part of this claim is obviously true and I will not dispute it: if God knew yesterday that I will mow my lawn tomorrow then it is <u>true</u> that I will mow my lawn tomorrow. (This is no special property of God, however: if <u>anyone</u> knew yesterday that I will mow my lawn tomorrow it is true that I will mow my lawn tomorrow.) But the rest of the claim - that I am therefore not free not to mow my lawn tomorrow - does not appear to me to follow from what precedes it, and thus I wish to dispute it.

One way in which this argument for the inconsistency of (3) might be expressed is as follows:

(6)   God believes that Jones will do x.

(7)   It is not possible for God to believe a falsehood.

(8)   Therefore, it is not possible for Jones not to do x.

Now this argument is ambiguous - it might be interpreted in one of two ways, but unfortunately neither produces a convincing result. The two interpretations turn on the meaning of (7). On the one hand, we might take (7) to mean that the proposition 'God believes p and p is false' is necessarily false. On this interpretation (7) may be true, but the argument is invalid - (8) does not follow from (6) and (7) (interpreted in this way) [2]. On the other hand, we might take (7) to mean, 'If God knows p then not-p is not possible.' And if we take (7) in this way the argument is valid, [3] but there seems to be no reason to grant that (7) (interpreted in this way) is true. For (7) now says that God believes only necessary truths, which is obviously implausible.

But a much stronger argument against (3) (where the term 'God' in (3) refers to an essentially omniscient being) has been formulated by Nelson Pike[4]. Essentially, Pike asks us to consider the following propositions:

(9)   God existed at T1, and God believed at T1 that Jones would do x at T2, and it was within Jones's power at T2 to refrain from doing x.

(10)   It was within Jones's power at T2 to do something that would have brought it about that God held a false belief at T1.

(11)   It was within Jones's power at T2 to do something that would have brought it about that God did not hold the belief he held at T1.

(12)   It was within Jones's power at T2 to do something that would have brought it about that any person who believed at T1 that Jones would do x at T2 (one of whom was, by hypothesis, God) held a false belief and thus was not God - that is, that God (who by hypothesis existed at T1) did not exist at T1.

What Pike claims is that (9) implies either (10), (11) or (12), all of which are contradictory or otherwise unacceptable, and that (9) must therefore be rejected. Now Pike's (9) seems closely related to or at least consistent with my (3), and if (9) must be rejected, then undoubtedly (3) must be rejected too, and my attempt to reconcile divine omniscience and human freedom collapses.

But I believe Alvin Plantinga has successfully rebutted Pike's claim[5] . Using a possible worlds ontology, he denies that (9) entails either (10), (11) or (12). In the next four paragraphs, let me briefly summarize Plantinga's argument. First, does (9) entail (10)? It does not seem that it does: had Jones refrained from doing x at T2 it would follow that a proposition which God <u>did in fact believe</u> would have been false, but this is surely unproblematical. What does not follow is (as (10) implies) that God (who is by hypothesis omniscient) <u>would have believed</u> that Jones would do x at T2 under these conditions. So (10) does not appear to follow from (9). What does appear to follow is:

> (10') It was within Jones's power at T2 to do something such
>   that if he had done it, then a belief that God <u>did hold</u>
>   at T1 <u>would have been</u> false.

But how does (10') create a problem? It certainly does not entail that Jones can make God hold a false belief. What (9) says is that God believes that Jones will do x at T2 and that Jones has the power not to do x at T2. And of course it follows that if God knows at T1 that Jones will do x at T2 then Jones <u>will</u> do x at T2 (as I admitted earlier). But if it is still logically possible at T2 for Jones to refrain from doing x - as (9) suggests that it is - we can capture this possibility by bringing in the modal notion of possible worlds.

Imagine a possible world W, different from the actual world, where Jones refrains from doing x at T2. Let us call the actual world 'Alpha'. Now in W, a belief that God holds in Alpha is false: so if, instead of Alpha, W had been actual, then a belief God holds in Alpha would have been false (and either (10), (11) or (12) would follow). But it does not follow that in W God holds the false belief that Jones will do x at T2 - unless it is true that an omniscient being must hold the same beliefs in all possible worlds. But this is obviously not true: since God is omniscient we can be quite sure that had W and not Alpha been actual he would have held the correct belief that Jones will refrain from doing x at T2. Thus it does not appear that (9) entails (10), i.e. that (9) entails that Jones has the power to make God hold a false belief.

What about (11) - does it follow from (9)? The problem is that (11) is ambiguous. It is unclear which of the following properly explicates (11):

> (11') It was within Jones's power at T2 to do something such
>   that if he had done it, then at T1 God would have held
>   a certain belief and also <u>not</u> held that belief.

> (11") It was within Jones's power at T2 to do something such
>   that if he had done it, then God would not have held a
>   belief that in fact he did hold.

(11') entails that Jones can bring about a contradictory state of affairs, but it does not appear that (9) entails (11'). (11") does appear to follow from (9), but is perfectly innocuous: it does not follow from (11") that God did hold a belief that he didn't hold.

And finally, what about (12) - is it entailed by (9)? Again it seems not. What (9) actually entails is:

> (12') It was within Jones's power to do something such
>   that if he had done it, then anyone who believed
>   at T1 that Jones would do x at T2 would not have
>   been God.

That is, if Jones had not done x at T2, and if God had believed at T1 that Jones would do x at T2, then God would have held a false belief and would not have been God. But in a world W where Jones does not do x at T2, God does not have to hold the same beliefs that he does in Alpha, and in this case, he certainly won't.

Perhaps the basic intuition behind this critique of Pike can be expressed as follows. It is obvious that the following propositions are quite different:

> (13)   Jones will not mow his lawn tomorrow,

and

> (14)   Jones cannot mow his lawn tomorrow.

I believe that (13), but not (14), is entailed by 'God knew yesterday that Jones will not mow his lawn tomorrow.' Nor is (14) entailed by (13). There simply is no acceptable rule of logic that allows these entailments.

This point can be argued for in another way as well. Take the following argument:

> (15)   God knows at T1 that Jones will do x at T2.
> (16)   Therefore, Jones will do x at T2.

This argument is valid, as I have admitted all along: if (15) is true then (16) is true. Now Pike claims that the problem of omniscience and human freedom is created by the doctrine of God's essential omniscience, that is, the doctrine that it is part of God's essence to be omniscient or that he is omniscient in all possible worlds. Human foreknowledge and non-essential divine foreknowledge do not create the problem, he says. But contrary to Pike, I believe the difficulty is caused by (16), not by (15), nor by the claim that God is essentially omniscient. For if (15) did not entail (16) (or if the doctrine of God's essential omniscience did not entail propositions like (16)), there would be no problem of reconciling divine foreknowledge and human freedom.

So the problem can be stated in this way: is (16) compatible with the following proposition?

(17) It is within Jones power not to do x at T2.

I believe that (16) and (17) are consistent, for notice the following proposition:

(18) It is within Kucheman's power not to allow Bruno to
       enter his office, but Kucheman will allow Bruno to
       enter his office.

This, I believe, is a clear, logically unproblematical proposition that no one would have difficulty understanding. But (18) entails both

(19) Kucheman will allow Bruno to enter his office

and

(20) It is within Kucheman's power not to allow Bruno to
       enter his office.

If (18) is consistent (as I believe it is), then (19) and (20) are consistent. But (19) and (20) are logically parallel to (16) and (17) (with 'at T2' omitted). Thus, (16) and (17) are consistent.

But Pike has now answered Plantinga[6]. What he says is that other considerations beside logical considerations must come into play in deciding on the truth value of propositions like

(21) It is within Jones's power to refrain from doing x
       at T2.

That is, in order to prove propositions like (21) it will not do merely to show (as Plantinga has done) that it is logically possible for Jones to refrain from doing x at T2, that there is a possible world in which Jones refrains from doing x at T2. Pike says:

> The question is not whether there is just some possible world
> or other in which Jones refrains from doing x at T2. What must
> be asked is whether there is a possible world, having a history
> prior to T2 that is indistinguishable from that of the actual
> world, in which Jones refrains from doing x at T2. The answer is
> that there is not.[7]

In no world in which God believes at T1 that Jones will do x at T2 does Jones refrain from doing x at T2. Thus, Pike concludes, it is not within Jones's power to refrain from doing x at T2.

It is easy to see that at least part of what Pike is claiming is correct (nor is there any reason to think Plantinga would dispute it). It is true, for example, that the claim 'It is within my power to do x' means more than 'It is logically possible for me to do x.' It is logically possible for me to run the mile in twenty seconds flat, but this is not within my power. Roughly, let us say that an act is in my power if my doing it is both logically and non-logically possible. Pike never spells out the notion that I am calling 'non-logical possibility' (perhaps it is something like causal possibility), but his claim that logical possibility is not enough is surely correct. And Pike is also correct in saying that in any possible world in which God believes at T1 that Jones will do x at T2, Jones <u>will</u> do x at T2. That is, there is no possible world in which God believes at T1 that Jones will do x at T2 and Jones fails to do x at T2. Let us call all the possible worlds in which God believes at T1 that Jones will do x at T2 <u>P-worlds</u>. Then it is true that in all P-worlds Jones does x at T2.

But does it follow from this that in no P-world is it within Jones's power to refrain from doing x at T2? That is, does it follow that there is no world in which God believes at T1 that Jones will do x at T2 and in which it is within Jones's power to refrain from doing x at T2? Pike appears to believe that this does follow, but I cannot see how it does.

What Pike claims is that Plantinga erred in failing to restrict his analysis to P-worlds. That is, he says, the claim that it is within Jones's power to refrain from doing x at T2 (despite God's belief at T1 that Jones will do x at T2) is not a claim about all logically possible worlds but is a claim about all P-worlds. But it is difficult to see precisely how this restriction represents an advance in solving the present problem. For it is quite beyond dispute that in all P-worlds Jones <u>will</u> do x at T2; Pike and Plantinga can agree on this point. But merely asking us to reduce the scope of our interest to P-worlds does not seem to me to show that it is not within Jones's power to refrain from doing x at T2 (though this power, if he has it, will obviously not be exercised). For surely the following inference is invalid:

(22) In no P-world will Jones refrain from doing x at T2.

(23) Therefore, in no P-world is it within Jones's power to refrain from doing x at T2.

If Pike does wish to claim that (22) entails (23), he can ask us to accept the principle that it is not in my power to do a given act y if doing y is not logically possible for me. Thus he can argue as follows:

(22) In no P-world will Jones refrain from doing x at T2.

(22a) Therefore, in no P-world is it logically possible for
Jones to refrain from doing x at T2.

(23) Therefore, in no P-world is it within Jones's power to
refrain from doing x at T2.

But if this argument is valid, a strange universal fatalism seems to
follow, which many (including Pike, I assume) will not be prepared to
accept. Let us define an A-world as any possible world in which Jones
freely raises her arm at T3. Now notice this argument:

(24) In no A-world will Jones refrain from raising her arm
at T3.

(25) Therefore, in no A-world is it logically possible for
Jones to refrain from raising her arm at T3.

(26) Therefore, in no A-world is it within Jones's power to
refrain from raising her arm at T3.

This seems a strange result indeed, for (26) seems to contradict the
stipulation that A-worlds are worlds in which Jones freely raises her
arm at T3. Now since any action can quite apparently be described in
some such way as this, it follows that no one is ever free, that
everything we ever do is done under circumstances in which no other
act is within our power.

What has gone wrong here? Clearly it is not the second step of the
above arguments (the derivation of (23) from (22a) and (26) from
(25)). For the principle that if doing a given act is logically impossible
for me it is not within my power to do it seems quite reasonable.
Thus the problem must be in the initial step. Now I agree that

(27) In no possible world do I do y

entails

(28) It is logically impossible for me to do y.

But I do not agree that

(29) In no Z-world do I do z

(where Z-world is defined as a possible world in which I refrain from
doing z) entails:

(30) It is logically impossible for me to do z in a Z-world.

The reason for this is that (29) merely says, 'In no world in which I refrain from doing z do I do z.' And this certainly does not entail (30).

The problem here is that the logical possiblity or impossibility of acts is a function of what occurs or does not occur in <u>all</u> possible worlds, not just some. To make statements like (30) is like saying 'If I walk home I cannot fail to walk home' or 'If Teddy Kennedy is ever elected president he cannot fail to be elected president.' Such statements as these, if true, would entail the fatalistic, but false, doctrine that all truths are necessary truths. In fact, they are simply misleading and confused ways of talking.

But leaving this aside, we must still wonder what sort of difficulty Pike has in mind when he says that (15) and (21) cannot both be true.

(21) It is within Jones's power to refrain from doing x at T2.

(15) God knows at T1 that Jones will do x at T2.

I have called it a non-logical difficulty, but what sort of non-logical difficulty is it supposed to be? Pike does not clearly say. Perhaps it is what might be called (using some of Pike's terms) a 'fact-infested' difficulty, or a difficulty that concerns 'actualities not just logical possibilities'. But it is still not clear to me precisely how these propositions are supposed to be inconsistent.

Perhaps we can advance a bit further than this. Pike asks how we might decide whether the following statement is true or false:

(31) It is within my power to jump a ten-foot fence.

His answer, which I believe is quite correct, is that it is inadequate merely to show that my jumping a ten-foot fence is logically possible. What we must look to, he says, are factors like the physical condition of my body, the general scientific principles governing the behaviour of bodies, etc. Let us use the term <u>causal possibility</u> for this. Roughly, let us say that an act is causally possible if it violates no natural law. (My jumping a ten-foot fence is causally impossible because it would violate certain natural laws about gravity and the jumping ability of beings of a certain degree of strength, agility, weight, etc.) Thus it is logically but not causally possible for me to leap a ten-foot fence or run the mile in twenty seconds flat. Is this what Pike means? Perhaps so. But if so, I am still in the dark as to the precise nature of his latest argument, for I do not see what natural laws dictate that it is not within Jones's power to refrain from doing x at T2 even if God does indeed know at T1 that Jones will do x at T2.

But perhaps this is not the end of the matter. Perhaps Pike-like arguments for the incompatibility of (1) and (2) are at heart motivated by the conviction that the past cannot be changed. Perhaps those who advance such arguments believe that this conviction will have to be given up if (1) and (2) are compatible. But fortunately this is not true, as we can see by the following argument in which the conviction that the past cannot be changed is made explicit.

(32)   It is true at T1 that God knew at T1 that Jones will do x at T2.

(33)   T1 is in the past.

(34)   No past truth can be changed.

(35)   The truth at T1 that God knew at T1 that Jones will do x at T2 cannot be changed.

(36)   No one is ever able to do something that cannot be done.

(37)   Jones is not able to do anything that would change the truth at T1 that God knew at T1 that Jones will do x at T2.

(38)   If Jones is able to refrain from doing x at T2 Jones is able to change the truth at T1 that God knew at T1 that Jones will do x at T2.

(39)   Therefore, Jones is not able to refrain from doing x at T2.

The reason this argument is instructive is that it is invalid for the very reasons that Plantinga points out. Premise (38) is the culprit. Why say Jones is able to change a past truth? Why not just say Jones is able at T2 to do something which entails that God held a different belief at T1 than he in fact did hold at T1? As long as it is clear that this is an ability which in this case Jones does not exercise, there appears to be no major problem[8].

The only way I can see that (39) can validly be derived is via two new premisees, the first of which is entailed by (32):

(32a) Jones will do x at T2,

and

(37a) It is never in anyone's power to do something that he or she will not do.

That is, the following argument appears to be valid:

(32)   It is true at T1 that God knew at T1 that Jones will do x at T2.

(32a) Jones will do x at T2.

(37a) It is never in anyone's power to do something that
he or she will not do.

(39) Therefore, it is not in Jones's power to refrain from
doing x at T2.

But the obvious problem here is that if (37a) is true, fatalism is true.
Fortunately, however, (37a) is not only false but obviously false.

Of course it might be objected to this fatalistic version of the (32)-
(39) argument that the truth value of propositions cannot be dated,
that is, that propositions are either timelessly true or timelessly
false, while God's beliefs can be dated (as they are in (9)-(12)). Now I
am not in favour of the view that all truth values are timeless, but
this is a controversial and thorny issue (see Chapter 2), and I do not
wish to raise it again. Fortunately we do not need to, for the
following similar argument for fatalism will do the job equally well:

(40) It is timelessly true that Jones will do x at T2.

(41) It is not in anyone's power to make a timeless truth
false.

(42) If it is Jones's power to refrain from doing x at T2
it is in Jones's power to make a timeless truth false.

(43) Therefore, it is not in Jones's power to refrain from
doing x at T2.

This argument, in my opinion, is no more sound than its predecessor.
But if it is the conviction that the past cannot be changed that
motivates Pike-like arguments for the incompatibility of (1) and (2),
we can now see that such arguments do not differ essentially from
certain classical arguments for fatalism.

It is quite true, of course, that the past cannot be changed. Neither
Plantinga nor I have said anything that denies this. But it now appears
that the principle that the past cannot be changed cannot be
exploited by Pike for his purposes. Again I conclude that a rational
person can believe in both divine omniscience and human freedom.

The second objection against (3) is that it appears to allow that an
event can cause something to happen prior to it - or, alternately, that
an event can be caused by something that will happen after it. It
seems, that is, that (3) says roughly that 'what I will freely do
tomorrow' causes 'God to know yesterday what I will freely do
tomorrow'. But this is incoherent: obviously (as Hume claimed and as
all our intuitions seem to confirm), a cause must be temporally prior
to its effect. And since (3) appears to violate this basic intuition, (3)

must be rejected, along with my attempt to use (3) to reconcile (1) and (2). But this objection is surely confused. (3) doesn't claim that it is what I will do at T2 that causes God to know something at T1 (i.e. what I will do at T2) - that would be incoherent. What (3) claims is that it is God's ability to foreknow, exercised at T1 that causes God to know at T1 what I will do at T2 - and this does not make the effect prior to the cause.

But perhaps the criticism is more subtle than this. Perhaps the critic is interpreting (3) as claiming that God's exercising at T1 his ability to foreknow is caused by what I will do at T2. And this, the critic might say, is clearly incoherent because it violates Hume's principle that causes must antedate their effects. But the answer to this is that the relationship is contingent upon is not the same thing as the relationship is caused by. (3) does indeed claim that an event that occurs at T1 (God's foreknowledge) is contingent upon an event that occurs at T2, but this is not the same thing as saying that it is caused by that event. And Hume's causal principle does not seem to hold in cases of contingency relationships; earlier events or states of affairs can be logically contingent upon later ones. Take for example the statement, 'Davis will be a grandfather.' I believe this statement is at present either true or false. It might be true and it might be false; but its truth value is now unknown to me and, I believe, to all non-omniscient knowers. But whichever truth value it now has is clearly contingent upon certain events that will or will not occur in the future.

Of course someone might claim that this sort of knowledge of an event before it occurs is precisely what is incoherent or that this sort of foreknowledge just cannot occur. But that is another matter entirely. What we are concerned with here is the compatibility of foreknowledge with human freedom. And if divine foreknowledge is possible, it looks as if the second objection to (3) also fails.

Now someone might claim at this point that it is precisely the truth of (1) that (causally) rules out freedom here. That is, it might be claimed that it is precisely God's foreknowledge that Jones will do x at T2 that causes Jones to do x at T2. I find this view extremely puzzling: I cannot see how knowledge, even divine foreknowledge, can be causally efficacious in the required way. Surely human foreknowledge does not have this quality. If I now know (as I believe I do) that 'Tomorrow will be Saturday', this foreknowledge surely does not cause it to be Saturday tomorrow. Doubtless divine foreknowledge is quite different from human foreknowledge, but how does this affect the case?

Aquinas is sometimes cited as holding that divine foreknowledge causes future events,[9] but I believe this is in error. What Aquinas says is not that God's foreknowledge per se causes things to happen, but that 'the knowledge of God is the cause of things when the will is joined to it' [10]. He does begin the 'I answer that' section of the relevant article with the bold claim, 'The knowledge of God is the cause of all things' [11]. But he then gives an illustration that makes us wonder if this is exactly what he means: 'The knowledge of God', he says, 'is to all creatures what the knowledge of the artificer is to things made by his art.' The reason we wonder about this is because it surely does not seem that the potter's knowledge of how to make a pot is a sufficient condition for a pot to be made. There may be no clay in the neighborhood, for example. And happily it turns out that this is not what Aquinas is claiming, either for potters or for God. What he apparently means is that God's knowledge causes things to happen when he also wills them to happen.

Aquinas cites Origen, who had claimed that God knows future events because they are future and not that they are future because he foreknows them. In response to this, Aquinas says: 'Origen spoke in reference to that aspect of knowledge to which the idea of causality does not belong unless the will is joined to it.' And this last admission is crucial, for if there are such things as _free_ acts (as defined earlier), God's will is _not_ joined to his knowledge in these cases. It may or may not be true, as Aquinas would claim, that God's foreknowledge causes certain sorts of future events to occur -namely those that are also predetermined or caused by God's will. But since we are concerned with free events here (where causality is ruled out), we are left without any clear way of understanding how God's foreknowledge that Jones will do x at T2 causes Jones to do x at T2, where this is a free act. Accordingly, I will reject this claim.

To return to the general point for which I am arguing here, I should note that there is one sort of case where God's foreknowledge of a future event is inconsistent with the claim that the event is free. This is where God's foreknowledge is what I will call 'inferential foreknowledge', i.e. where he deduces or infers what is going to happen in the future by extrapolating from what is happening in the present by use of causal laws (or by some other procedure). Where events are brought about and made inevitable by sufficient antecedent conditions, and where God inferentially knows that they will happen, there freedom (as defined earlier) is ruled out. But where there are no sufficient antecedent conditions, i.e. where the agent bringing about a future event is free to do one thing or another given the same antecedent conditions, there God cannot have inferential knowledge of the future, for there are no sufficient antecedent conditions for him to infer from. He must have some other sort of knowledge. I will call this other sort of knowledge 'future vision', and it does not (I believe) rule out freedom.

Richard Taylor [12] argues that if God foreknew at T1 that Jones will do x at T2 Jones cannot genuinely deliberate about x. (Let us say that Jones can only genuinely deliberate about x if Jones is free - as defined earlier - in doing x.) Taylor makes this claim because he assumes that God's knowledge of the future must be inferential knowledge: if God has inferential knowledge of what will occur at T2, then there are sufficient antecedent conditions for the occurrence of x, and Jones cannot genuinely deliberate about doing x.

But if God has future vision, he does not need to know the future inferentially: he simply 'sees' the future, just as we see the present and have seen the past. He knows the future intuitively or immediately, not inferentially. I should note that the claim that God has future vision does not entail that he is timeless. As I argued in Chapter 2, God is 'in' time, i.e. is a temporal being, just as I am: he too has a past, present and future; today is '9 June, 1982' for God just as it is for me. But none of this rules out the claim that God has complete knowledge (memory) of what happened in the past, complete knowledge of what is happening in the present, and complete knowledge (future vision) of what will happen in the future.

Thus, retaining Taylor's notion of deliberation, God can foreknow at T1 a deliberated decision Jones will make at T2. He knows not on the basis of sufficient antecedent conditions, for if Jones was genuinely deliberating, there were none. Rather he simply 'sees' by future vision what the decision will be. Perhaps an analogy will help: consider the difference between an omniscient computer designed to predict the future and a crystal ball. The computer works by being programmed with the present state of all the things in the universe and all true natural laws. By computing these factors it can predict the future state of any of these beings - except states that will occur apart from sufficient antecedent conditions (if there are any such states). It cannot, that is, predict a decision that is reached by genuine deliberation, a free decision. A crystal ball, however, can. For it does not worry about present states and causes and natural laws but rather simply 'peers into' the future. Its 'picture' of the future includes deliberated decisions because it 'sees' rather than computes or deduces, what will happen[13].

Thus my argument is that if God foreknows the future, and if human beings are sometimes free, God's 'seeing' of future events will include free decisions and is not incompatible with their existence.

Where does all this leave us? I believe we can now conclude that Christians are within their intellectual rights in holding that (3) is possibly true and therefore that (1) and (2) are consistent. That is, a rational person can believe in both divine foreknowledge and in human freedom. Of course there may be senses of 'free' held by some people where freedom really is incompatible with divine foreknowledge. For example, nothing prevents a person from saying, 'I'm sorry, but in my sense of the word, a person is 'free' if and only if the outcome of a free decision is in principle not foreknowable - by God or anyone else.' I do not know why anyone would want to hold such a view of freedom - it certainly is not required to make moral responsibility possible - but this does not prevent a person from defining 'free' in this way. All I claim to have done in this chapter is to have reconciled divine foreknowledge with the sort of freedom defined earlier.

5 Omnipotence

It is clearly part of the biblical tradition that God is all-powerful or, as philosophers and theologians usually put it, omnipotent. For example, Job says of God

> I know that thou canst do all things, and that no purpose of thine can be thwarted. (Job 42:2)

The psalmist says

> Our God is in the heavens;
> he does whatever he pleases. (Ps. 115:3; cf. also 135:6; Dan. 4:35)

Jeremiah says to God: 'Nothing is too hard for thee' (32:17; cf. also 32:27; Gen. 18:14). Jesus said: 'With God all things are possible' (Matt. 19:26; cf. also Mark 14:36; Luke 1:37). And Paul speaks of 'the immeasurable greatness' of God's power (Eph. 1:19).

However, the Bible nowhere offers a systematic account of God's power, and it is not clear precisely what the various biblical statements on divine power such as those cited above imply. My aim in this chapter is to arrive at a theologically and philosophically tenable understanding of omnipotence. My account will be influenced by biblical teachings, Christian tradition, and the questions philosophers have raised about omnipotence. The chapter will be divided into two parts. In the first I will attempt to solve two paradoxes that philosophers have found in classical Christian accounts of divine power. In the second I will try to arrive at an acceptable definition of the term 'omnipotent', noting the many difficulties encountered by philosophers and theologians who have tried to define it.

Much recent discussion of omnipotence among philosophers has centred around certain paradoxes that have to do with the nature of the control that an omnipotent being is said to have over other beings. I will argue that there are two separate issues here, though they have sometimes been treated as one. Following Mackie and Flew, I will call the first the 'paradox of omnipotence'. It asks whether an omnipotent being can create a being it subsequently does not control, i.e. decides not to control. Let us say that 'A does not control B' (where A is a being that can have desires) roughly means 'It is causally possible for B to do things A does not want B to do'.

Mackie and Flew argue that the nature of omnipotence, properly understood, precludes God's creating a being he does not control. Thus the so-called paradox of omnipotence is an attempt to show that Christianity is inconsistent to the extent that it holds both that God is omnipotent and that human beings are free (in the sense of the word 'free' stipulated in Chapter 4).

Discussion of an issue that I believe is quite separate has centred around the so-called paradox of the stone, and I will refer to this second issue by that name. This paradox asks whether an omnipotent being can create a being it subsequently <u>cannot</u> control, e.g. a stone it cannot lift. Let us say that 'A cannot <u>causally</u> control B' (where A is again a being that can have desires) roughly means 'It is not in A's power to prevent its being in B's power to do things A does not want B to do'. The paradox of the stone is best interpreted as an argument to the effect that the notion of omnipotence is incoherent, i.e. that it is logically impossible for there to exist an omnipotent being.

Let us consider the paradox of omnipotence first. At the outset it will be best if I sketch out the view I wish to defend, and treat the arguments of Flew, Mackie and others as criticisms of that position. As I will argue in Chapter 7, my view is that God freely decided, for reasons he knows best, to allow human beings moral freedom vis-a-vis his wishes. This means he created them with the ability to disobey as well as obey him. Of course God can intervene any time he wants in order to prevent people from disobeying him, but not without negating their freedom. Thus it is logically impossible for God to make us such that we are caused by him to be both free and obedient. God then <u>permits</u> things to happen that he does not <u>want</u> to happen.

Perhaps it is not unlike a human father who knows he can force his son to clean his room but who, for reasons the father knows best, decides to allow the son to decide for himself whether to clean the room. In this case the father <u>permits</u> but does not <u>will</u> that the room not be cleaned. Analogously, God's omnipotence entails that he <u>can</u> control every event in the world's history if he wishes (at the price, of course, of abrogating human freedom), but not necessarily that he <u>does</u> control every event. I admit that the statement 'God allows x to occur' is far from clear. I have no rigorous analysis of it to offer - let us roughly say it means 'God desires that x not occur; God does not prevent x's occurring; and x occurs.'

Antony Flew argues strongly against this scheme, and although his arguments are based more on the Christian doctrine of God as the creator than on omnipotence, they merit our attention. Flew first emphasizes that according to the Christian tradition God not only brought all things into existence but is the 'constant and essential sustaining cause' of everything in the universe. This rules out the distinction between allowing and causing, he says.

As Creator he could not decide simply to leave to their own devices creatures already autonomously existing. He both designs

and makes them in full knowledge and determination of all that
they will ever do or fail to do. As Creator he must be the first
cause, prime mover, supporter, and controller of every thought and
action throughout his utterly dependent universe. In short: if
creation is in, autonomy is out.[1]

We decide what a man - any man, including ourselves - really wants
by determining what he would do if all obstacles were removed.
But to creative omnipotence there are no obstacles. So what he
really wants must be whatever actually comes about, and that goes
for everything that is happening, including whatever we are
doing . . . . All our actions must, in the primary sense, be according
to God's will.[2]

But this surely does not follow. I am one who wishes to hold that
God is both creator and sustainer of everything that exists. Buy why
cannot God create a free being and sustain the undesirable acts that
this being decides to do? Why cannot an omnipotent creator, because
of a decision on his part to make human beings free, allow and sustain
events he wishes had not occurred? I fail to see an argument here
that rules this out. Certainly other agents can do analogous things -
e.g. the father who in a sense 'sustains' his son's decision not to clean
his room. Similarly, I argue, without God's sustaining power our sins
would not exist. But how does Flew's conclusion follow? I agree with
the doctrine Flew is discussing, namely that nothing happens save by
God's 'ultimate undetermined determination and with his consenting
ontological support'. But this surely does not entail the rigid
predestinarian model - God as the 'Supreme Puppet-master with
creatures whose every thought and move he arranges'[3] - that Flew
says it entails. Why cannot God give his 'consenting ontological
support' to actions to which he does not give his moral support? I
believe he can do this very thing, and does.
　　Flew might respond to this, however, as follows. He might claim
that the two cases of 'permitting' we have here, that of God and the
human father, are not anaologous. The difference, he might say, is
that the father need not take any action in order to permit the room
not to be cleaned; he can allow the room not to be cleaned simply by
remaining inactive. But in the case of God (at least on the standard
theological notion of 'sustaining'), the world and the undesirable
actions of its human denizens cannot exist unless God acts, that is,
takes actual steps to sustain them. This seems to me a fair
distinction: the two cases are not precisely analogous. But the
response I am imagining Flew making does not save his argument. I
still see no reason why God cannot decide to sustain, that is, take
actual steps to continue in existence, certain human actions he would
prefer not to occur.
　　In an article entitled 'Omnipotence', J. L. Mackie argues that 'If
God can make it to be that x, but it is that not-x, he has chosen to let

it be that not-x, and therefore he has made it to be that not-x. Anything that God could have made otherwise, but leaves it as it is, he in effect makes as it is'[4]. The common distinction between allowing and causing applies well to non-omnipotent beings, Mackie says, but not to God. Allowing but not causing something to happen is typically based on either lack of effort or a degree of inadvertance: things that are under our control and that we do not want to happen do indeed sometimes happen, but only if we do not try to prevent them or do not realize they will occur.

> But the more completely the matter is within our power, the less clear does the first ground of the distinction become. If it is something that we can either bring about or prevent with negligible effort, allowing it to happen is less completely differentiated from bringing it about. And similarly the more completely the matter is within our knowledge, the less clear does the second ground of the distinction become; if it is something we cannot help attending to, allowing it to happen cannot be marked off by the criterion of inadvertance. It seems, then, that as power and knowledge increase, this everyday distinction fades out, and for a being with unlimited power and unlimited vision it would not hold at all.[5]

This entails, Mackie says, that any being that is omnipotent is also omnificent, i.e. is the cause of everything that is.

But again I do not think this follows, as we can see by returning to the father-son analogy. The father may be able to cause the son to clean the room with minimal effort - for example, by simply saying 'Please clean your room'. He may also have full knowledge of what is happening - for example, he may actually be in the room, fully aware of what the room looks like and of the activity of the son. But it is still possible for him to allow something to happen that he does not want to happen and that he certainly does not cause to happen, namely, the room's not being cleaned. And even with the distinction between action and inaction made earlier, I see no reason to say that an omnipotent being cannot do this same thing with free creatures he has made.

Douglas Walton argues that 'If Al has the power to make the chalk drop then Cal cannot at the very same time (or over the same period) genuinely have the power to bring it about that the chalk does not drop. One agent or the other has merely the illusion of control' 6 But this does not appear to be true. Al can genuinely have the power to make the chalk drop at the same time that Cal has the power to bring it about that the chalk does not drop, i.e. the chalk can actually drop because of a decision of Al's as long as Cal does not exercise his power to prevent the chalk dropping. And this is just what Christians believe God does: he has the power to prevent disobedience, but chooses not to exercise this power and in so doing allows us to be free.

Walton further says: 'It seems inconceivable that Almighty God could be said to bring about a state of affairs that would impair his power'[7] Is this true? Well, there is of course a difference between a being reducing its power and simply deciding not to exercise it. I do not find it inconceivable that God do either, but it is the second that Christians believe God has actually done so far as human free choice is concerned. It is true that on my understanding of what God has done, God must 'concur with' or 'consent to' every event that occurs, even the wrong acts we do. What this simply means is that such acts could not occur unless God allowed them to occur. In an indirect sense, then, God is indeed responsible for our sins (as I will admit in Chapter 7); he could prevent them if he wished (although it would be at the cost of depriving us of our freedom). But it does not mean that God agrees with or likes or causes what we do.

Thus I see no serious difficulty for Christianity in the paradox of omnipotence. It does not appear to be inconsistent to hold both that God is omnipotent and that human beings are morally free.

But let us now turn to the paradox of the stone, which is much more intractable. Savage states the paradox as follows:

(1)   Either x can create a stone which x cannot lift, or x cannot create a stone which x cannot lift.

(2)   If x can create a stone which x cannot lift, then, necessarily, there is at least one task which x cannot perform (namely, lift the stone in question).

(3)   If x cannot create a stone which x cannot lift, then, necessarily, there is at least one act which x cannot perform (namely, create the stone in question).

(4)   Hence, there is at least one task which x cannot perform.

(5)   If x is an omnipotent being, then x can perform any task.

(6)   Therefore, x is not omnipotent.[8]

Since x is any being, Savage says, the paradox apparently proves that it is logically impossible for any being to be omnipotent, i.e. it proves that the notion of omnipotence is incoherent.

The deep question here is whether an omnipotent being can create a thing it subsequently causally cannot control. Formerly we were asking whether God can create creatures whom he cannot control without violating their freedom. Here we are asking whether he can create things he subsequently cannot control at all, e.g. a stone he cannot lift, an iceberg he cannot melt, a universe he cannot control.

Another way of asking this question (at least if I am correct in some of the things I will say below) is: Can God take away his own omnipotence? My intuitions say yes - that God can indeed do this if he chooses - which is one of the reasons I am suspicious of the doctrine that God is not just omnipotent but essentially omnipotent. My intuitions, for example, say that a God who can voluntarily take away his own omnipotence is more powerful than a God who cannot. But part of the difficulty here is that the reverse intuition can be supported too: that a God whose omnipotence is, so to speak, unstable and potentially fleeting is less powerful than a God whose omnipotence is, so to speak, inviolate. Perhaps one's intuitions on this deeper question influence the answer one chooses to give to the paradox of the stone.

Nearly everyone who writes about the paradox of the stone believes there is a solution to it, but, interestingly, the 'solutions' that have been suggested differ widely. Three main approaches have been taken. The first is to say that God cannot create a stone he cannot lift because to ask an omnipotent being to do such a thing is to ask for something that is logically impossible. I will call this the Mavrodes solution[9]. The second agrees that God cannot create a stone he cannot lift, but the reason given is quite different. It is claimed that the words 'God cannot create a stone he cannot lift' imply no lessening of divine omnipotence because no one act is in fact named here that an omnipotent being cannot do. I will call this the Savage solution[10]. The third is to say that God can create a stone he cannot lift but that this does not lessen divine omnipotence unless God does in fact create a stone he cannot lift. I will call this the Swinburne solution[11]. Let us now look at each approach in more detail.

Several philosophers have taken a Mavrodes-like line on paradox[12]. The basic strategy here is first to point out, following Aquinas, that omnipotence does not include the ability to do the logically impossible. Then it is claimed that the phrase 'a stone to heavy for God to lift' means 'a stone too heavy to be lifted by him who can lift anything'[13]. And this description, it is then claimed, is incoherent. That God cannot make a stone which logically cannot be made does not lessen his omnipotence or entail that the notion of omnipotence is incoherent. But this solution has been criticized. As Savage points out, even if we assume that God is omnipotent, the phrase 'a stone too heavy for God to lift' is self-contradictory only if the sentence 'God is omnipotent' is necessarily true. And it begs the question against the person who poses the paradox, Savage says, to assume that an essentially omnipotent God exists, since this person is attempting to show precisely that it is logically impossible for such a being to exist[14].

However, perhaps Mavrodes's solution is not so easily refuted as Savage implies. For one thing, there is a significant 'burden of proof' issue here. Suppose Savage is arguing against a person who (a) believes that God is essentially omnipotent and (b) accepts Mavrodes's solution to the paradox of the stone. Savage can't properly claim to refute this person by arguing that God can perform a given task - e.g. make a stone he can't lift - which is logically impossible if God is essentially omnipotent. Perhaps to do that would be to beg the question. Such a person will rightly respond: 'Since I believe that God is essentially omnipotent, your argument - which only succeeds if God is contingently omnipotent - doesn't affect me'.

Savage also claims that Mavrodes's solution does not apply to Savage's version of the paradox (the one cited above). But this is not true. Mavrodes can claim that premise (5) in Savage's statement of the paradox is false - what it should say is something like:

(5a) If x is an omnipotent being, then x can perform any task the description of which does not involve a contradiction.

And Mavrodes can claim that when 'x' in the statement of the paradox is replaced by the term 'God' (understood as an essentially omnipotent being), premise (3) names a task - namely, God creating a stone which God cannot lift - which involves a contradiction. Thus the paradox fails.

But while I accordingly believe that Mavrodes can defend himself against Savage in this way, Mavrodes's solution is not available to me since I do not hold that God is essentially omnipotent. I certainly believe that God is omnipotent, but I see no good reason to say that Yahweh would not be Yahweh or would not be divine if there were some consistent act he couldn't do, e.g. make the Pentagon levitate. Now I believe Yahweh can do this very thing, but suppose he couldn't -why would it then follow he would no longer be divine? (Of course, if inability to perform this one consistent act portended more serious inabilities, Yahweh's divinity might well be endangered. But there is no reason why it logically must do so.) So I must look for another solution. Let us then turn to Savage's own approach.

Savage's basic line on the paradox has also been taken by several philosophers [15]. What he does is deny the truth of (3). He claims that while it is true that an omnipotent being cannot create a stone it cannot lift, this is a logically necessary characteristic of rather than a limitation on omnipotence. For the statement, 'God cannot create a stone that God cannot lift' does not entail that there is any sort of stone that God cannot make or any sort of stone that God cannot lift. All the statement in fact means is, 'If God can create a stone, God can lift it' [16]. No limitation on God's creating or lifting power is implied here, for no one act is in fact named that an omnipotent being cannot do. God can still make stones of any size and lift stones of any size. It simply follows, as a matter of logic, that a being whose stone-creating and stone-lifting powers are unlimited 'cannot create a stone he cannot lift'. Thus the paradox fails to show that it is logically impossible for there to exist an omnipotent being.

Criticism of Savage's article has centred around his claim that the paradox fails to endanger omnipotence because no one act is named that an omnipotent being cannot do. Some have argued, for example, that the one coherent act the paradox shows that an omnipotent being cannot do is make an unliftable stone. The unliftableness of the stone may have nothing to do with its great weight. It could be unliftable for any number of reasons - great bulk or great slipperiness, for example. That is, an omnipotent being can create a stone with any consistent property he likes (e.g. weight, colour, shape, etc.); it is just that he will always subsequently be able to lift it. So what it is that he cannot do, according to the paradox, is make a stone to which he gives the power subsequently to resist his own lifting power [17]. There is clearly an analogous task human beings can do - make things they subsequently cannot lift - but an omnipotent being cannot do it. Thus an omnipotent being is not omnipotent, i.e. it is logically impossible for there to exist an omnipotent being.

I have some sympathy for Savage's solution to the paradox. Even if it turns out that Savage is incorrect in his claim that the paradox names no one act an omnipotent being cannot do, I believe there is still a fair reply he can make. He can say, that is, that the paradox merely teaches us some interesting new things about omnipotent beings (i.e. that there are more things they cannot do for logical reasons than we may originally have imagined). It does not show, he can say, that the notion of omnipotence is incoherent. Nevertheless, I will discuss Savage's solution no further because it is Swinburne's solution that seems to me most illuminating.

Let me introduce Swinburne's solution by citing an argument from J. L. Cowan:

> Since no one can make something he cannot lift unless he cannot lift everything, everyone (including God) will be limited either with respect to his making or with respect to this lifting or both.[18]

This sort of argument seems presupposed in much that is said in discussions of the paradox of the stone, but it appears to be quite mistaken. There may well be beings who can both make things they cannot lift and lift anything that exists. They can have both powers quite easily as long as the things they can make that they cannot lift do not in fact exist, i.e. as long as they refrain from exercising their power to make them. (For all I know, Cowan may have recognized this. Perhaps by the term 'everything' he meant not 'everything that exists' but rather 'everything that can possibly exist'.)

This, in effect, is what Swinburne says about the paradox of the stone: an omnipotent being can 'make a stone he cannot lift', but this creates a problem for him only if he does in fact make such a stone. He remains omnipotent only as long as he refrains from doing so. Swinburne says:

True, if an omnipotent being actually exercises (as opposed to merely possessing) his ability to bring about the existence of a stone too heavy for him subsequently to bring about its rising, then he will cease to be omnipotent . . . But the omnipotence of a person at a certain time includes the ability to make himself no longer omnipotent, an ability which he may or may not choose to exercise. A person may remain omnipotent forever because he never exercises his power to create stones too heavy to lift, forces too stong to resist, or universes too wayward to control.[19]

The point is that an omnipotent being becomes non-omnipotent in respect of his lifting power only if there actually exists something he cannot lift. His omnipotence is not lessened or taken away if he (or anybody else, for that matter) merely <u>has the power</u> to make something he cannot lift[20].

There is an objection that can be raised against this argument. It follows from the argument that it is logically possible for God, if he is omnipotent, not to be omnipotent. That is, it follows that God is neither <u>essentially</u> omnipotent nor strongly immutable. But I do not find this point bothersome. I have already (in Chapter 3) argued against the claim that God is strongly immutable. And as noted earlier, I have no wish to hold that God is essentially omnipotent - only that he is omnipotent.

My intuitions are such that God can, if he wishes, take away his own omnipotence, and this is something he cannot do if he is essentially omnipotent and strongly immutable. Someone may object that necessary omnipotence is part of the concept of God, but the only reply this objection requires is to insist that it is not part of my concept of God, nor do I see any reason why it must be part of the Christian concept of God. Furthermore, the doctrine of the incarnation (see Chapter 8) seems to me to require Christians to say that God has the power voluntarily to limit his power.

Some might argue that this makes God's omnipotence fleeting and precarious: there is some possiblity he will no longer be omnipotent at some point in the future. But since it is clear that we are talking about a voluntary resignation of omnipotence on God's own part, I see no difficulty here. There is nothing in the Swinburnian approach I am adopting that entails that God's continued omnipotence depends on decisions to be made by <u>other</u> beings.

I conclude, then, that Swinburne's solution does indeed solve the paradox of omnipotence. An omnipotent being <u>can</u> create a stone he cannot lift and an iceberg he cannot melt and a universe he cannot control - and he remains omnipotent only as long as he refrains from doing so.

Having dealt with the two main paradoxes connected with omnipotence, I will now try to arrive at an acceptable definition of the term. As noted earlier, it is difficult to say precisely what omnipotence is. We can say, of course, that it has to do with creative power or power to do or power to bring about of great magnitude. But more than this is not easy to say. The typical approach is to define omnipotence in terms of power or ability to do things, but some have recently argued that it is best to take another approach. P. T. Geach, [21] for example, prefers to define omnipotence in terms of having power over things. Richard Swinburne [22] prefers to define it in terms of power or ability to bring things about. As procedural stipulations, I have no objection to these suggestions. In fact, I will follow Swinburne in defining omnipotence in terms of power to bring about. But I do not believe it ultimately makes much difference which approach one takes. This is because the kinds of powers both Geach and Swinburne speak about seem to reduce on analysis to power to do. To have power over x can surely be analysed as having power to do certain things, e.g. to do certain things to x or to make x to certain things[23]. To have power to bring x about can surely be analysed as having power to do certain things, e.g. to bring about that someone or something does x or to do the general act of 'bringing about x'.

My method in this section of the chapter will be the same as that used by many others who write about omnipotence, namely, to propose various possible definitions of the word 'omnipotent', beginning at the strongest, and to discuss possible objections to each definition, in hopes of arriving at an acceptable one. To count as adequate, let us say that a definition of 'omnipotent' must, first, be coherent, i.e. not contradictory or confused or open to telling objections; second, it must roughly agree with our intuitions or pre-analytic beliefs about what omnipotence is (some of these intuitions might have to be given up, but they should be given up only with great caution); and third, for the Christian philosopher at least, it must agree with what is found in the Bible and Christian tradition about divine power.

One obvious way to begin is to say that a being B is omnipotent if and only if

(A)   <u>for any state of affairs s, B can bring about s.</u>

This is the strongest definition of the term, and definitions like it have at times been defended. But with the possible exception of Luther and Descartes, all Christian philosophers and theologians have recognized it as too strong. For definition (A) entails that an omnipotent being can bring about even contradictory states of affairs, e.g. Jones's being a married bachelor, 2 + 2's equalling 5, God simultaneously existing and not existing. And any definition that entails that such states of affairs can obtain is surely incoherent and thus fails to satisfy our first criterion. Furthermore, we know from logic that a contradictory proposition entails any proposition at all, i.e. from a contradiction any proposition whatever logically follows. Thus the proposition, <u>God simultaneously exists and does not exist</u>, a contradiction, entails any proposition anyone cares to name, even the proposition, <u>B is omnipotent if and only if B can do nothing but sit and stare idly at toothpicks</u>. And if we were required to accept this proposition, where would we then be?

Despite this, some might want to defend definition (A) via the following argument:

> It is true that definition (A) leads to <u>what we understand</u> as contradictions. But surely our minds are limited in comparison to God's infinite wisdom. Surely there are systems of logic God can understand but we can't in which what seem to us to be contradictions make perfectly good sense. Thus God can create states of affairs like those puzzling ones mentioned above, and our definition of 'omnipotent' must reflect this ability.

I do not wish to deny that much of this is true. Our minds are limited. But there are still good reasons not to accept definition (A). Now there are in fact many systems of logic, but for the sake of argument, let us say that there is one system of logic that nearly every rational human being understands and in which logically contradictory propositions are recognized as unacceptable. Let us call this system 'L'. Now in L the proposition <u>Jones is a married bachelor</u> is contradictory and thus there is no question of its being true or describing an actual state of affairs.

Now perhaps the above argument in favour of definition (A) amounts to something like this: there is a system of logic L' which God understands and we do not in which <u>Jones is a married bachelor</u> is not only coherent but true. And this is what I have no wish to deny, though of course I have not the vaguest idea how the system L' would work. But my general point against this argument is just this: we have no present grounds for affirming the present claim about L' and thus no present grounds for accepting definition (A). There is precious little in Scripture, Christian tradition, or human reason that gives us good reason to affirm (A), and so I will not do so[24]. Furthermore, we have a very good reason not to affirm it, namely the fact that the notions of L' and of there being married bachelors are incoherent and thus nonsensical to us. And it is irrational under any circumstances to affirm that incoherent claims are true.

So let us try a slightly weaker definition. Let us now say that a being B is omnipotent if and only if

(B)   <u>for any logically possible state of affairs s, B can bring about s.</u>

At this point Plantinga[25] argues that definitions like (B) are deficient because the act of 'making a table no omnipotent being made' is a logically possible act, but an omnipotent being cannot do it. Now I do not believe this argument succeeds as it stands. In my study at home there exists a table that was not made by an omnipotent being (I happen to know who made it). But at the time it was made I believe my table (that very table, not another just like it) could well have been made by an omnipotent being. So I think it is logically possible, in this sense, for an omnipotent being to make a table no omnipotent being made. But Plantinga's argument succeeds admirably as long as we are talking about a table which has the property of not having been made by an omnipotent being essentially. The state of affairs of there existing a table which is essentially unmade by an omnipotent being may or may not be a logically possible state of affairs, but even if it is, no omnipotent being can bring it about. Our definition of 'omnipotent' must not require that B be able to create a possible state of affairs which in no possible world is created by God.

Thus our definition should now say: a being B is omnipotent if and only if

(C)   for any state of affairs s such that there is a possible world in which B brings about s, B can bring about s.

(I've omitted the term 'logically possible' that appeared in (B) because the phrase in (C) about 'a possible world' covers the same considerations that lead us to insert the term in (B).) This is an interesting and helpful modification. Let us see if it is adequate. Definition (C) is designed to rule out any requirement that B is able to bring about logically impossible states of affairs such as those discussed above. But I should point out that it also rules out B bringing about logically necessary states, e.g. the state of affairs of 1 + 1's equalling 2, or the state of affairs of all bachelors being unmarried. Since it is logically impossible for these states of affairs not to obtain, it is incoherent for us to imagine that any being causes them to obtain. The states of affairs that an omnipotent being can bring about, then, are all contingent states of affairs.

How do we set out to discover whether a state of affairs is coherent? For it is surely true that many actions which are incoherent on some descriptions, e.g. the act of creating a square circle, are apparently coherent on other descriptions, e.g. the act of creating what I am now thinking about (where I am thinking about a square circle). And the same thing will surely be true of states of affairs as well as actions. Let us stipulate that a state of affairs is coherent if and only if none of its true descriptions is incoherent (where a 'true description of x' is a true statement or set of true statements about x) and that a state of affairs is incoherent if and only if any of its true descriptions is incoherent.

It should be pointed out that definition (C) is quite similar to the definition of 'omnipotent' Aquinas arrives at in Summa Theologica, I,

25, 3[26]. He first says:

> Since power is said in reference to possible things, this phrase, <u>God can do all things</u>, is rightly understood to mean that God can do all things that are possible; and for this reason He is said to be omnipotent.

These words seem at first glance to fit (B) rather than (C), but Aquinas goes on to say:

> Everything that does not imply a contradiction in terms, is numbered among those possible things, in respect of which God is called omnipotent: whereas whatever implies a contradiction does not come within the scope of divine omnipotence, because it cannot have the aspect of possibility.

Now since the notion of an omnipotent being making a table which has the essential property of not having been made by an omnipotent being implies a contradiction, perhaps Aquinas's definition of 'omnipotent' in this passage fits definition (C).

However, definition (C) becomes inadequate when we raise considerations of time. Here, for example, is a logically possible state of affairs: <u>Stephen T. Davis first catching mononeucleosis in 1982</u>. It may seem quite possible for an omnipotent being to bring about this state of affairs until I add a complicating detail - the fact that I contracted mononeucleosis for the first and (I sincerely hope) only time in 1962. Thus we seem to have here a state of affairs that not even an omnipotent being can <u>now</u> (i.e. in 1982) bring about. Since the past is unchangeable, not even God can bring it about now that I <u>first</u> catch mononeucleosis in 1982. Prior to 1962 he could have done so, but now it is too late. It is not logically impossible for me first to catch mononeucleosis in 1982 (because it is not necessarily true that I first catch mononeucleosis prior to 1982); it is just that it is logically inconsistent with contingent events that have occurred prior to 1982.

No definition of 'omnipotent' will be acceptable, then, if it entails that an omnipotent being must be able to change the past - either directly, e.g. by bringing it about today that Hitler was assassinated in 1938, or indirectly, e.g. by bringing it about that next week I will shake hands with the person who assassinated Hitler in 1938. A necessary condition for a state of affairs being 'bringable about' at a certain time, then, is that it be logically compatible with everything that occurred prior to that time. Let us therefore add a temporal indicator to definition (C)[27]. Let us now say that a being B is omnipotent at time t if and only if

(D) <u>for any state of affairs s after t such that there is a possible world sharing the history of the actual world up to t in which</u>

B brings about s, B can bring about s.

Now (D) is the definition of 'omnipotence' which I consider adequate and wish to defend. However, it and definitions like it have been criticized in several ingenious ways in recent years, and a good many philosophers have abandoned it in favour of other more elaborate definitions. Let me now discuss what I take to be the three most serious objections that can be raised. None seems to me decisive.

The first criticism is that definitions like (D) do not apply to non-bodily beings like God. Since God is supposed to be a spiritual or incorporeal being, it is said, there are certain logically possible things God cannot do, e.g. do twenty push-ups, run a mile, get a headache[28]. But this is surely incorrect. If God, a spiritual being, is truly omnipotent as defined in (D), there is no reason why he cannot first become embodied and then do twenty push-ups, run a mile, and get a headache. Some might want to argue that God is an essentially spiritual being, i.e. that he cannot become embodied and remain divine or remain the being that he is. But (1) if God is essentially spiritual then by (D) (and earlier definitions of 'omnipotent' as well) it does not diminish God's power to say that he cannot get a headache, etc., since these are things an essentially spiritual being cannot possibly do. And, more importantly, (2) Christians can hardly accept the claim that God is essentially spiritual anyway; they believe that God not only can become incarnate in a body, but did (see Chapter 8, where I discuss this further).

The second common objection to definitions like (D) can be stated as follows: suppose there is a man for whom it is an essential property that the only thing he can do is scratch his ear. Then he is apparently omnipotent by definition (D). For of any other act that can be named, say the act of wriggling his toes, the sentence that states that he does it is incoherent, since it is essential to him that scratching his ear is the only thing he can do. But the claim that such a man is omnipotent violates our pre-analytic conception of omnipotence, and so must be rejected. (There is no such problem if it is an accidental property of this man that he can only scratch his ear, for then the sentence 'The man who can only scratch his ear creates the world' is false but coherent.)

But can there exist a being for whom it is an essential property that all he can do is scratch his ear? Obviously not: any being who can scratch his ear also has many other properties as well (namely, those that are entailed by his ability to scratch his ear), e.g. ability to scratch, ability to scratch something, ability to scratch part of his body, ability to move (an immobile being can't scratch), ability to be truthfully referred to as 'a being who can scratch his ear', etc.

But perhaps this objection to definition (D) can be restated in a more acceptable way. Perhaps it can be said that on definition (D) we must falsely consider omnipotent the following being: a being for whom it is an essential property that all he can do is scratch his ear and do anything else that is entailed by scratching his ear. But I have serious doubts about the coherence of this notion as well. Let us call the person who has the property in question 'Joe'. It is, then, an essential property of Joe that all he can do is scratch his ear and anything else entailed by scratching his ear. I would argue that no such being as Joe can possibly exist. Of course if we understand the word 'do' as covering only conscious or overt acts we can imagine a being that has the property in question <u>accidentally</u>, e.g. a being who for a certain period of time somehow happens to be totally paralysed except for his right index finger, which can move and which happens to be resting on his ear. This seems perfectly possible. But I can't imagine this property being <u>essential</u> to any being. Why would Joe no longer be Joe if, say, his paralysis slackened a bit and he was able to scratch his temple too? Surely it is false to claim that we can mention just any property we can think of and then claim that there is a possible being who has it essentially[29]. Thus it does not appear that the objection we are dealing with gives us good reason to reject definition (D)[30].

The third objection to definitions like (D) is much more complicated and will take longer to unravel. It has to do with random events which are, so to speak, 'unbringable about' or events brought about by free agents which are 'unbringable about' by any being other than the free agent in question. Suppose an event will occur in five minutes that can truly be described as random or uncaused (e.g. the swerve of an electron as described in quantum mechanics). It follows, then, that definition (D) of omnipotence is too strong, for it requires that an omnipotent being be able to bring about this event, which it clearly cannot do if the event is, as stipulated, random. Or suppose I am correct in my belief that some human choices are free (in the sense discussed in Chapter 4). That is, suppose some events are brought about by the free choices of agents and are thus 'unbringable about' by any other being. If this is true, it follows that the logically possible state of affairs, <u>Jones freely deciding to blow his nose,</u> cannot be caused by God (where Jones is not God). For if it were caused by God Jones would not be free in the stipulated sense. So it seems that (D) is too strong; it apparently requires that an omnipotent being be able to bring about events such as these.

But perhaps (D) is immune to this difficulty. The question is quite tricky - it raises issues larger than randomness and freedom - and must be looked at carefully. Definition (D) might be defended via the following argument:

> If it is necessarily true that an event e is random, then there is no possible world in which B brings about e, and so (D) does not require that B be able to bring about e; and if it is contingently true that e is random, then there is a possible world in which B brings about e (unless, of course, B has the property of not bringing about e essentially). Likewise, if it is necessarily true that an event

f is freely brought about by an agent Jones (where Jones is not B), then there is no possible world in which B brings about f, and so (D) does not require that B be able to bring about f; and if it is contingently true that f is freely brought about by an agent Jones (where Jones is not B), then there is a possible world in which B brings about f (again, unless B has the property of not bringing about f essentially). Accordingly, (D) still stands.

However, a powerful argument can be mounted at this point - an argument to the effect that if (D), together with the above interpretation of (D), is accepted, then everybody is omnipotent. Surely any state of affairs you can think of that I won't in fact bring about - say, the state of affairs of my oldest son awakening tomorrow morning (let's assume he will wake up on his own) - can truly be described in such a way that it becomes incoherent to imagine my bringing it about. There are, of course, possible worlds in which I bring about my oldest son's awakening tomorrow morning, but none in which I bring about the following state of affairs: <u>my oldest son's awakening tomorrow morning and my not bringing about my oldest son's awakening tomorrow morning</u>. When described in this way it seems <u>logically impossible</u> for me to bring about the described state of affairs. But since by (D) my inability to do so does not count against the claim that I am omnipotent, I may well be omnipotent. The moral is this: in the case of any agent whatever (however powerful or powerless), with a bit of ingenuity we can think of an accurate but incoherent description of the agent's bringing about any state of affairs that the agent will not in fact bring about. So it turns out that the agent logically <u>cannot</u> bring it about. Now since according to (D) states of affairs an agent logically cannot bring about do not count against the claim that the agent is omnipotent, it follows that everyone is omnipotent[31].

Is this a good argument? I do not think so. Let me begin my reply to it by pointing out the obvious fact that there are several ways of describing one and the same event. To pick a different example, suppose that tomorrow morning a dog named Max in Alta Loma, California will scratch. Let us call this event 'g'. Now clearly g can be correctly described in many ways:

D1:   Max will scratch
D2:   Max, a dog from Alta Loma, California, will scratch.
D3:   Max will scratch tomorrow morning.
D4:   Unbeknownst to Jimmy Carter, Max will scratch tomorrow morning.
D5:   Max will scratch tomorrow morning, and Max's scratching will not affect the price of gold in Zurich.

Can I cause Max to scratch tomorrow morning? Well, I suppose I could. If I wanted to do so I could certainly drive to Alta Loma tomorrow morning and place some fleas on Max's body. That would undoubtedly do the trick. But now notice that if it is in fact true that I will <u>not</u> cause Max to scratch tomorrow morning, the event g that we have been talking about can also be described as follows:

> D6:   Max will scratch tomorrow morning and S. T. Davis will not bring about Max's scratching tomorrow morning.

But surely it is implausible to say that D6 describes a state of affairs I logically <u>cannot</u> bring about. This is because D6 and D3 (assuming I will not bring about Max's scratching tomorrow morning) both describe g, i.e. one and the same event. If it is in my power to bring about the event described in D3 (as I certainly think it is), then it is also in my power to bring about the event described in D6. That is, if it is <u>contingently</u> true that I will not bring about Max's scratching tomorrow morning, it does not magically become <u>necessarily</u> true that I will not bring about Max's scratching tomorrow morning just because we choose to describe g by the use of D6 instead of D3.

Is it true that everyone is omnipotent? Obviously not. Is it true that (D) entails that everyone is omnipotent? Of course not. Just because we can take a state of affairs I don't bring about and correctly add to its description the words, 'and Davis does not bring it about' does not make it logically impossible for me to bring it about. As I argued in Chapter 4, statements like 'g is not brought about by Davis' are quite compatible with statements like 'It is in Davis power to bring about g'.

Definition (D) accordingly only makes me omnipotent if it is <u>necessarily true</u> that I do not bring about all the states of affairs that I do not bring about, i.e. if it is essential to me or to the states of affairs themselves (if states of affairs can have essential properties) that I do not bring them about. If there are possible worlds having a history similar to the actual world in which I defeat Ali in boxing (as there are) and if it is not in my power in the actual world to do so (as it is not), then I am not omnipotent. Our ability correctly to describe a given state of affairs as 'Ali's being defeated in boxing and Davis not defeating Ali in boxing' does not affect this result. I am still not omnipotent. And since this is just what (D) entailed in the first place, (D) still stands[32].

Incidentally, this shows the error of those who hold that God is the cause of everything that occurs. If my interpretation of the Christian claim that human beings are free is correct, it follows that there are many things that God doesn't cause, e.g. my free choices. As we saw earlier in this chapter, some philosophers deny that free agents can co-exist with an omnipotent being. But, again, I see no reason to say this. Being omnipotent does not imply having all the power that there is. Nothing prevents an omnipotent being - so to speak - from delegating some of its power to lesser creatures. This is just what the doctrine of human freedom says God did, and our definition of omnipotence will have to reflect this. What does seem intuitively to be required is that the omnipotent being's power be overriding, i.e. that the being be more powerful than any other being and can, if so inclined, take away any power previously granted to other beings. (Obviously, I am claiming that this is a necessary condition of omnipotence, not sufficient.)

(D), then, is the definition of the term 'omnipotent' that I believe is theologically and philosophically acceptable. It is immune at least to the more obvious difficulties that can be raised and it seems to me consistent with Christian intuition about the doctrine of divine omnipotence. If God is omnipotent, then on definition (D) at any point in time he can bring about any state of affairs that is logically possible for him to bring about and that is compatible with everything that occurred prior to that time[33].

6 Benevolence

That God is good is affirmed throughout the Bible and is universally accepted by Christians.

> For the Lord is good;
>   his steadfast love endures forever,
>   and his faithfulness to all generations. (Ps. 100:5)

> O give thanks to the Lord,
>   for he is good;
>   for his steadfast love endures forever. (Ps. 107:1)

> And Jesus said to him, 'Why do you call me good? No
> one is good but God alone.' (Mark 10:18)

Let us take the statement 'God is good' to mean that God is wholly or perfectly good. He is not a mainly good being with a slight demonic side: rather, he has no evil in him at all. Let us say that 'God is good', in this sense, means that God never does what is morally wrong; all his intentions and actions are morally right. If it is always morally wrong, say, needlessly to break a promise, this is something God never does. If it is always morally wrong to cause needless suffering, this too is something God never does. Connected with this is the notion that God is benevolent: he loves us, cares for us, forgives us, and never acts malevolently toward us. Within the limits of the freedom he has given us, he works to achieve his gracious desires for us.

This naturally leads us to ask an old question about the freedom of God. If God is good, as defined above, it follows that he never in fact does evil. But we can still ask whether he is free or able to do evil (a freedom or ability which, if he has it, he never in fact exercises). For example, is it in God's power or ability to break a promise or cause needless suffering? Or is he in a sense constrained to be benevolent, not to do evil? There is no question that God is free to do what seems to some or even all human beings to be evil but in fact is good. As long as the apparently evil things God does are really good or are necessary to produce greater goods, there is no difficulty in continuing to affirm his goodness. The real question is whether God is free or able to do genuinely evil things.

Christian tradition is divided here; some theologians say yes and some say no. I will argue for the affirmative side, that God is able to do evil (although in fact he never does evil). However, let us begin with those who deny that God is free to do evil. There are two quite different ways of arguing to this conclusion. One is to be found classically in Anselm and Aquinas and has been recently presented by Richard Swinburne. The second is suggested, among others, by William of Ockham.

The Anselm-Aquinas-Swinburne argument seems to revolve around the central insight that God is in a sense limited by his own holy nature. He cannot do evil, for if he did he would no longer be God (or at least the God in which Christians believe). Anselm sees the problem as arising in this way: he believes that God is omnipotent and yet he also believes that there are certain things God cannot do, e.g. tell a lie. He wonders how this can be. His solution is to argue that the capacity to do things like lie or be corrupted

> is not power, but impotence. For, he who is capable of these things is capable of what is not for his own good, and of what he ought not to do; and the more capable of them he is, the more power have adversity and perversity against him; and the less has he himself against these.[1]

The argument appears to be this: to do evil is to be corrupted by forces other than oneself. Evil acts are enslaving, and in fact grow out of impotence rather than power. The more evil acts that moral agents do the more power forces like adversity and perversity have over them and the less power they have (to do good). Thus an omnipotent being, who by definition cannot be enslaved by alien forces, cannot do evil.

Is this a good argument? It does not seem so; in fact, it seem sophistical, for the obvious counter-example looks equally compelling: The more good that moral agents do the less power and freedom they have, for the more forces like goodness and compassion have power over them and the less power they have (to do evil). Furthermore, evil may well be enslaving to human beings in the sense that the more evil acts they do the more evil acts they are bound to do, but why must this be true for an omnipotent being as well? So there seems to be no good reason here to deny that God can do evil.

Aquinas similarly argues that God cannot do evil because sin is repugnant to omnipotence:

> To sin is to fall short of a perfect action; hence to be able to sin is to be able to fall short in action, which is repugnant to omnipotence. Therefore it is that God cannot sin, because of his omnipotence.[2]

Here Aquinas defines sin as <u>falling short of perfect action</u>. But an omnipotent being surely cannot 'fall short in action'. Thus God, who is omnipotent, cannot sin. But this argument too surely fails; it seems to be based on an equivocation on the term 'falling short'. 'Falling short', where this means something like 'trying one's best but doing less than can be done' is 'repugnant to omnipotence'. But sinning is surely not 'falling short' in this sense. Sin is not, for example, like trying one's best but lifting only 100 pounds in a weight-lifting contest when lifting more is possible. Biblically, sin is 'falling short' in the sense of 'missing God's declared standard of righteousness' (as revealed, say, in the moral law of the Old Testament). But this does not seem repugnant to omnipotence. There seems to be no reason here to deny that an omnipotent being can break a promise or cause someone to suffer needlessly. If God were to do such things he would indeed fall short of his own revealed standard of righteousness, but why could he not do just this?

As noted in Chapter 5, Aquinas's official position on omnipotence seems to be that an omnipotent being can do anything that does not entail a contradiction. But Aquinas seems also at times to work with a second position, namely that the power any being can have must always be understood in terms of its basic nature. He says:

> Power is predicated of God not as something really distinct from His knowledge and will . . . The knowledge or will of God, according as it is the effective principle, has the notion of power contained in it. Hence the consideration of the knowledge and will of God precedes the consideration of His power, as the cause precedes the operations and effect.[3]

This can perhaps help us to understand why Aquinas calls sin 'falling short in action', but I do not believe it will improve his argument that God cannot sin. Aquinas's point is that divine power is always expressed in the context of God's will, which is essentially morally perfect. Divine omnipotence just is God's ability to act on his omniscience and perfect will. Thus God can only sin if he lacks power, i.e. power to do what his perfect will directs. Since divine omnipotence covers the ability to do only what God wills, and since God's morally perfect nature entails that he only wills what is good, God can only sin if he is non-omnipotent. As long as he remains omnipotent, he cannot sin.

I will not explore the interesting question whether the view of omnipotence presupposed here is consistent with Aquinas's official position. But it is clear that Aquinas has not proved, even on this more sympathetic interpretation of his 'falling short in action' doctrine, that God cannot sin. For those who think that God can sin will deny Aquinas's main premise that God's will is essentially perfect. That, after all, is the basic question here: do we have any good reason to believe that God's nature is essentially morally perfect? Aquinas has apparently not supplied us with such a reason.

In a separate argument in the Summa Contra Gentiles, Aquinas says:

> The will never aims at evil without some error existing in the reason, at least with respect to a particular object of choice. For, since the object of the will is the apprehended good, the will cannot aim at evil unless in some way it is proposed to it as a good; and this cannot take place without error.[4]

This argument can perhaps be more easily evaluated if we organize it as follows:

(1)   Agents always will to do what they see as good
(2)   To see evil as good is to be in error
(3)   Agents only will to do evil if they see evil as good
(4)   God cannot be in error
(5)   God cannot see evil as good
(6)   Therefore, God cannot do evil.

But the problem here is that premise (1) is ambiguous. 'Good' here might mean 'beneficial to the agent' or it might mean 'morally good'. If it means the latter, premise (1) certainly seems untrue for human agents, and even if it is true of God that he always in fact <u>does</u> will to do what he sees as morally good, this does not settle the question whether he is free or able to will to do what he sees as moral evil. If 'good' means the former, i.e. beneficial to the agent, premise (1) might be true for human agents, but even if it is true of God that he cannot be in error (which I will grant), it does not follow that it is never beneficial to God or in his best interest to do evil. Since if Christianity is true human agents cannot do evil with impunity (ignoring notions like repentance and forgiveness), it is perhaps true that it is never in our best interest to do evil. But God certainly can do evil with impunity if he can do evil at all, so it is not clear why a sin on God's part must be based on an error of some sort.

What I take to be a version of this last Thomistic argument has recently been presented by Richard Swinburne. He argues that it is logically impossible for omniscient and perfectly free beings to do evil. What does it mean to say of agents that they are 'perfectly free'? To Swinburne it apparently means two things: first, that they always do what they think there is an overriding reason to do, what (in some sense) they regard as good; and second, that their choices are only influenced by rational factors, never by non-rational ones. Thus, Swinburne says:

> An omniscient person who is also perfectly free will necessarily do right actions and avoid wrong ones - since . . . being perfectly free, he will necessarily do those actions which he believes right and avoid those which he believes wrong, and . . . being omniscient, he will hold true beliefs in this field. A man may fail to do his duty

because he does not recognize what his duty is or because he yields to non-rational influences outside his control. But neither of these possibilities is a possibility for a perfectly free and omniscient person. It is logically necessary that a perfectly free and omniscient person be perfectly good.[5]

Is this a good argument? I do not think so. In fact, I believe it fails for the same reason that Aquinas's last argument fails. This can be seen clearly if we state Swinburne's argument as follows:

(7)   God is perfectly free
(8)   God only does actions he believes are right (i.e. what he believes he has an overriding reason to do)
(9)   God is omniscient
(10) All God's beliefs are true beliefs
(11) If God believes that an action is right it is right (i.e. if God believes he has an overriding reason to do an action he has an overriding reason to do it)
(12) Therefore, God only does right actions.

The problem here is with premise (8), which is ambiguous. 'Right' here might mean 'beneficial to God' or it might mean 'morally right'. If the former, (12) does not follow from the premises above if (12) is to be interpreted as supporting Swinburne's claim that God cannot do moral evil. If the latter, (8) does not follow from (7) and the argument fails. It is true that God, like any agent, must always act for a purpose, must always do what in some sense he considers right. But I see no reason here to deny the logical possibility that the purpose be gratification of an evil desire of his. It is true in some sense that God must always do what there is an overriding reason to do, but, again, that overriding reason might be gratification of an evil desire of his. Swinburne seems to be assuming that it can never be rational to do something immoral. This may be true, but Swinburne certainly hasn't shown that it is true. Thus, his argument gives us no good reason to deny that God can do evil.

Once in discussion I encountered what amounts to the following argument for the conclusion that God cannot do evil (perhaps it also appears somewhere in the literature):

(13) Only beings that have unsatisfied desires can sin
(14) God has no unsatisfied desires
(15) Therefore, God cannot sin.

The argument is valid but unsound - neither premise is true, in my opinion. Against (14) it need only be pointed out that God apparently has lots of unsatisfied desires, e.g. the desire that I never sin. (The line from the Lord's Prayer - 'May your will be done on earth as it is in heaven' - seems to presuppose that God's will is not being done on earth.) Against (13) it need only be noted that the possibility of God having a desire that is both satisfied and morally evil has not been ruled out.

A second quite different argument for the conclusion that God cannot do evil can be constructed from the writings of William of Ockham. I say 'can be constructed' because Ockham's actual views on this subject are more subtle than the argument I will present might be taken to imply. The one supreme absolute in ethics for Ockham is our duty to obey God. Obeying God is the one act which can never be sinful, no matter what God commands us to do (even to disobey him). Conversely, disobeying God is the one act that can never be virtuous, no matter what God commands us to do (even to disobey him). (It is logically possible for God to command us to disobey him but it is impossible for us to obey such a command since in obeying it we would be disobeying it.) Aside from this one absolute, right and wrong depend entirely and only on the will of God, on what he decides to command us to do. Furthermore, God's will is completely free. With God, Ockham says, 'a thing becomes right solely for the reason that he wants it to be so'[6]. In other words, God's willing that Jones do x is a sufficient condition for it to be morally right that Jones do x. It follows from this that God logically cannot do evil (assuming that it is logically impossible for God to do something that God does not will that God do). God is under obligation to the will of no superior being. He is, so to speak, the author of morality; whatever he does (again, assuming he always does what he wills that he does) is <u>by definition</u> good. What is good is just what God wills or does; thus, again, God cannot do evil.

This is a powerful and intriguing argument. Perhaps Kierkegaard was flirting with it when he asked whether God's command to Abraham that he sacrifice his son Isaac should be considered a 'teleological suspension of the ethical'[7]. But I believe there are two serious problems with it[8]. The first point is that on the view we are considering the word 'good' is being used in an unusual way - so much so that we have no clear understanding of the sentence 'God is good'. We can understand what it is for Jones to be good - Jones is good if and only if Jones does what God wills that Jones do. But in what sense is God good? If and only if God does what God wills? But this is surely unsatisfactory. We certainly cannot understand the word 'good' in the sentence 'God is good' in the same way we understand it in such sentences as 'Jones is good.' For Jones is not good if Jones robs, murders and lies, but on the view under consideration God is good no matter what he does. It turns out, then, that 'God is good' is no more informative a sentence than 'God is God'. But surely, as I will argue later, Christians do mean something significant and non-tautological when they affirm the goodness of God.

The second problem with the Ockhamite view we are considering is that it allows for the possibility that God is a being whom we have no moral reason to worship. Why should we worship him if he is not morally good in at least a roughly similar way (though to an infinitely exalted degree) as are morally good human beings? Of course there is nothing in Ockham's view that requires its defenders to say that God actually wills robbery, murder and lying - it only requires them to say that even if God willed such things he would still be good. But this seems seriously problematical. Since on Ockham's view God's will is always free, that is, God can will robbery and murder, I would argue that if God willed such things he would no longer be morally good (as I understand the term). Consequently, I would have no moral reason to worship him.

Given God's power, of course, I might have strong prudential reasons to worship a God whose will is by definition good - he might punish me if I fail to do so. But given a desire on God's part that I worship him for moral reasons, i.e. because I believe morally he deserves or merits my worship (a desire I believe God has), God is obliged to use notions like 'good', 'morally right', etc. in ways I can understand. That is, he must use them in ways at least roughly similar to the ways in which I use them. To say things like 'Jones's murder of Smith is morally right just because God willed that Jones murder Smith' is to use words in a confusing way. It leaves us wondering why any being who wills that a murder occur would expect me to consider him worthy of worship. When the Bible and Christian people call God 'good' they mean (among other things), I believe, that God does not do things like commit murder, steal property, tell lies, or break promises. For these two reasons, then, I must reject the theory that God cannot do evil because whatever God wills is by definition good.

Peter Geach denies that we rightly decide whether God is lovable or admirable by appealing to the criteria standardly used for judging whether human beings are lovable or admirable. To the objection that we have no good moral reason to love and admire God if he is not at least as virtuous as a virtuous human being, he replies that the objection is perverse:

> What is being asked for is that God should be admired and loved for his great glory, for being God, for being utterly unlike man in nature . . . . God is to be loved and admired above all things because he is all truth and all beauty . . . . The protest that we ought not so to love and admire him if he does not share the mortal perfections proper to his creatures is a mere impertinence.[9]

Even if God were to allow the human race to continue in its sinful ways and destroy itself, Geach says, 'we could still praise God for his great glory: for being there, for being God'[10].

I believe Geach is quite correct that we would have several compelling reasons to admire God even if he were (by human standards) evil. We could admire, for example, his great power and wisdom and skill in creating the universe. It is also true that in judging God's moral character we cannot use precisely the same criteria we use in judging human beings: as Geach correctly points out, several human virtues have no application to the life of God, e.g. courage and chastity. But it still seems clear that if God were evil in relation to such typical human standards as truth-telling and promise-keeping we would have no good moral reason to admire him (and perhaps no good reason at all to love him). If God were (by human standards) evil, and especially if he were (by human standards) malevolent, one would think the proper responses to him would be suspicion and fear rather than love and admiration. So it still seems that if God wants us to love and admire him for moral reasons (as I believe he does) he must be good in an analogous way to morally good human beings. That is, he must, for example, tell the truth, keep his promises, and refrain from causing needless suffering.

It looks, then, as if neither way of arguing for the conclusion that God is unable to do evil suffices. Let us then turn to the view that God is free to do evil. Now if God is free to do evil we can ask whether he ever in fact does evil. Some Jewish and Christian thinkers say that he does, that there is an evil or demonic side to God. But I find this view biblically and theologically objectionable; I believe that God is wholly good. What I want to say, then, is that God is free to do evil (for reasons I will specify below) but doesn't and won't. That is, it is both logically possible and within God's power to do evil, but he doesn't do evil and won't.

Jonathan Harrison argues that even for those who say that doing evil is in God's power there can be a sense in which doing evil is not logically possible for God. If perfect goodness is an essential property of divinity, then God cannot do evil and remain divine, and the sentence 'God does evil' is necessarily false. Still, Harrison says, it can be within the power of the person we now think of as God, i.e. the actual creator of the universe, to do evil. It is just that if he did evil he could no longer properly be called God [1].

Here we see at work a distinction (to be discussed in more detail in Chapter 8) between two uses of the term 'God'. On the one hand, the term might be a proper name referring to a given being (Yahweh) who actually is the omnipotent, omniscient creator of the world. On the other hand, the term might be a title for or definite description of any divine being (Yahweh or anybody else who happens to be the omnipotent, omniscient creator of the world). Harrison is saying that doing evil is possible for Yahweh but not for a divine being - if Yahweh did evil he wouldn't be divine. (In other words, the statement 'God cannot do evil' is false when understood de re but true when understood de dicto.)

However, the problem I have with this argument is that I do not believe that perfect goodness is an essential property of God in either sense of the term 'God' (though I certainly hold that perfect goodness is a property of God in both senses). How could anyone know that Yahweh, if he exists, has perfect goodness as an essential property, i.e. that he logically cannot do an evil deed? How could anyone know that Yahweh, if he exists and is divine, would no longer be divine if he did one evil deed? I do not think anybody knows these things. That does not, of course, show that they are not true. But it does suggest that those of us who reject them are within our rights. I do hold that Yahweh will never exercise his power to do evil: but that is not the same as saying that Yahweh does not have such power or has the power but would no longer be God if he exercised it. Accordingly, I will not follow Harrison's line.

If it is both logically possible and within God's power for him to do evil, must we then say that there is some probability he will do evil, however infinitesimally small? Not at all. I believe we can be quite sure God will never do evil. God abstains from doing evil precisely because he wills not to do evil. Doing evil is in his power but he will not do evil. Analogously, I believe it is within my power intentionally to poison my neighbour's cat, but I will not do it. The probability is not zero (I am not morally perfect, as God is) but very near it. I have no desire to do it; I choose not to do it. Doing evil, then, is simply contrary to God's choices. Nelson Pike's phrase is apt: God 'cannot bring himself to do evil' because doing evil would contradict a 'firm and stable feature of his nature', i.e. his moral strength and goodness [12].

Is there any reason to take this line, aside from the difficulties connected with the view that God is unable to do evil? Yes, I believe so. One good reason has to do with the religious phenomenon of praising God. The Bible is shot through and through with the injunction that we praise God; Christians accordingly engage in praise of God whenever they gather to worship him.

> Praise the Lord!
> O give thanks to the Lord,
>   for he is good;
> For his steadfast love endures forever! (Ps. 106:1)

> Enter his gates with thanksgiving,
>   and his courts with praise!
> Give thanks to him, bless his name! (Ps. 100:4)

But I see no good reason to praise God for his moral goodness if God is unable to sin; likewise, I see no good reason to thank god for his benefits to us and answers to our prayers if it is not in his power to be malevolent toward us.

Perhaps this is too hasty. We can easily imagine some good reasons to praise an essentially morally perfect being for his goodness. For one thing, our praise might be justified on the grounds that it will

serve to inspire us or others to imitate the perfect being's behaviour.
For another, as noted earlier, our praise might be justified on the
grounds that it is prudent: if praise is what God wants from us, he
might punish us if we fail to praise him. But neither constitutes the
sort of moral praise we give a person whom we think merits it. And it
is this sort of praise, I believe, both that Christians want to give to
God and that God wants from us.

If God is actually unable to do evil it is no more morally apt to
praise him for his goodness than it is apt to praise the refrigerator
for keeping the food cold or a spider for refraining from telling lies.
Refrigerators are designed to keep food cold; they aren't agents who
make choices; it isn't praiseworthy that they keep food cold. Spiders
just aren't able to tell lies; it isn't praiseworthy that they don't. If
God's nature causes or determines him to do good in such a way that
doing evil is not in his power, I would conclude that he is not a free
and responsible moral agent and thus is not a fit object of the praise
and thanks of his people.

Geach sneers at this argument as a startling and ridiculous way of
commending God's morals,[13] but he does not argue against it.
Perhaps Geach is again thinking that God is laudable just for being
God, i.e. for his non-moral qualities like power and wisdom and
creative skill. If so, I agree with him. But I believe God is also
laudable for being morally good, and I cannot see how a being who is
unable to do evil can be laudable for being good. Of course, if we
adopt a soft determinist notion of divine freedom, we can have God
being both causally unable to do evil and morally responsible for his
goodness. (In speaking of God's being 'causally unable to do evil' I do
not mean to imply that those who believe that God cannot do evil
believe that God is caused not to do evil by forces external to him -
rather that his own morally good nature causally prevents him from
doing evil.) But I believe this notion of freedom is unsatisfactory. If
God is to be morally responsible for his goodness he must be causally
able to do evil.

Geach also argues that Christianity collapses unless we can be sure
that God cannot lie or break promises[14]. But this surely is not true.
Christianity only collapses if we cannot be sure that God has not or
will not lie or break promises - not if it is merely in God's power to
do so. I believe we can be sure that God never has and never will lie
or break a promise. This is enough; why must we be sure he cannot do
so? Geach further says:

> Well, as regards a man it makes good sense to say: 'He has the
> bodily and mental power to do so-and-so, but he certainly will not,
> it would be pointlessly silly and wicked.' But does anything
> remotely like this makes sense to say about Almighty God?[15]

Geach clearly thinks it does not. But aside from the problem of a disembodied being like God being spoken of as having 'bodily power', I see no difficulty here. Why cannot we say that God has the ability to do certain things which in fact he will never do?

(16)   God has the ability to make Walter Cronkite stutter nervously on national television, but he never will.
(17)   God has the ability to hide a can of vegetable soup in my office, but he never will.
(18)   God has the ability to tell a lie, but he never will.
(19)   God has the ability to break a promise, but he never will.

All four sentences, in my opinion, make good sense.

Thus the doctrine of God's perfect goodness can now be taken to mean that God is a consistently good being despite the freedom he has at any point to do evil. This makes him a morally free and responsible agent. This makes his consistent benevolence morally praiseworthy. And this, in turn, makes him a fit object of the adoration and worship Christians give him.

7 Evil

The problem of evil, in my opinion and in the opinion of many others, is the most serious intellectual difficulty that Christians and other theists face. I will distinguish between two forms of the problem, what I will call the 'logical problem of evil' (LPE) and the 'emotive problem of evil' (EPE), and I will try to say something in response to each. The LPE is perhaps the most common form. It is usually stated in such a way as to imply that theism is in some sort of logical difficulty.

As we have seen, Christians affirm both the following propositions:

(1) God is omnipotent

and

(2) God is good.

We discussed omnipotence in Chapter 5 and goodness in Chapter 6. I have nothing to add here on omnipotence. Regarding divine goodness let me repeat that I take the statement 'God is good' to mean 'God is wholly good'. It follows from this statement, I believe, that God never causes any sort of suffering unless it will lead to a greater good. This is obviously vague and in need of explication, but what I am excluding is the notion that God is a mainly good being who nevertheless has a demonic side.

Now nearly everyone, Christian or not, is willing to affirm a third proposition (and, indeed, this proposition seems crucial to Christianity and other forms of theism), namely,

(3) Evil exists.

The LPE is just this: The conjunction of (1), (2) and (3), which we can call

(4) God is omnipotent and God is good and evil exists

is apparently logically inconsistent. That is, (1), (2) and (3) are an inconsistent set; they cannot all be true; the truth of any two of them apparently implies the falsity of the third. For if God is omnipotent it seems he is <u>able</u> to prevent evil; and if God is good it seems he is <u>willing</u> to prevent evil. Why then does evil exist? Thus Christianity is in logical difficulty because all three propositions are and must be held by Christians. That is, (4) is essential to Christianity and (4) is necessarily false; thus Christianity is contradictory. This, then, is the LPE.

Let us distinguish between two sorts of evil, <u>moral evil</u> and <u>natural evil</u>. Roughly, moral evil is wrongdoing or suffering brought about by moral agents such as human beings. Moral evil is often called 'sin'; it includes such things as pride, envy, lying, murder, selfishness, robbery, greed, etc. Roughly, natural evil (sometimes called physical evil) is pain and suffering brought about directly by such natural events as earthquakes, diseases, famines, floods, etc.

There are two basic strategies a Christian might adopt in response to the LPE. The first is to give up one of the three propositions that create the problem. One possibility is to deny that God is omnipotent; we might say that God is very powerful but is simply not able to prevent evil; he tries his best but evil exists because he is not powerful enough to overcome the forces that oppose him. Another possibility is to deny that God is wholly good; he is omnipotent, it might be said, but has an evil or demonic side that sometimes expresses itself in malevolent acts. Or, thirdly, we might deny that evil exists - claim that it is 'an illusion of the material sense', or some other sort of metaphysically unreal thing.

But apart from any philosophical objections that might be raised against these views, this general strategy will not seem theologically attractive to Christians. As I mentioned, (1), (2) and (3) all seem essential to Christianity as normally understood. Giving up one or another of these three propositions seems a terribly high price to pay. Christians, then, will be attracted by the other strategy, which is to try to argue, in one way or another, that (1), (2) and (3) are not an inconsistent set, that the truth of (3) does not entail that (1) and/or (2) must be false.

Many versions of this strategy have been suggested in the history of Christian thought, but most seem (to me, at least) weak and unable to solve the LPE. The one line of argument that seems promising is the 'free will defence' (or FWD, as I will call it). It was first presented with great vigour by Augustine (A.D. 354-430) and has recently been skilfully defended by Alvin Plantinga. I will now explain its major themes.

What were God's aims in creating the universe? According to the FWD, he wanted two things. First, he wanted to create the best universe he could, i.e. the best possible balance of moral and natural good over moral and natural evil. And second, he wanted to create a world in which created rational agents (e.g. human beings) would decide <u>freely</u> to love and obey him. Accordingly he created a world in which there originally existed no moral or natural evil, and he created human beings with the facility of free moral choice.

Recalling the argument of Chapter 4, let us say that persons are free moral agents if and only if in the case of the decisions they make

(5)   Their choices are not coerced or causally determined

and

(6)   They have genuine alternatives, i.e. it is actually in their power, under the same antecedent conditions, to do something or not do it.

Obviously, in making humans free God ran the risk that they would choose evil rather than good. The possibility of freely doing evil is the inevitable companion of the possibility of freely doing good. Unfortunately this is just what human beings did: they chose to go wrong; they fell into sin. So God is not to be blamed for the existence of evil in the world - we are. Of course God is indirectly responsible for evil in the sense that he created the conditions given which evil would come into existence (i.e. he gave us free choice), and he foreknew the evil choices we would make. But even given these conditions, it was not inevitable that evil exist. The non-existence of evil was quite possible; humans could have chosen to obey God. Sadly, they didn't.

Why then did God create free moral agents in the first place? Does it not look as if his plan went wrong, as if his righteous desires were thwarted? Not so, say proponents of the FWD. God's policy decision to make us free was wise, for it will turn out better in the long run that we act freely, even if we sometimes err, than it would have turned out had we been created innocent automata, programmed always to do the good. God's decision will turn out to be wise because the good that will in the end result from his decision will outweigh the evil that will in the end result from it[1]. Though John Hick is not an advocate of the Augustinian FWD, his emphasis on the eschatological character of Christianity is quite correct and can be used by free will defenders. Free will defenders claim that in the eschaton it will be seen that God chose the best course. And, furthermore, they will claim that this favourable balance of good over evil was obtainable by God in no other way.

In response to the problem of evil, some theists have argued that this is 'the best of all possible worlds'. Must the FWD make this claim? I believe not. In the first place, it is not clear that the notion 'the best of all possible worlds' is coherent. Take the notion 'tallest conceivable man'. This notion is incoherent because no matter how tall we conceive a tall man to be we can always conceptually add another inch and thus prove that he was not, after all, the tallest conceivable man. Just so, it may be argued, the notion 'the best of all possible worlds' is incoherent. For any possible world, no matter how much pleasure and happiness it contains, we can think of a better one, i.e. one with slightly more pleasure and happiness[2]. Accordingly, there logically cannot exist such a world, and the FWD need not claim that this world is the best of all possible worlds.

But even if this argument is incorrect, even if the notion is coherent, the FWD still need not claim that this is the best of all possible worlds. Better worlds than this world are conceivable, in my opinion. For example, so far as I am able to tell, this world would have been morally better (would have contained less moral evil) had Hitler not hated Jews. The death of six million Jews in the Holocaust, I believe, was based on decisions made by free and morally responsible human agents, Hitler and others. So the FWD must in a sense say that the amount of good and evil that exists in the world is partially up to us and not entirely up to God. If so, it then becomes easy to imagine worlds better than this one - e.g. a world otherwise as much as possible like this one except that no Jews are ever murdered. Thus this is not the best of all possible worlds.

What the FWD must insist on is, first, that the amount of evil that in the end will exist will be outweighed by the great goods that will then exist; and second, that this favourable balance of good over evil was obtainable by God in no other way that was within his control. (Free will defenders need not claim, incidentally, to be able to explain how or why each evil event that occurs in history helps lead to a greater good. As regards the Holocaust, for example, I confess I am quite unable to do so.)

But let us return to propositions (1), (2) and (3), which the LPE critic says form an inconsistent set. Is this true? How does the FWD answer this charge? Let me restructure the problem slightly. It will be less cumbersome to work with two rather than three propositions, so let us now ask whether

(3)   Evil exists

is consistent with the conjunction of (1) and (2), which we can call

(7)   God is omnipotent and God is good.

Those who push the LPE will claim that (3) and (7) are inconsistent - if one is true the other must be false. Is this true?

Well, Alvin Plantinga has used in this connection a recognized procedure for proving that two propositions are logically consistent[3]. Let us see if it is usable here. We can prove that (3) and (7) are consistent if the FWD can provide us with a third proposition (which I will call (8)), which is consistent with (7) and in conjunction with (7) entails (3). Here is an analogy. It might initially appear that the following propositions are inconsistent:

(9)   Kucheman wants Bruno to stop barking and Kucheman has the power to make Bruno stop barking.

(10)   Bruno does not stop barking.

But they are consistent, despite appearances. We can see this via a third proposition:

(11)   Kucheman allows Bruno to decide whether to stop barking; Kucheman wants Bruno to decide whether to stop barking more than he wants Bruno to stop barking; and Bruno decides not to stop barking.

(11) is possibly true; (11) is consistent with (9); and the conjunction of (9) and (11) entails (10). Thus (9) and (10) are consistent.

Now what is the proposition that the free will defender can use to show that (3) and (7) are consistent? Let me suggest the following:

(8)   All the evil that exists in the world is due to the choices of free moral agents whom God created, and no other world which God could have created would have had a better balance of good over evil than the actual world will have.

What this says is that God's policy decision to create free moral agents will turn out to be wise and that it was not within God's power to have created a better world. Now (8) certainly seems possibly true (the question of its truth will come up later); I can detect no contradiction or incoherence in (8). And (8) does seem consistent with (7) - I see no reason to call them inconsistent, at any rate. And the conjunction of (7) and (8) does indeed entail (3). Thus (3) and (7) are consistent and the LPE is apparently solved. A rational person can believe that God is omnipotent, that God is good, and that evil exists. It is apparently false to claim that the LPE shows that Christianity and other forms of theism are contradictory.

It is important to emphasize here the liberatarian notion of moral freedom that the FWD is based upon. This is because the FWD can quite easily be refuted if a different notion of freedom is smuggled into it. Indeed, this very strategy has been used by some critics. Steven Boer, for example, argues that people are morally free if they are able to try to do evil deeds, i.e. make evil choices and formulate evil intentions, whether in fact they are ever able to succeed. Boer says:

Free will has nothing intrinsically to do with the question of whether or not a given agent succeeds in doing what he 'willed' to do, unless the intended action pertains to certain kinds of immediate control over his body . . . . In short, freedom of the will is freedom of opportunity: it is a license to choose and try, not a warranty of success. [4]

This allows Boer to argue that God could have made us both free (in the sense stipulated) and unable, because of systematic divine interventions, to succeed in doing the evil deeds we intend. That is, God could have prevented the doing of evil deeds without compromising anyone's free will. That he obviously has not done so, Boer says, exposes the failure of the FWD.

But surely Boer's notion of freedom is a strange one; and it is certainly not the notion of freedom that the FWD is based upon. The logic of the situation is this: free will defenders wish to argue that

(12)   God creates a world W in which persons have free will

is inconsistent with

(13)   God brings it about that persons in W do no evil.

In so doing, they supply a notion of 'free will' and a line of argument which allow them to make two points: first, that (12) and (13) are inconsistent because it is necessarily true that if a person is _free_ in doing something, no one else - not even God - can bring it about that that person does it; and, second, that it is logically possible that the actual world in the long run will turn out better than would any alternative world in which persons were not free (in the sense of the term used by free will defenders).

Surely, then, it is the responsibility of people like Boer to criticize the FWD on the basis of its own definition of the term 'free will', not some other. (Of course the FWD fails if it can be shown that people cannot possibly be free in its sense of the word, but Boer has not shown this, nor, to my knowledge, has anybody else.) Obviously, if critics are allowed to read their own notion of free will into the FWD, they can easily make the argument look pretty silly. Suppose someone holds that people have 'free will' if and only if all their actions are caused by God. Then it would be easy to show that (12) and (13) are consistent and that the FWD fails. But of course this would not constitute much of an argument against the FWD, since free will defenders do not hold this view of free will.

In this connection, I must insist that the biblical sense in which persons have free will, as well as the sense of this term found in the writings of free will defenders such as Augustine and Plantinga, is not Boer's 'free to will but not to do' sense. We are morally free agents, according to the FWD, if we are free to do evil deeds, not just to will to do them. Boer can reply that the FWD's notion of free will is illusory or somehow mistaken. But it seems far more plausible than his notion. If God were systematically to prevent our doing evil deeds, as Boer suggests, would we really be morally free? Surely I am a morally free agent only if I can actually do evil deeds as well as will them.

If this is not the case, we are in the perfectly absurd position (as Boer's argument really seems to entail) of having to say, for example,

that we are all free to fly like the birds because we can will to fly
like the birds! In fact, many children entertain this very fantasy.
Some even try to fly, e.g. by jumping off fences while flapping their
arms vigorously. But they soon learn that it is causally impossible to
fly in this way, and so they stop willing to do it too - for the
perfectly acceptable reason that it is quite useless to try. Clearly, if
God were systematically to intervene to prevent evil deeds, or so to
arrange the world that evil deeds never causally followed upon evil
intentions, soon no one would try to do evil deeds any longer. If
people learned that attempts to insult or injure or kill always failed,
they would soon stop trying. They would then most certainly not be
morally free.

However, there are several objections more serious than this that
must be dealt with before we can consider the LPE solved. I will
mention three.

The first can be stated as follows:

If the whole creation was originally perfectly morally good, then
human beings, as orginally created, were perfectly morally good.
But then how do we explain the fact that people sin? A fall into sin
seems logically impossible for a perfectly morally good being; a
being sins only if it has a moral flaw. Since humans do sin, it
follows that they were not originally created perfectly morally
good, and thus God is directly responsible for moral evil[5].

Several things here are true. I agree that a perfectly morally good
being will never sin. I agree that there was no evil in God's original
creation. And it is also true that Genesis 1:31 says of God's entire
creation (which obviously includes human beings) that 'it was very
good'. But despite this, the answer to the above objection is that the
FWD is not committed to the view that humans were created
perfectly morally good. The biblical expression 'very good' quite
obviously does not mean 'perfectly morally good' - how could created
things like the moon or Mount Baldy or the eucalyptus tree outside
my office be perfectly morally good? Clearly they cannot, and so
'very good' must mean something else. I would suggest God judged his
creation to be very good in that it was a harmonious, beautiful,
smoothly-working cosmos rather than the ugly, churning chaos over
which the Spirit of God had moved (Gen. 1:2). Human beings too were
created good in this sense, but not perfectly morally good. Since God
wanted them to be free moral agents, he must have created them as
spiritually immature, morally neutral creatures, capable of choosing
either good or evil. And this is just what the FWD says he did.

The second objection asks why an omnipotent being couldn't have
created free beings who always freely choose the good. If this is
logically possible, a good creator who was able to do so would

certainly have done so. Since he obviously did not do so, at least some of the claims theists make about God must be false. Thus J. L. Mackie argues as follows:

> If God has made men such that in their free choices they sometimes prefer what is good and sometimes what is evil, why could he not have made men such that they always freely choose the good? If there is no logical impossibilitiy in a man's freely choosing the good on one, or on several occasions, there cannot be a logical impossibility in his freely choosing the good on every occasion. God was not, then, faced with a choice between making innocent automata and making beings who, in acting freely, would sometimes go wrong: there was open to him the obviously better possibility of making beings who would act freely but always go right. Clearly, his failure to avail himself of this possibility is inconsistent with his being both omnipotent and wholly good.[6]

Mackie appears to be making two claims here - first, that there is no logical impossibility in a free moral agent always freely choosing the good; and second, that God can create free moral agents such that they will always freely choose the good. (Mackie also appears to believe that the first entails the second.) Now if these claims are true, they constitute a refutation of the FWD. For their effect is to falsify a crucial assumption of the FWD, namely, that it is impossible for God to create moral agents such that they are both free and will always choose the good, that the possibility of doing evil is the inevitable companion of the possibility of freely doing good.

I have no wish to dispute Mackie's first claim. Though it seems highly improbable, it does seem logically possible that all free moral agents always freely choose the good. 'Jones is a free moral agent and Jones never sins', is not necessarily false. Of course, given the definition of 'free' stated earlier, it follows that had this possibility been actualized, i.e. had the moral agents whom God created never sinned, it would have been what might be called a 'pleasant accident'. God would not have brought it about, nor would he be responsible for it. For if the agents were really free no one could have caused or coerced them to behave as they did.

Thus Mackie's second claim - that it is logically possible for God to create free moral agents and ensure that they always freely choose the good - is false and does not follow from the first. 'Jones is a free moral agent whom God creates in such a way that Jones never sins', is necessarily false. There is a logical tension betwen an agent's being free vis-a-vis certain acts and that agent's somehow being influenced by God always to behave in a certain way regarding those acts. Again we see that given God's decision to create free moral agents, it follows that it is in part up to those agents and not entirely up to God what the world will be like. There are some logically possible worlds that God cannot create. If there is a given free moral agent, say

Jones, who in a given situation will freely decide to sin, it is not in God's power to create a world in which Jones is free, the situation is exactly the same, and Jones does not sin[7].

But an objection might be raised here: 'I am surely free to torture and kill my pet dog, but I am perfectly sure that I will never do so. Why couldn't God have created all moral agents with both freedom to sin and the same aversion to sin that I have to torturing and killing my dog?' The answer to this is that it is a wrong sense of 'free' that is being used here. It is certainly logically possible and, apart from my desires and beliefs, causally possible for me to torture and kill my dog. But it is precisely my desires and beliefs that causally prevent me from doing so. And had God created moral agents who had analogous desires and beliefs that prevented them from sinning, they would not have been _free_ moral agents, i.e. free to obey or disobey God.

The third objection has to do with the distinction between moral and natural evil. Now the FWD, as I have formulated it, relies on (8), which begins with the claim that 'All the evil that exists in the world is due to the choices of free moral agents whom God created'. But this seems clearly false (so this objection would run). If the FWD works at all it is perhaps a solution only to part of the LPE, namely, that part that concerns moral evil. But how can such natural evils as earthquakes, disease and famine be attributed to moral agents? This seems absurd, which is precisely why we call such evils natural rather than moral in the first place. Thus (8) is clearly false, and the FWD fails.

For years I would have been inclined to agree with the substance of this objection. I was of the opinion that the FWD solved the problem of moral evil but not the problem of natural evil. I felt that other arguments beside the FWD had to be appealed to when dealing with natural evil, although I confess none of these arguments seemed particularly convincing to me. But in recent years Alvin Plantinga has suggested that the FWD can indeed solve the problem of natural evil. He appeals to an often neglected aspect of Christian tradition, which was also used by Augustine in his writings on the problem of evil, namely, the notion of Satan or Lucifer as the cause of natural evil. Augustine, Plantinga says,

> attributes much of the evil we find to Satan or to Satan and his cohorts. Satan, so the traditional doctrines goes, is a mighty nonhuman spirit who, along with many other angels, was created long before God created man. Unlike most of his colleagues, Satan rebelled against God and has been wreaking whatever havoc he can. The result is natural evil. So the natural evil we find is due to the free actions of nonhuman spirits. [8]

What is to be said about this? Plantinga admits many people find belief in the devil preposterious, let alone the idea that the devil and his cohorts are responsible for whatever natural evil we find. But this does not amount to much of an argument against Augustine's thesis, Plantinga insists. Truth is not decided by majority vote. However, Plantinga's main point against those who object to his luciferous defence is to insist that to do the job of solving what I am calling the LPE, proposition (8) (which, as we have seen, claims that all evil is due to the choices of created free moral agents) need only be possibly true. And this seems quite correct. As we saw, in order to solve the LPE, (8) need only be consistent with (7) and capable of entailing (3) when conjoined with (7). Now if (8) is consistent with (7), i.e. if it is logically possible for both (7) and (8) to be true, then (8) itself is possibly true. Later, when dealing with the EPE, we will have to raise the question of the truth of (8), which means we will have to ask about the truth of Plantinga's luciferous defence. But as far as the LPE is concerned, Plantinga seems to be correct, and I confess he has convinced me. It certainly does seem <u>possible</u> that natural evil is due to the choices of Satan and his cohorts. Thus the luciferous defence can solve the LPE as concerns natural evil.

All three objections to the FWD as a solution to the LPE fail. Those who push the LPE argue that Christians and other theists contradict themselves by believing in the omnipotence and goodness of God and the existence of evil. We can now see that this is not true. The FWD successfully rebuts this charge.

But even if it is true that theism is logically consistent, there is another difficulty that remains, namely, what I call the EPE. This difficulty too concerns this proposition that is believed by Christians:

(4)   God is omnipotent and God is good and evil exists.

Now against (4), someone might say something like this:

I admit there is no logical inconsistency in (4), but the problem of evil, when grasped in its full depth, is deeper than a mere logical exercise. A cold logical approach that merely shows the consistency of (4) fails to touch the problem at its deepest nerve. To show, as a sheer logical exercise, that (4) is consistent does nothing to convince people to believe (4). To show that (4) is <u>possibly true</u> does not show that it is <u>true</u> or even <u>probably true</u>, i.e. it does nothing to show that people should believe in God's omnipotence and goodness[9].

There is much that must be sorted out in these words. What exactly does the EPE come to? This is not altogether clear in the above lines, and perhaps it might help to suggest some possible interpretations.

Words such as those above are sometimes expressed with deep emotion. Perhaps the EPE means something like this: the existence of evil in the world somehow makes us deeply feel that

(7)   God is omnipotent and God is good

is false. That is, the existence of evil in the world makes us deeply feel that (1) and/or (2) must be rejected or modified. Because of evil, we find (7) hard to believe. Now there are obviously people about whom this could truly be said. Albert Camus comes to mind. So does Elie Wiesel. But despite this, it is hard to detect any real difficulty for Christianity here. By itself, this seems no more serious an objection to Christianity than, say, the following comment: 'You Christians believe in God but somehow I can't'.

But perhaps the EPE means something more than this. Perhaps the claim is that the existence of evil makes (7) improbable or implausible, that the existence of evil constitutes strong evidence against (7). But the problem with this is that it is difficult to see how any probabilistic judgements can be made here. And this is for the obvious reason that we do not seem to be in a position to make a probability judgement about the truth of the FWD. As I have claimed, the FWD claims that (4) is consistent because the following proposition is possibly true:

(8)   All the evil that exists in the world is due to the choices of free moral agents whom God created, and no other world which God could have created would have had a better balance of good over evil than the actual world will have.

If we knew that (8) was false or improbable we might have good reason to deny (7). But in fact we do not know that (8) is false or improbable (at least I am aware of no good argument or evidence that falsifies (8)), and so we do not seem to be in a position to say that (7) is false or improbable.

There seems to be no way for us to argue analogically either. We might be able to do so if the following proposition were known to be true:

(14)   There are ninety universes in which evil exists but no good, omnipotent God, and only ten universes in which evil and a good, omnipotent God both exist.

If (14) were known to be true we might be able to make a probability estimate - someone might claim, at any rate, that (14) renders the probability that (7) is true .1. But in fact (14) is not only not known to be true - it does not even appear to make good sense. Since the term 'universe' is all-inconclusive (nothing except perhaps God lies outside 'the universe'), there are no 'other universes' than ours with which we can compare it[10].

But perhaps there is another way of stating the 'probability' interpretation of the EPE.

> If you were the Christian God - the omnipotent and good creator of
> the world - what sort of world would you create? One thing is for
> sure: you wouldn't create this sort of world. You wouldn't create a
> world containing cancer, atomic bombs, child abuse and famine.
> You would create a world without these evils. Thus it appears
> highly improbable that the world was created by the Christian
> God [11].

I will say some things later that are relevant to this objection, but
for now I wish simply to insist that I have not the vaguest idea what
sort of world I would create given the stated conditions, nor do I
believe anyone else does. Of course my general aim would be to
create a world with the best possible balance of good over evil. Would
eliminating natural evil or free moral agents achieve this end? I just
don't know, and I do not believe anyone else does either. Of course it
is <u>possible</u> that if I knew all relevant facts I would create a world
very different to this one. But it is also possible that I would create a
world as much like this one as I could. I just don't know enough to say,
and neither does anyone else, in my opinion.

Of course, the best judgement we can make is that natural evils
like cancer and earthquakes are evil and should be fought against
with all our power. My point, however, is that: (1) we do not know all
the causal connections between things and so are not in a perfect
position to discern good and evil (I remember my amazement when as
a child my father told me that it was a good thing that flies existed);
and (2) God, who according to the Christian tradition is omniscient
and infinitely wise, <u>is</u> in such a position. So I fail to see how the
existence of evil in the world (or the existence of a large amount of
evil in the world) renders (7) improbable. At best, we must await the
skeptic's explanation of precisely how the existence of evil renders
(7) improbable. It is not clear at this point that it does [12].

Let me clarify one point. I am not saying that all evil is only
apparent. I am sure there are some events which the world would
have been better without. Nor am I saying that no probabilistic
judgements can be made about the goodness or evilness of events. I
am saying four things: (1) We are sometimes wrong in making such
judgements. (2) It is very difficult for us to make such judgements
about huge, complex events like, say, the Second World War, and
virtually impossible for us with the facts we know to make such
judgements about the 'omni-event' of the history of the universe
(nothing can stand in a probabilizing relationship to the universe). (3)
Some events we now consider evil - perhaps even the Holocaust - may
turn out on balance good (though in the case of the Holocaust I again
confess I do not see how). (4) Even if some ineradicably evil events
occur (because of the freedom God gives his creatures), these events
while retaining their evilness will either be used by God to produce

the eschaton or else will be overcome in it.

Possibly there are other interpretations of the EPE that are more threatening to Christianity than the ones we have been discussing. I cannot think of any, however, and so I conclude that the EPE poses no philosophical difficulty for Christianity. If the Christian's problem when confronted with the LPE is the apologetic task of responding to the critic's charge that Christianity is inconsistent, then if the LPE can be solved (by the FWD or any other argument) I see no added philosophical problem for Christianity in the EPE. I believe I have shown that (4) is consistent, and so believe that this defensive apologetic task has been accomplished.

But perhaps there is still a residual feeling that the problem of evil has not been completely disposed of. I confess to having such a feeling, and perhaps other Christians will too. But I believe this residual feeling that somehow still not all is well is based on no philosophical difficulty but rather on what might be called the 'evangelistic difficulty' that the problem of evil poses for Christians and other theists. This difficulty is not the negative apologetic task of responding to a philosophical criticism, but rather the positive evangelistic task of convincing people to believe (7).

I have been using the term 'philosophical difficulty'. There exists what I call a philosophical difficulty for a belief if there is some reason to consider it either logically inconsistent or disconfirmed by the preponderance of available evidence. Thus all philosophical difficulties are also 'evangelistic difficulties', for it is usually hard to convince someone to accept an apparently inconsistent or apparently ill-founded belief. But some evangelistic difficulties are clearly not philosophical - e.g. the difficulty we might have trying to convince a patient in mental hospital to accept the belief that he is not Napoleon.

Now trying to convince people to believe

(7)   God is omnipotent and God is good

may indeed be a serious difficulty. But evangelism is not philosophy. If philosophers have successfully defended theism against the charge that

(4)   God is omnipotent and God is good and evil exists

is inconsistent or improbable, it is difficult to see what else they can or must do. They may not be able to convert a person who says, 'I'm sorry, but because evil exists I just can't see how a good, omnipotent God can exist'. But they can point out that this person's inability to believe does not in itself constitute a good reason for Christians to give up their belief. Thus, I conclude, the EPE may pose difficulties for Christianity, but not philosophical difficulties.

One obvious weakness of many theodicies is that they cannot account for the huge <u>amount</u> of evil that apparently exists in the world. For example, some theodicists claim that pain and adversity are really good because they help people rise to new moral and spiritual heights in overcoming them. No doubt this is true in some cases - the athlete who improves performance because of a rigorous and painful training regime, the novelist whose works are more deeply insightful into human nature because of early struggles, say, with poverty and rejection notices from unappreciative publishers. But this theodicy simply cannot account for the amount of suffering that we see in the world. How can the murder of six million Jews in the Second World War lead people to new and otherwise unobtainable heights? The very thought seems absurd, almost obscene.

At first glance, the FWD seems less embarrassed than other theodicies by the amount of evil that exists in the world: the free will defender will simply say of all evil events that they are due not to God (or at least not directly to God) but rather to created free moral agents who choose to do evil. But at a deeper level, the FWD still seems open to this objection. For when we consider people like Hitler and events like the Holocaust we are bound to wonder whether the facility of free moral choice, which the FWD says God gave human beings, has turned out to be worth the price. Even if we grant that it is a <u>prima facie</u> good that God created us free moral agents rather than causally determined automata, we can still wonder, to put it in economic terms, whether this freedom has turned out to be cost-effective. Surely some will say (perhaps one of the millions of surviving Jews who lost family and friends in the Holocaust), 'I wish God had created a world of more determinism and less murder'.

The notion of our being less free than the FWD claims that we are seems to make perfectly good sense. For example, I am not now free to destroy the planet Saturn: apparently God has not given me that ability. But then why couldn't God have created me with an analogous inability to commit murder? Why didn't God, for example, place us in an environment that provided fewer opportunities or temptations to go wrong than he in fact did? Or why didn't he create us with a stronger psychological endowment - say, a stronger desire to do good or a weaker desire to do evil?

There are two points I wish to make about this. First, we do not know whether freedom is cost-effective. Let us be clear what it is we are evaluating: it is the policy decision God made (according to the FWD) to allow human beings moral freedom, i.e. freedom to do right or wrong without interference. Obviously, a correct decision on whether or not a given policy is cost-effective cannot be made till the results of the policy are in and can be evaluated. But how can we now correctly decide whether freedom will turn out to be cost-effective if we have no idea how human history will turn out? Perhaps it is true, as Christians believe, that the eschaton holds in store for us such great goods that all pre-eschaton evils will be outweighed. We do not know whether this claim is true, and so we do not know whether God's policy will turn out to be cost-effective.

Of course decisions often have to be made on the basis of inconclusive evidence. Perhaps it is true that each person, here and now, must decide whether to believe that freedom is cost-effective, just in the sense that each person must decide, here and now, whether to believe in a good, omnipotent God despite the presence of evil in the world. And such a decision can obviously be made only on the basis of evidence that is presently available (although some people believe there is evidence that the Christian eschaton is coming). But even if, for pragmatic reasons, such a decision must be made here and now, it can still be seen that it is ultimately unfair to try to make - at this time and with the evidence we now have - a correct judgement about the cost-effectiveness of God's policy. Only when the drama is finished can a fair judgement be made whether applause is warranted. If there turns out to be no Christian eschaton, or if history ends in a violent bang or a desperate whimper, then we will see that freedom is not cost-effective. But we cannot see that now.

The second point is that only God knows whether freedom will turn out to be cost-effective. Only he knows how human history turns out, what our destiny is. Furthermore, only God is in a position to weigh huge goods and evils against each other in order to make correct judgements about whether, say, the Second World War was, on balance, a morally good or morally evil event. Thus only God is in a position to judge whether moral freedom will turn out to be worth the price.

Of course it may be difficult for Christians and other theists to convince people that freedom is cost-effective. But this reduces to the evangelistic difficulty, which, as I said, is not a philosophical difficulty. Questions about the cost-effectiveness of freedom do not succeed in showing that Christianity is inconsistent, nor do they give the Christian any good reason to doubt that freedom is cost-effective. Thus, so far as I can see, they raise no philosophical difficulties for Christianity.

I mentioned earlier that we would return to the question of the truth and not just the logical possibility of the Augustinian answer to the problem of natural evil. In so doing, we will be facing a broader question: Are the general claims made in the context of the FWD true and not just possibly true? I believe they are, but can I convince someone else? Can the evangelistic difficulty be solved? Of course, in answering the LPE all I needed was possibly true, i.e. logically consistent, statements. But if I am able to solve the evangelistic difficulty of the EPE I must show that they are true. For if I can show people that they are true I have done about all I can do to evangelize them, i.e. to convince them to belive that God is omnipotent and good. The rest is up to them. But, sadly, I do not believe I can do so, for reasons I will now point out.

Let us return to

(8)   All the evil that exists in the world is due to the choices of
free moral agents whom God created, and no other world
which God could have created would have had a better
balance of good over evil than the actual world will have.

What are we to make of this statement? Is it true? probably true?
probably false? false? or are we unable to say? Perhaps it is best to
ask this: Do we have any evidence against (8)? Some people might
claim to know or reasonably believe that a better world would have
ensued had God not created the sort of free moral agents we find in
this world. But, as we have seen, we have no way of knowing whether
this is true. The strongest thing we can reasonably say, I believe, is
that we just don't know.

Some might want to claim to have evidence that natural evil is not
caused by the devil on the grounds that we seem to be able to give
perfectly satisfactory scientific explanations of disease, earthquakes,
famine, etc., without even mentioning the devil. But, as Plantinga
points out, 'this is relevant only if their having natural causes
precludes their also having nonnatural causes'[13]. In point of fact, he
says, we have no reason to deny that such events are to be ascribed
to the free activity of moral agents. Perhaps we have no evidence for
the claim, but we certainly seem to have no evidence against it
either.

Are there then theological objections that can be raised against the
luciferous defence? Perhaps so. Unlike some contemporary believers,
I do not wish to deny the existence of Satan. And the luciferous
defence does seem consistent with orthodox Christian tradition: the
thesis that Satan is the 'ruler of this world' is taught in the Bible (see
1 John 5:19; John 12:31; 14:30) and is affirmed by many theologians.
But is it theologically wise for a Christian to attribute natural evil to
Satan? One might wonder, for example, what precisely is the
connection, causal or otherwise, between Satan's evil choices and
natural evil.

This is not easy to say. One possible suggestion is this: natural evil
is God's punishment for our sins. That is, God uses Satan's ability to
cause natural evil as a way of punishing us for our sins. Augustine
takes this line, and it does seem to constitute a clear causal
connection. But I believe it is theologically unacceptable because it
makes God unfair. It does not seem that natural evils justly fall on
those who deserve them. The righteous quite apparently suffer from
disease, floods, etc., as much as sinners. 'But we all deserve
punishment', a strict Calvinist might want to say here, 'we are all
sinners who deserve to contract cancer or suffer in a famine, and it is
only God's grace that rescues some from their just desserts'. But this

too is unfair. Suppose I catch my two sons in the process of deliberately trampling my wife's rare flowers; they are equally guilty, but I punish one severely (as he deserves) and let the other go free (as an act of grace). Is this fair? Of course not. A loving God should no more act this way than I should.

A second possible suggestion is this: Satan's fall, by a kind of natural necessity, was a cataclysmic event that shattered the harmony and natural goodness of creation. That is, before Satan's fall, the earth was Eden-like - there were no diseases, hurricanes, floods, etc. But Satan's original sin ruined all that and produced natural evil; the universe was no longer a paradise. This provides not as clear a casual connection between Satan and natural evil as does the first answer: it is hard to see how the sudden presence of natural evil by itself (i.e. apart from a desire on God's part to punish the original sinners) can affect natural laws and processes. But even if we waive this difficulty, we must still wonder why God created the relevant laws of natural necessity and not others. Why didn't he create a more stable Eden-like world - one whose processes and laws would not be disrupted by the presence of moral evil in it? That he did not do so will be taken by some as evidence against the Christian claim that he is both omnipotent and wholly good.

Finally, there is this: Satan is a malevolent being; he goes about causing suffering in any way he can. Like the first, this seems a clear connection between Satan and natural evil. But the difficulty here is that causing people pain does not seem to be part of Satan's programme as we learn about it in the Bible and Christian tradition. What he wants to do, according to the tradition, is separate people from God, get them to ignore or disobey or curse God. Why then waste his time causing earthquakes and all the rest? Of course, natural evil does apparently cause some people to deny God. But in the case of others, suffering and adversity seem to bring them closer to God. So if causing natural evil is supposed to be a way of accomplishing the devil's aim of separating people from God, it seems at least in part counterproductive. Now perhaps Satan is not entirely rational: perhaps he is slightly confused about how best to accomplish his aims. Or perhaps natural evil really is an effective Satantic strategy, but we just can't see why. Is this third answer acceptable, then? I believe it is the best of the three, but even it is not entirely satisfactory. Too many questions are left unanswered. Plantinga's luciferous defence may be both true and theologically satisfactory, but at least it is not clear that it is [14].

To solve the evangelistic aspect of the EPE would in general require two convincing arguments - first, that natural evil is caused by the choices of free moral agents such as Satan, and second, that God's policy decision to create free moral agents is wise because freedom will turn out to be cost-effective. All Christians believe the second and many Christians believe the first. But the difficulty is that these are revealed propositions; they are objects of faith, not knowledge. Private evidence would typically be appealed to by Christians in explaining why they believe them. I do not see how they can be substantiated by means of public evidence.

This same result appears when we consider the final objection to the FWD that I will discuss. It comes in several forms, but since all forms question the compatibility of the FWD with the doctrine of divine foreknowledge, I will call it the 'foreknowledge objection'. To facilitate matters, let me speak of several categories of possible free human agents. Let A be the set of all free human agents who if created are always morally perfect, i.e. who never sin. Let B be the set of all free human agents who if created are morally imperfect, i.e. who sometimes err. Let B1 be the subset of B called the Blessed, i.e. those who if created will spend eternity with God in heaven. Let B2 be the subset of B called the Damned, i.e. those who if created will spend eternity apart from God in hell. And, finally, let B2a be the subset of B2 who if created will be by all accounts moral monsters who cause great human suffering, e.g. people like Hitler.

Now we can pose the various forms of the foreknowledge objection as a series of questions: first, why didn't God foresee which persons, if created, would belong in category A and which in category B and then choose to create only those who would belong in A? Second, if there is some reason why morally imperfect people must exist, why didn't God at least foresee which persons among those in the B group would belong in B1 and which would belong in B2 and then choose to create only those who would belong in B1? Third, if there is some reason why the Damned must exist, why didn't God at least foresee which of the Damned would belong in the B2a group and then refrain from creating them? These, then, are the various forms of the foreknowledge objection. Let me attempt to deal with them in turn.

In response to the first question, I have already admitted that it is logically possible for free moral agents never to sin - I only insisted that if this happened it would be a sort of happy accident from God's perspective, not attributable to him. Now in response to this first form of the foreknowledge objection, Plantinga raises the possibility of what he calls 'transworld depravity' [15]. This is the property of any being which does at least one morally wrong action in every world which God could have actualized. Plantinga says that it is logically possible that every free human agent whom God could have created suffers from transworld depravity. This seems to me quite correct - it is possible and does indeed help to show that the LPE can be solved.

But in the context of the EPE, we must ask whether the claim that all possible free human agents suffer from transworld depravity is not just possible but true. And I believe the answer is that it is not. There are, in my opinion, possible worlds in which even Hitler never sins, e.g. those in which he dies at the age of two days. However, there is a weakened kind of transworld depravity from which I believe all free human agents do indeed suffer. I believe in transworld depravity for all free human agents (1) who live long enough to make a significant number of moral choices, and (2) who live in worlds relevantly similar to the actual world. And the main relevant similarity I have in mind here is that the world be one which God has designed with the same purpose in mind that I claimed earlier in this chapter he in fact has for the actual world. I believe it is highly probable that any free human agent who must make a significant number of moral choices in a world like ours will eventually go wrong.

So the answer to the first question is: given God's aims and desires in creation, i.e. his aim to create a world in which free human agents would freely say yes to him, it may well be that category A turns out to be an empty set (i.e. is permitted though perhaps not desired by God to be an empty set). Given the pervasive influence of evil in the actual world, I seriously doubt that any free human agent who reaches an age of moral and spiritual responsibility (whatever it is) will remain morally innocent for long. It may be that there is no free human agent who, once created in these circumstances, remains morally perfect. Of course God could have ensured that evil would have no pervasive influence in the world, but given his aims in creation he ran the risk that evil would run rampant, and unfortunately it did.

The second question asks why God didn't create only those whom he could see would be blessed and not those whom he could see would be damned. As is well known, John Hick answers this objection by denying that there are any damned: we can be sure, he says, that all people will eventually be saved[16]. Much as I would like to follow Hick here, I do not believe any biblical Christian should do so. Universalism is too clearly inconsistent with the testimony of scripture to constitute a viable option to those who have high regard for its theological authority.

The quick answer to the second question is: I do not know. I do not know why God created those whom he knew would be damned and not just those whom he knew would be blessed. But fortunately this is not all that can be said. For one thing, I believe there are serious problems of personal identity here. Perhaps these problems can be solved; but my point can be made in this way: suppose John Jones, Sr, is in the actual world part of the Damned and his son, John Jones, Jr, is in the actual world part of the Blessed. Now the second form of the foreknowledge objection can be seen as asking why God, foreseeing this, didn't choose to create John Jones, Jr, but not John Jones, Sr, his father. But John Jones, Jr, just is the son of John Jones, Sr. Could John Jones, Jr be John Jones, Jr without being the son of John Jones, Sr? If individuals pre-exist their embodied lives - as disembodied souls, for example - and can at birth be packaged, so to speak, in any number of ways, perhaps so, But the notion looks seriously problematical if, as I believe, human persons are created de novo at conception or birth and become who they are in large part through their heredity. If so, it follows that John Jones, Jr could not have existed unless John Jones, Sr existed.

But the main point I wish to make in response to the second form of the foreknowledge objection is that the existence of hell is quite compatible with the existence of a good God, once we rid ourselves of common misconceptions about it. I do indeed believe that there is a place called hell but I do not believe it is a place where, à la Dante, protesting people are led against their will to be tortured vengefully. I believe the people who will end up separated from God freely choose hell and would be unhappy in God's presence. Having lived their lives apart from God, they will choose to go on doing so. Furthermore, I do not believe hell is a place of suffering or torture. Biblical metaphors that seem to suggest so are metaphors. They suggest, I believe, the deep regret the citizens of hell will feel that they are not able to live in the presence of God, the source of all life, light and love in the universe. Though they freely choose hell and could not be happy in paradise, I believe they will clearly understand what they have chosen to miss.

The third question asks why God didn't avoid creating those free human agents whom he foresaw would be moral monsters. Again I must say here that I do not know. It is similar to what I said earlier about particularly heinous events in world history: Christians need not feel that they can explain why God allowed such events to occur. Ultimately it comes down to trust. Some people trust in God and some do not: the ones who do not trust in God choose not to question him inordinately (Isa. 45:9-11). They believe he has the answers to many questions that now appear to us unanswerable. Christians, then, believe, though they cannot prove, that God had a good reason for allowing evil people to exist and evil events to occur. Christians do not claim to know what that reason is, but they trust in God.

Thus, again, we see that there is an aspect of the emotive problem of evil that remains a problem: the difficulty the believer has in convincing the non-believer to believe in God's goodness and omnipotence. This leads me to conclude as follows about the problem of evil: on a philosophical level, the LPE can be solved, but the evangelistic aspect of the EPE cannot. That is, I have no philosophical tools for convincing a person who, because of the existence of evil, denies God's omnipotence and/or goodness instead to affirm God's omnipotence and goodness. Perhaps there are other tools at my disposal; perhaps I can preach to this person. But it is at this point that Christian philosophy comes to the end of its tether and can do no more for faith.

So my main claim in theodicy is that God will emerge victorious and in the end will redeem all evil. This does not mean he will make it such that the evil events we have seen in the world's history never occurred (it is too late for God or anyone else to do anything about that) or even that precisely all of them will turn out to be causally necessary to produce God's victory (though some will be). It means that God's giving us moral freedom was necessary to the goods that will exist in the eschaton; that some of what now seems evil to us will be used by God to help produce the eschaton (though in the case of some evils I cannot now explain how he will do so); and that all evil will be redeemed by God in the sense that the goods that will exist in the eschaton will outweight all the evils that have ever existed and will make them pale into insignificance. Thus God's policy decision to create us with moral freedom will be shown to be wise; the end result will have been achievable through no other policy.

8 Incarnation

In A.D. 451 the Council of Chalcedon declared that Jesus Christ is:

> at once complete in Godhead and complete in manhood, truly God
> and truly man, consisting of a reasonable soul and body; of one
> substance with the Father as regards his Godhead, and at the same
> time of one substance with us as regards his manhood; like us in all
> respects, apart from sin; one and the same Christ, Son, Lord, Only-
> begotten, recognized in two natures, without confusion, without
> change, without division, without separation; the distinction of the
> two natures being in no way annulled by the union, but rather
> characteristics of each nature being preserved and coming together
> to form one person and subsistence.[1]

These words formed the basis of the orthodox Christian doctrine of
the incarnation, a doctrine which has been nearly universally believed
by Christians ever since. The main idea is that Jesus Christ is one
person in whom two natures co-exist, a divine and a human; these
natures are neither confused nor separated in him; he is 'truly God
and truly man'. (Let me parenthetically note that because of its
familiar use in the Chalcedonic formula cited above, I will in this
chapter frequently use the term 'man', despite its sexist
connotations.)

But is this claim that Christ is 'truly God and truly man' coherent,
i.e. is it logically possible? Theologians have typically classified it a
mystery or paradox, i.e. a difficult doctrine that puzzles us, stretches
our minds, and always remains in part unfathomable. For example,
Thomas Aquinas, speaking of the unity of the two natures of Christ,
says: 'To explain this union perfectly is beyond man's strength'[2]. And
William Temple says: 'If any man says that he understands the
relation of Deity to humanity in Christ, he only makes it clear that
he does not understand at all what is meant by an incarnation'[3].

But is the claim that Christ is 'truly God and truly man' also
incoherent, i.e. is it a statement which cannot possibly be true? Is it,
for example, an explicit contradiction (like the statement 'Jones is
standing and Jones is not standing') or, if not this, at least a
statement which for other logical reasons cannot be true (like the
statement 'The tallest conceivable man just left the room')? Some
would say it is. For example, John Hick has recently argued in The
Myth of God Incarnate that the orthodox doctrine has no clear
content and thus no non-metaphorical meaning. The doctrine

remains a form of words without assignable meaning. For to say, without explanation, that the historical Jesus of Nazareth was also God is as devoid of meaning as to say that this circle drawn with a pencil on paper is also a square.[4]

Thus Hick is saying that it is logically impossible for Jesus to have been 'truly God and truly man' and that the statement 'Jesus Christ is truly God and truly man' is therefore necessarily false.

This is obviously a topic in which Christians are crucially interested. The furore that accompanied the appearance of The Myth of God Incarnate both in Britain and in America attests to that. Not only is the classical Christian understanding of the incarnation at issue here - so perhaps is Christianity itself. For the doctrine that 'God became man in Jesus Christ' is universally recognized by Christians as being at the heart of their faith. The theological stakes could not be higher.

Is Hick correct, then? Is the orthodox doctrine incoherent? Obviously this will depend on what the words 'truly God and truly man' mean. What I wish to do in this chapter, therefore, is to explore several possible interpretations of these words and arrive at an interpretation that is both coherent and theologically acceptable. I will argue that the words 'Jesus Christ is truly god and truly man' have a coherent meaning and that this sentence is therefore possibly true. I will not present arguments that it is true, though I believe it is. Thus this chapter is mainly a philosophical prolegomenon to christology rather than a christology per se. The importance of this prolegomenon ought not be underestimated, however. For if the orthodox christology is incoherent it must be rejected no matter how many arguments can be amassed in its favour.

To prove that a given statement, s, is coherent is theoretically easy: one must simply show that it is entailed by another coherent statement t (or coherent set of statements). However, in practice this is often difficult. That t in fact entails s might be disputed; so might the coherence of t itself [5]. I am going to try to show that the statement 'Jesus Christ is truly God and truly man' is coherent. The coherent statement which I will claim entails it is in fact a whole series of statements, namely, the interpretation of the incarnation I will submit later in the chapter. Now in the case of complicated series of statements it is often difficult to see whether they are coherent and whether they entail some other statement. Nevertheless, I hope to present a convincing case that 'Jesus Christ is truly God and truly man' is entailed by a coherent statement or series of statements.

In order to put the issue presented by Hick's arguments in as clear a focus as possible, I am going to ignore certain problems that are surely relevant. For example, I am going to pretend that all parties to the dispute will agree that God is an omnipotent and omniscient necessary being. I am also going to pretend that there are no serious difficulties involved in attributing properties to God, i.e. that we all clearly know what is meant by such statements as 'God is omniscient'. I mention this because some will perhaps claim that Hick's argument cannot properly be evaluated unless puzzles about theological predication are first solved, and others might want to exploit our unclarity about the divine nature in order to answer Hick[6].

There is one other methodological point that must be mentioned before proceeding. When we ask whether the incarnation is possible, i.e. whether God can become man while remaining God, we must specify in what sense we are using the term 'God'. One possibility is that the term 'God' is a proper name, i.e. a term denoting Yahweh, the being who alone (so Christians believe) is divine. Another possibility is that the term 'God' is a title or descriptive term for any divine being. In the sentence, 'God alone is God', the first occurrence of the term 'God' is a proper name while the second is a title or descriptive term. What the sentence means is: 'Yahweh alone is divine'. Unless otherwise indicated, the term 'God' in this chapter will be used in the second way. I will be asking the question: <u>Can any truly divine being also be truly human</u>? (Of course, if it is true that Yahweh alone is divine, I will in effect also be asking whether the individual Yahweh can be truly human, but that is not how I will pose the question.)

Let us begin by asking specifically what the words 'Jesus Christ is truly God and truly man' mean. In order to answer this, we first need a notion of what it is <u>to be something</u>, as in being a horse or being truly man. I believe that this notion can most simply be analysed in terms of having certain properties. Surely if a thing has all the properties of a horse it is a horse; if a thing has all the properties of a man it is a man[7].

If so, the first interpretation that will occur to us is probably something like this: <u>Jesus Christ has all the properties of God and all the properties of man</u>. But this will not do; it is far too vague. Which human properties are we talking about here? Some human beings are right-handed and some are left-handed: which was Jesus? Again, some human beings have the property of preferring blueberries to strawberries and some have the property of preferring strawberries to blueberries: which human property did Jesus have? The difficulty here is that this interpretation is too inclusive of properties. It seems to require that Jesus have all the properties humans can possibly have. And many of them, of course, will be inconsistent with each other, like preferring blueberries to strawberries and preferring strawberries to blueberries.

To remedy this difficulty, a second interpretation can easily be suggested: <u>Jesus Christ has all the essential properties of God and all the essential properties of man</u>. Or, more precisely: he has all the properties that are essential to the divinity of any divine being and all the properties that are essential to the humanity of any human being. (I am supposing, as a kind of minimum definition, that an essential property of x is a property a thing cannot fail to have and be x.) This is a much better interpretation than the first and must be examined carefully.

Let us look here at Hick's example of the square circle. Would it be coherent to claim that there exists a thing that is (imitating the language of Chalcedon) 'truly a square' and 'truly a circle'? Clearly Hick is correct: such a claim would be incoherent. But why? Let us say that a thing is a square if it is a geometrical figure with four equal sides and four equal angles. And let us say that a thing is a circle if it is a closed geometrical figure all of whose points are equidistant from the centre. Now we can see what a thing would have to be if it were 'truly a square' and 'truly a circle'. It would have to be a closed geometrical figure with four equal sides, four equal angles, and all its points equidistant from the centre. And this clearly is incoherent. It is logically impossible for a thing to have four equal sides, four equal angles, and all its points equidistant from the centre. Hick is correct.

How does this apply to the theological question at hand? Can a being be truly divine and truly human? Or, to put it another way, can God take human form and actually be human while remaining God? The apparent problem with the interpretation of 'truly God and truly man' we are discussing is that some divine properties are inconsistent with some human properties. (I take the sentence 'properties a and b are consistent' simply to mean that one and the same being can simultaneously have both a and b, as a horse can be simultaneously both ill-tempered and slow.) Some properties, of course, can be held in common by God and man - e.g. the property of being able to think, the property of not being canine, the property of being mentioned in this book. But others apparently cannot, and this is precisely what accounts for the paradoxical character of the incarnation as interpreted by Chalcedon.

For example, the following properties seem characteristic of God, as understood in theism:

(1)   Being omniscient
(2)   Being omnipotent
(3)   Being necessary
(4)   Being creator of the world.

And the following properties seem equally characteristic of human beings:

(5)   Being non-omniscient
(6)   Being non-omnipotent
(7)   Being contingent
(8)   Not being creator of the world.

But obviously the properties in the first list are inconsistent with those in the second. Apparently no being can simultaneously have all the above properties.

The interpretation of the phrase 'truly God and truly man' that we are discussing mentions the notion of an <u>essential</u> property. Now to focus for a moment on properties (3) and (7), suppose it is essential to divine beings that they be necessary beings, i.e. beings that depend for their existence on no other beings. And suppose it is an essential property of human beings that they be <u>contingent beings</u>, i.e. beings that depend for their existence on other beings. It seems to follow from this that God cannot become man and remain God, for no being can be both necessary and contingent. If the orthodox statement that 'Jesus Christ is truly God and truly man' means that Jesus Christ simultaneously has <u>all</u> the essential properties of God and <u>all</u> the essential properties of man, and if necessary existence is an essential property of God and contingent existence is an essential property of man, then Hick is apparently correct. The claim looks incoherent, as was our earlier example of the square circle. For we want to say that no being can be both necessary and contingent.

But is this - the claim that Jesus Christ possesses all the essential properties of God and all the essential properties of man - a live option for Christian belief? Certainly not if (as some would argue) properties (1)-(4) are all essential to God, for the claim seems inconsistent with things that are clearly said about Jesus Christ in the New Testament. For example, omniscience is often said to be an essential property of God. God would not be God - so it is argued - if he were even partly ignorant. And the New Testament makes it clear that Jesus Christ was not omniscient. Mark's Gospel has him at one point expressing ignorance of who had touched his garment (Mark 5:30) and at another place admitting ignorance of the date of the parousia (Mark 13:32).

There are two routes a believer in Chalcedonic orthodoxy can follow at this point. One is paradoxically to say that Jesus Christ in some sense did indeed have both sets of properties - and that it is precisely in virtue of his having both that he is truly God and truly man. Here, naturally, tricky moves must be made concerning the <u>way</u> he possessed these properties, for as we noted, those in the (1)-(4) list do not seem consistent with those in the (5)-(8) list. One proposal might be to say that Jesus Christ was, for example, omniscient <u>as</u> God and non-omniscient <u>as</u> man[8]. Let us call this the <u>classical route</u> in christology. The other is what I will call the <u>kenotic</u> route. Its proposal is that in the incarnation Jesus plainly <u>did not have</u> the (1)-(4) properties (and any other divine properties that are inconsistent with humanity), and thus was 'truly man'. But he was still 'truly god' in virtue both of the divine properties he kept (those that were consistent with his humanity) and of the divine properties he once had (for example, (1)-(4)), temporarily gave up in the incarnation, and then regained in his ascension. This is the route I will follow. (The two routes are not mutually exclusive, however, and perhaps orthodox Christians must at points follow both.)

What is apparently needed, then, is an interpretation of 'truly God and truly man' that limits itself to divine and human properties that are logically consistent. Perhaps the interpretation we need is something like this: <u>Jesus Christ has all the essential properties of God that are consistent with his also being truly human and all the essential properties of man that are consistent with his also being truly divine.</u> I believe that this interpretation is on the right track, but it will have to be amended, for the notions of 'his also being truly human' and 'his also being truly divine' are not transparent and are in fact just what we are trying to explicate. They cannot be innocently smuggled into an interpretation of 'Jesus Christ is truly God and truly man' as if they were already understood.

Let us try to solve the problem in this way: <u>Jesus Christ has certain essential properties of God and certain essential properties of man and his divine properties and his human properties are consistent.</u> But this is problematical too. The definition is apparently satisfied if Jesus Christ has only one essential divine property and lacks all the others. Suppose omniscience is an esential property of God and suppose the only essential divine property Jesus Christ has is omniscience (ignoring the question whether it is essential to humans to be non-omniscient). That is, suppose he is a contingent, non-omnipotent being who also happens to be omniscient. Would he then be 'truly God'? Certainly not.

Thus we need to amend this definition slightly. Let us now say: <u>Jesus Christ has certain essential properties of God and certain essential properties of man; his divine properties and his human properties are consistent; the divine properties are sufficient to make him truly God and the human properties are sufficient to make him truly man.</u> I believe that this interpretation of the ancient formula 'truly God and truly man' is better than the others and will ultimately suffice. However, there is a serious objection that can be raised against it and that must be answered before we accept it.

The objection is this: how can Jesus Christ be 'truly god' if he lacks an essential property of God? I have pointed out that omniscience is often said to be an essential property of God (though - as I will explain - this is not my own view), and I have also noted that the New Testament picture of Jesus is apparently that of a non-omniscient being. How then can he be 'truly God'? Thus:

(9) 'An essential property of x' = df. a property that no being can fail to have and be x.

(10) 'An essential property of God' = df. a property that no being can fail to have and be God.

(11) Omniscience is an essential property of God.

(12)   No non-omniscient being is God.
(13)   Jesus Christ is non-omniscient.
(14)   Therefore, Jesus Christ is not God.

This argument appears valid; if it is, our recourse is to ask whether any of its premises can be challenged. Ignoring (11) for the moment, I am inclined to doubt both (12), which follows from (11) (at least in the way it must be understood if the argument is to be valid), and (13). As I will try to show, there are clear senses of (12) and (13) in which they are false.

Are the (1)-(4) properties essential to God? This is a difficult question. I certainly hold that they are properties of God, and I also believe that God (like all beings) must have certain of his properties essentially. But with most actually existing beings (as opposed, say, to mathematical entities like squares or segments) it is not easy to say which of their properties are essential to them. To take omniscience, a property we have already discussed in Chapter 2, is it true that God would not be God if he were not omniscient, e.g. if he had forgotten some fact? I don't see how anyone could know this. I cannot prove that omniscience is an accidental rather than essential property of God, but it seems so to me. What if God momentarily forgot where Steve Smith was born, and forgot how to deduce it from other things he knows? He would then of course no longer be omniscient, but would he then no longer be God? I don't see why. Furthermore, the fact that I believe both that Jesus Christ was God and that Jesus Christ was non-omniscient leads me to deny that omniscience is essential to God.

Accordingly, let me at this point say more about the nature of the incarnation. Then I will show how this casts doubt on the (9)-(14) argument. The point to notice is that the orthodox doctrine claims that God became man, not that man became God or that God and man somehow combined. This means, I believe, that the Second Person of the Trinity voluntarily and temporarily gave up those properties every divine being has that are inconsistent with being truly human[9]. Thus it is false to say that in the incarnation Jesus Christ had all the divine properties or was God simpliciter. Nor does the orthodox christology imply this; it only insists he was truly God. He was God as God can best be revealed in human form. Obviously, the fullness of the divine nature cannot be revealed to human beings and certainly not in bodily form. As Calvin says, pure God in our midst would only dazzle and frighten us; we would not comprehend such a revelation [10]. Nor does the orthodox doctrine imply that Jesus Christ was an ordinary man: obviously, he was no such thing. It only insists he was truly man.

Accordingly, we can reply to a fascinating conundrum Frances Young raises against those who believe in the incarnation and wish to produce evidence for it:

If Jesus was an entirely normal human being, no evidence can be
produced for the incarnation;
If no evidence can be produced, there can be no basis on which to
claim that an incarnation took place. [11]

There are two things that should be said here. (1) I doubt that any
believers in the incarnation, whatever the force of their desire to
avoid docetism, want to say that Jesus was 'an entirely normal human
being'. Evidently, had he been an entirely normal human being there
would today be no Christians or Christianity! Jesus is reported in the
Gospels as attracting disciples, speaking with authority, healing the
sick, forgiving sins, dying on a cross, and being raised from the dead -
none of them the sorts of things normal human beings do. Believers in
the incarnation will be quite happy to grant that it is not normal for a
human being to be God incarnate. They will want to affirm, then, not
that Jesus was an entirely normal human being but that he was truly
a human being. (2) Even if it were true that Jesus was an entirely
normal human being, what would follow is not that no evidence for
the incarnation of any sort could be produced but rather that no
evidence from Jesus' life could be produced. There certainly could be
other evidence - God could choose to reveal to us that he was
incarnate in Jesus, for example [12].

To return to my understanding of the incarnation, let us again note
that the orthodox doctrine is that Jesus Christ had two natures in one
person. During his earthly ministry there were doubtless certain
things Jesus could not have done unless he were God and certain
other things he could not have done unless he were a human being. He
could not have forgiven sins, for example, unless he were God and he
could not have died unless he were a human bieng. But of course he,
i.e. the one person Jesus Christ, both forgave sins and died [13].

This allows me to make two points in response to the (9)-(14)
argument. The first is this: just as skilled tennis players can choose to
play a game with their weak hand, so an omnipotent being can choose
temporarily to limit his power. Similarly, an omnipotent being who is
also omniscient can choose temporarily to be non-omniscient, i.e. not
to have access, so to speak, to all his knowledge. Though I doubt that
omniscience is an essential property of God, it may in some sense be
true that no being which is non-omniscient simpliciter (i.e. which is
not omniscient in any sense) can be God. But even if this is true, I do
not think that Jesus Christ was non-omniscient simpliciter. In other
words, I believe it is quite possible for an essentially omniscient being
temporarily to take non-omniscient form and all the while still be the
same essentially omniscient being. This is exactly what I believe God
did, or more precisely what the Second Person of the Trinity did, in
Jesus Christ. Thus premise (12), which says that no non-omniscient
being is God, is either false or radically misleading. There is a
relevant sense in which a non-omniscient being can be God.

Against this line of though Don Cuppitt says: 'Since the divine attributes belong to God not contingently but analytically it is logically impossible for the deity to doff one like a superfluous piece of clothing'[14]. I agree that if omniscience is an essential divine property, no divine being can lose omniscience and still be divine. But, as noted above, I doubt that omniscience simpliciter is an essential property of God, though I certainly believe that omniscience simpliciter is a property of God. And even if omniscience in some sense is an essential property of God, my theory affirms Jesus' omniscience in a relevant and in my opinion sufficient sense: he was an omniscient being who temporarily took non-omniscient form. Thus premise (12), which says that no non-omniscient being is God, is either false or radically misleading. (So, incidentally, is premise (11) from which (12) follows.) There is a sense in which a non-omniscient being can be God.

The second point has to do with my denial that Jesus Christ is non-omniscient simpliciter. The Second Person of the Trinity voluntarily and temporarily became non-omniscient in order to become truly man. At any point in his earthly ministry, I suspect, Jesus could have called on his omniscience (or omnipotence, for that matter - see Matthew 26:53), but had he done so, it would have been tantamount to his no longer being truly human. He would no longer have shared our human lot, which it was his intention to do. An omniscient being, he freely decided temporarily to abandon his omniscience and live only by what he could learn as a man and by what was revealed to him by the Father. (It was his acute sensitivity to God, rather than omniscience, I believe, that gave Jesus the prophetic insight into people's minds and the ability to foresee future events that he is recorded as having.)

There are two objections that might be raised here. The first is this: it seems quite unproblematical to speak of a powerful being deciding not to use some of its power. But is it equally unproblematical to speak of a knowledgeable being abandoning some of its knowledge? To say that Jesus was an omniscient being who decided to give up his omniscience sounds fishy. Can people choose not to know what they in fact know? In Mark 5:30, where Jesus asked who had touched his garment, was he just pretending not to know? No, I believe that he really didn't know who had touched his garment. But why is it that this notion of 'giving up knowledge' or 'deliberately forgetting' sounds suspicious? Perhaps it is because we just aren't used to the idea; humans apparently have no psychological mechanism for doing so. But surely there is no logical impossibility here; it is perhaps causally but certainly not logically impossible for people to give up some of their knowledge. But causal difficulties do not impede an omnipotent being. Thus the Second Person of the Trinity, an omnipotent being, could do just this (and, I believe, did).

The second objection is this: if Jesus was in fact ignorant but at any point was able to call on his temporarily abandoned omniscience to learn some fact he did not then know, he was not really human after all, for no human being has such an ability. But this argument is not compelling. It is quite true that no human being has such an ability, but this does not mean he was not really human. The central point is that he was in fact ignorant, just as we are. Whatever unused abilities he had, they do not change the fact that he did not use them; he truly was ignorant, for example, of the date of the parousia, just as we are. It was perhaps causally possible for him to come to know the date of the parousia, but it is causally possible for us to come to know it too: God might reveal it to us. Jesus was in fact non-omniscient; he knew no more than other people knew or at least could have known. This, in my opinion, is sufficient for him to have been truly human in his knowledge.

The notion that I am working with here - that of a being voluntarily abandoning some of its knowledge while retaining the ability to regain it - is not so mysterious as it might seem. I think it quite easy, for example, to imagine a being A, an item of knowledge p, and a procedure x whereby the following things could be said:

(15)   A does not know p;
(16)   A knows that A can know p if A does x;

and

(17)   A chooses not to do x.

(This sort of situation is actually quite common. Suppose you ask me if I know the sum of 5739 and 63201. I might well correctly respond: 'I know what to do in order to learn the answer, but I do not know it and choose not to know it'.) In cases where (15), (16) and (17) are all true, we might (in a slightly paradoxical but understandable way) say: 'A both knows and does not know p'. The sense in which A does not know p is this: A cannot at present truthfully answer relevant questions about p. The sense in which A does know p is this: A can answer them any time A wants to do so (by doing x).

Admittedly this is not exactly analogous to what I am saying about the incarnation - the part about abandoning knowledge is absent here. But the rest of it is, and if I was right in arguing earlier that the concept of voluntarily abandoning knowledge is coherent, then what we are allowed to say about Jesus is this: he <u>was</u> omniscient, i.e. he was an omniscient being who could have exercised his omniscience at any moment but freely decided to live for a time without it. There is also a sense in which he <u>was not</u> omniscient, i.e. for this brief time he did indeed carry out his resolve to live on the basis of limited knowledge. He knew no more than other human beings knew or at least could know, had they been as attuned to God as he was. The first, in my opinion, sufficed for him to retain his status as God and the second sufficed to make him man. Thus premise (13), which says that Jesus Christ is non-omniscient, is either false or radically misleading. There is a sense in which he was omniscient.

To sum up, my overall argument is this: in order to show that the orthodox christology is coherent we need not show that it is logically possible that Jesus was God <u>simpliciter</u> and man <u>simpliciter</u>. He was in fact neither, I believe. We need only show that it is logically possible that he was <u>truly</u> God and <u>truly</u> man. I take this to mean that we need only provide a legitimate sense in which we can truthfully (albeit somewhat paradoxically) say about him 'He is God' and a legitimate sense in which we can truthfully (albeit somewhat paradoxically) say about him 'He is man'. I have explained how such senses can be provided. Looking at the Jesus of the New Testament, Christians do indeed want to say about him 'He is God' and do indeed want to say about him 'He is man'.

All orthodox Christians affirm that 'Jesus Christ is truly God and truly man'. The problem is deciding exactly what this statement means. I do not claim that the approach taken in this chapter is entirely new. For example, it has points of connection with the christologies of the kenotic theologians of the nineteenth and early twentieth centuries - Thomasius, Dorner, Gore, Weston, etc. [15]. However, these theologians have been subject to considerable criticism, [16] and some of the specific ways they developed their christologies seem unacceptable. However, it now appears that kenotic theories are making something of a comeback, and I would like at this point to reply to two criticisms of kenosis that appear in the recent book <u>Incarnation and Myth</u>, edited by Michael Goulder.

First, Don Cuppitt mantains that kenosis 'is not a theory designed to account for the facts about Jesus, but a theory designed to explain how one can go on believing in the incarnation in a time when the old arguments have broken down' [17]. This is a puzzling criticism. Even if it were true it would not damage kenotic theories of the incarnation in the slightest. But in fact it is not true: the theory is primarily designed to account for the biblical picture of Jesus, especially the kenosis hymn in Philippians (see below) and the human and divine characteristics attributed to Jesus in the Gospels. If the theory also helps in the apologetic task of defending the incarnation (which is admittedly how I am using it in this chapter), I see nothing whatever wrong with that.

Second, Maurice Wiles argues against kenotic and other orthodox theories of the incarnation as follows:

> If it is logically conceivable for God to be actually identified with
> a human person without in any way taking away from the full and
> genuine humanity of that person, it follows that God does not, in
> fact, draw near to us as individual men and women or share our
> suffering as directly as apparently he could. [18]

The argument is not well put, but I believe something in the neighbourhood is correct: if it were true (not merely logically conceivable) that God is identified with one and only one human being, then it follows that God does not draw near to or share the suffering of the rest of us as directly as he could have (assuming it is possible for him to have done so).

In other words, if it is true (I am not saying it is) that God could have kenotically identified himself with any one or perhaps with all of us rather than just with Jesus, it does indeed follow that God could have drawn nearer to me and shared my suffering more than he did in fact do. He could have done so by choosing, say, my grandmother or even me (rather than Jesus) to be incarnate in. This much is true, but surely there is little here in the way of a criticism of kenosis or incarnation. Who says God must identify with everybody and share everybody's suffering as directly as possible? Why is this needed? Is it even possible? Why is it an argument against orthodox theories of the incarnation that on those theories he hasn't done so?

I wish now to make three final points. The first is the claim that the sentence 'Jesus Christ is truly God and truly man' is coherent. I can detect no contradiction or other sort of incoherence here, at any rate. The basic idea is this: <u>Jesus Christ failed to have some divine properties but was still God and had some divine properties but was still a human being,</u> and he failed to have some human properties but was still a human being and had some human properties but was still God. This is the account of the incarnation that I claim is itself coherent and entails the statement 'Jesus Christ is truly God and truly man'. I do not claim that no paradoxes remain, nor have I dealt with all the divine and human properties that are relevant to this issue. (I have dealt mainly with omniscience, but I believe similar arguments can be used for other relevant properties.) Nevertheless, I find the argument convincing; properly understood, the classical christological claim that Jesus Christ is truly God and truly man is coherent.

The second point is that this understanding of the incarnation seems consistent with some of the great christological passages of the New Testament. I am not able to show this in detail here; I will limit myself to a few comments. For example, Philippians 2:5-8 says:

Have this mind among yourselves, which you have in Christ Jesus, who, though he was in the form of God, did not count equality with God a thing to be grasped, but emptied himself, taking the form of a servant, being born in the likeness of men. And being found in human form he humbled himself and became obedient unto death, even death on a cross.

One traditional way of interpreting these words is this: Jesus Christ was 'in the form of God' as the Second Person of the Trinity, but at a certain point in time he 'emptied himself' both of his divine glory and of many of his divine properties, including omniscience, and took on 'human form', i.e. became a human being. If this is what Paul meant, it is certainly consistent with what I have been claiming (see also 2 Corinthians 8:9). Furthermore, my interpretation of the incarnation seems consistent with the theology of the prologue to John's Gospel, where 'the Word' which 'was with God and was God' 'became flesh and dwelt among us, full of grace and truth' (John 1:1, 14). Finally, something like my understanding of the incarnation seems presupposed in John 17:4-5, where Jesus prays:

> I glorified thee on earth, having accomplished the work which thou gavest me to do; and now, Father, glorify thou me in thy own presence with the glory which I had with thee before the world was made

Several things are evident here: (1) Jesus Christ once had divine glory and complete oneness with the Father (see also 17:11, 20-26); (2) he did not at the time of his prayer (i.e. during his earthly ministry) possess divine glory; and (3) he looked forward to regaining it. This seems entirely consistent with my claim that in his earthly ministry he voluntarily gave up some of his divine properties.

Nowhere does the New Testament make the precise statement that 'Jesus Christ is truly God and truly man'. Thus these words, which are from Chalcedon and not the Bible, can never take on scriptural authority for Christians. Nevertheless, centuries of Christian tradition attest to the adequacy of these words as best formulating the Christian understanding of the person of Jesus as he was historically encountered by the disciples, as he is read about in the Scriptures, and as he is spiritually encountered by believers today. Many theological distortions threaten - most of which, in my opinion, are spiritually dangerous and theologically unacceptable - that Jesus was just a very godly man, that he was God play-acting in the role of man, that he was half God and half man, etc. We must leave the door open that some superior way of expressing the nature of the person of Christ will be found. I have found no better way, however.

The third point concerns the christology, or the outline of a christology, that is implicit in the argument I have presented. What the Fathers at Chalcedon produced, I believe, was not an explanation of the incarnation (that was wisely left to individual theologians) but rather a guideline. It was a way of letting the church know what is acceptable and what is not acceptable to christology. In sum it says: any christology is acceptable that affirms the divinity, the humanity and the unity of the person of Christ. The christology that I here offer affirms all three and so falls within the boundaries of Chalcedonic orthodoxy.

Some may find this christology inadequate. Perhaps my views are at heart Docetist or Arian or theologically objectionable for some other reason. I do not believe such claims would be true, but the point I wish to make here is this: as long as the objections that are raised against my christology are theological rather than logical, and as long as it is granted that my christology at least falls within the boundaries marked out by Chalcedon, then perhaps my main claim is correct. It does after all seem logically possible that the orthodox christology is true.

I conclude, then, that the statement 'Jesus Christ is truly God and truly man' (1) is coherent, (2) is consistent with the New Testament witness to Jesus, and (3) is the most adequate way Christians have of saying what they want to say about Jesus. I recommend that Christians continue to affirm that 'Jesus Christ is truly God and truly man'.

9 Trinity

The Christian doctrine of the Trinity is notoriously easier to state than explain. Augustine states it as follows:

> There are the Father, the Son, and the Holy Spirit, and each is God, and at the same time all are one God; and each of them is a full substance, and at the same time all are one substance. The Father is neither the Son nor the Holy Spirit; the Son is neither the Father nor the Holy Spirit; the Holy Spirit is neither the Father nor the Son. But the Father is the Father uniquely; the Son is the Son uniquely; and the Holy Spirit is the Holy Spirit uniquely. All three have the same eternity, the same immutability, the same majesty, and the same power. [1]

The doctrine says in sum that the one God exists in three distinct and unconfused persons - Father, Son and Holy Spirit. The three persons are not three gods or even three parts or aspects of God but one God. No person is subordinate to any other; all are co-equally and co-eternally divine.

Not surprisingly, Christian theologians almost with one voice have stressed that this doctrine is a great mystery, perhaps the greatest mystery in Christian theology. Some even say that the doctrine cannot be adequately understood by human reason. My aim in this chapter is to take a look at and defend the doctrine from the point of view of analytic philosophy. I will discuss three recent attempts to clarify or rationalize the doctrine, and will conclude by discussing the concept of 'mystery' in theology. I will ask whether it is ever rational for a person to believe a mystery such as the Trinity, and will argue that it is.

It might be helpful to begin by asking where the doctrine came from - especially since it does not seem the sort of notion Christians would gratuitously invent. For one thing, the inherently paradoxical character of the doctrine would seem to make it singularly unattractive - unlike, say, the doctrine that God is omnipotent or the doctrine that god is loving. For another, the early Christians were Jews or at least saw themselves as inheritors of the Jewish view of God. They would have committed themselves to a doctrine that can easily (though erroneously) be interpreted as a step away from monotheism only for the strongest of reasons.

The answer, I believe, is that those who first believed the doctrine held that it was revealed to them by God. Despite the doctrine's problematical character, they accepted it because they believed God had made it known that his nature was that of a Trinity. Now it is often said that the doctrine of the Trinity is not found in the Bible. And this is certainly true; the Bible is not a treatise on systematic theology. But the building blocks of the doctrine, the basic notions it consists in, <u>can</u> be found in the Bible. And it was obviously under their influence that the doctrine was formulated.

First, the Bible makes it clear that there is only one God.

Hear, O Israel: The Lord our God is one Lord (Deut. 6: 4)

I am the Lord, and there is no other, beside me there is no God (Isa. 45: 5)

We know that 'an idol has no real existence' and that 'there is no God but one'. For although there may be so-called gods in heaven or on earth . . . yet for us there is one God, the Father, from whom are all things and for whom we exist. (1 Cor. 8: 4-6).

It is clear, then, that the doctrine of the Trinity must not be interpreted as tri-theism. Any step in that direction is heresy, for there is but one God.

Now some philosophers deny that we can legitimately speak of the oneness of God because, not being a spatially locatable type of thing, God is not identifiable or locatable by his relations with things or events that are spatially locatable. Thus the category of number has no relevance to God. As Keith Ward says, 'God cannot be said to be one in the ordinary sense, that he is one among (possible) others; that he is a distinguishable individual, of which there could be two or more'[2]. Part of this is certainly true: we are not able to look about us and count the numbers of Gods in the neighbourhood, as we can do with things like sheep or trees. But surely God - if God exists - <u>can</u> count the number of Gods in the universe. And surely if God knows that he is unique, that no other existing thing is like him, nothing prevents him from revealing this fact to us. This is just what Christians believe he has done: they hold that God is unique because they believe God has revealed that he is unique. Furthermore, just because we say 'God is one' it does not follow that there might be others, i.e that it is logically possible that there are other beings in the same category. Take the category 'tallest man ever to live on earth'. Now there might not be anything that fits this description, but if there is something that fits it there is only one thing that fits it. The description itself entails that if it is instantiated it is only instantiated by one individual. The same is true, Christians believe, of the category 'God'.

Second, despite the Bible's commitment to the notion of God's absolute uniqueness, it also seems unhesitatingly to speak of the

Father, the Son and the Holy Spirit - as if they are separate things and as if they are God. Here are four biblical texts which are often pointed to by Christians as containing seeds of the doctrine of the Trinity:

> And when Jesus was baptized, he went up immediately from the water, and behold, the heavens were opened and he saw the Spirit of God descending like a dove, and alighting on him; and lo, a voice from heaven, saying 'This is my beloved Son, with whom I am well pleased'. (Matt. 3: 16-17)

> And Jesus came and said to them, 'All authority in heaven and on earth has been given me. Go therefore and make disciples of all nations, baptizing them in the name of the Father, and of the Son, and of the Holy Spirit'. (Matt. 28: 18-19) β]

> Now there are varieties of gifts, but the same Spirit; and there are varieties of service, but the same Lord; and there are varieties of working, but it is the same God who inspires them all in every one. (1 Cor. 12: 4-6)

> The grace of the Lord Jesus Christ and the love of God and the fellowship of the Holy Spirit be with you all. (2 Cor. 13: 14)

Obviously, I do not claim this is anything like a thorough review of those biblical texts that are relevant to the doctrine of the Trinity (see also Luke 1: 35; John 14: 16-17; 1 Peter 1: 2). But perhaps it is enough to indicate why Christians have always believed they should hold the doctrine - because they believe it is the best available analysis of what was given them by God in the Scriptures about his own nature.

The early Christians also believed they experienced God in three persons. The Son was experienced as incarnate in Jesus of Nazareth on earth; he was seen as God fulfilling his redeeming mission among human beings. The Father was experienced as the one who sent the Son and who reigns transcendently as creation's sovereign. And the Holy Spirit was experienced as God who dwells immanently in the world and in the lives of Christians, empowering, guiding, convicting, illuminating.

But is the doctrine of the Trinity coherent? Is there any good reason for a Christian to believe it? Let us say that the doctrine consists at heart of five statements:

(1)   The Father is God.
(2)   The Son is God.
(3)   The Holy Spirit is God.

(4)   The Father is not the Son and the Son is not the Holy Spirit
       and the Holy Spirit is not the Father.
(5)   There is one and only one God.

The problem is that these statements seem to constitute an
inconsistent set, i.e. a set of statements whose members cannot all
be true. Indeed, this can be shown easily, for (1), (2), (3) and (5)
entail:

(6)   The Father, the Son, and the Holy Spirit are one thing,

and (4) entails:

(7)   The Father, the Son, and the Holy Spirit are separate things.

But, obviously, (6) and (7) are inconsistent. Thus (1)-(5) is an
inconsistent set of statements; apparently, the set cannot rationally
be believed. If Christians are really obliged to affirm both (6) and (7),
as it seems they are, it seems to follow that they are obliged to
contradict themselves.

But I believe the real mystery of the Christian doctrine of the
Trinity is not the apparent inconsistency of (6) and (7). For it is
obvious that Christians have a move they can make here, one that is
designed to show that what we are talking about is perhaps a mystery
but not quite an explicit contradiction. What they can say is that the
sense in which the Father, the Son and the Holy Spirit are distinct
things is a different sense than the sense in which they are one thing.
And as far as it goes (which is not far) this seems a perfectly fair
reply. For the ontological boundaries of what constitutes a 'thing' are
vague, loose, flexible and overlapping.
    Notice:

(8)   Joseph, Mary and Jesus are separate things and
       Joseph, Mary and Jesus are one thing.

This sentence seems inconsistent until we realize that the sort of
thing referred to in the first conjunct is a person and that the sort of
thing referred to in the second is a family. Again:

(9)   Lines AB, BC and CA are separate things and lines AB, BC
       and CA are one thing.

This sentence too seems inconsistent until we realize that the sort of
thing referred to in the first conjunct is a line and that the sort of
thing referred to in the second is a triangle. Joseph, Mary and Jesus
can well be separate persons and one family; lines AB, BC and CA
can well be separate lines and one triangle.
    But these examples unfortunately do not help us much with the

Trinity (which is why I said this move does not carry us far). For they do nothing to tell us what sorts of things Father, Son and Holy Spirit are as separate things and what sorts of things they are as one thing. Father, Son and Holy Spirit are three what and one what? Here, I believe (following Augustine[4]), is the real source of mystery of the Trinity: not that God is three-in-one (lots of things - like triangles and families - can legitimately be described as three-in-one) but that with God we have no ready answer to the questions: three what? and one what? That is, we have no ready ontological categories in which to place God.

It is tempting merely to repeat the classical terminology and say, 'God is three persons and one substance', pretending that that solves the problem. But the patristic and medieval categories - three persons in one substance, three hypostases in one essence, etc. - seem obscure and problematical. Perhaps these categories satisfied curious people of long ago. But is is only with great difficulty that we today can come to understand what the Fathers and the Scholastics meant by them,[5] and I fear such terms are unhelpful even to those who have taken the trouble to understand, them, let alone the average person who for some reason wonders about the Christian doctrine of the Trinity.

If we had apt categories at hand we could show that the doctrine of the Trinity is coherent, just as the categories 'person' and 'family' showed that (8) is coherent and just as the categories 'line' and 'triangle' showed that (9) is coherent. It is not surprising, then, that Christian theologians have typically gone to great lengths to find 'analogies' of the Trinity. The Trinity, it has been said, is something like human memory, intellect and will, or like the liquid, solid and gaseous state of water, or like the roots, trunk-branches and fruit of a tree, or like the three dimensions of solids, or like that which loves, that which is loved and love. Unfortunately, all seem utterly inadequate. 'God is not like that', we feel like saying each time.

Let me illustrate the difficulties involved in explaining or rationalizing the doctrine of the Trinity. I will refer briefly to three recent discussions by people - two philosophers and a theologian - who face the central problem of the doctrine's apparent contradictoriness.

William L. Power, in his article 'Symbolic Logic and the Doctrine of the Trinity', construes the three persons of the Trinity as 'the eternal identifying characteristics of the members of a class which can only have one member'[6]. The doctrine states, he says, the God is Father (or Creator), Son (or Revealer), and Holy Spirit (or Sanctifier). Thus if the predicate constants 'C', 'R' and 'S' respectively abbreviate 'Creator', 'Revealer' and 'Sanctifier', the doctrine can be stated as follows:

$(\exists x) \; [\; (Cx \; \& \; Rx \; \& \; Sx) \; \& \; (y) \; [\; (Cy \; \& \; Ry \; \& \; Sy) \; \rightarrow \; (x=y) \;] \;]$.

If x is God, we then have it that God is the one and only Creator, Revealer and Sanctifier. And suppose we further specify that 'Creator' means 'necessary condition for all beings including itself' and that 'Revealer' means 'necessary condition for all aims, rationality and order including its own' and that 'Sanctifier' means 'necessary condition for all value including its own'. It then follows, Power says, that God is the one and only member of the set of all creators, revealers and sanctifiers.

Power goes on to claim that this analysis of the Trinity is not vulnerable to the charge of modalism, 'For I have asserted that the unique identifying attributes of God are eternal or necessary attributes or attributes which could not be otherwise. In more traditional language, these characteristics of God are modes of presentation of the eternal economy of the Godhead rather than the temporal economy of God'[7]. But this claim does not seem to me correct. To the extent that Power's analysis does not help us see how God can be both three and one, to that extent it may not be open to the charge of modalism, but to the extent that it does, it is so open.

We can see this as follows. Despite the fact that he makes the three persons of the Trinity eternal and necessary modes of the Godhead (they are not just three aspects of how God appears to us), it is still true that Power's statement of the doctrine of the Trinity does not rule out the heretical possibility that the three persons are not ontologically distinct from each other. The claim that the Father <u>is not the same thing</u> as the Son, etc. (premise (4) above) is crucial to the orthodox doctrine and is absent in Power's analysis. This raises the distinct possibility, since he stresses the oneness of God, that the three persons are merely three different views of himself which God must necessarily show to us (like the three sides which a spinning triangle must show to an adjacent observer in two-dimensional space). Thus Power does not solve our essential puzzle - how a being can be both three and one[8].

A. P. Martinich, in his recent article 'Identity and Trinity', argues that the central problem with the doctrine is its claim that the three persons of the Trinity are somehow both identical and not identical. Thus the doctrine is apparently inconsistent. However, the doctrine cannot be believed by a rational person if it is contradictory, Martinich says, and so he tries to show, via a discussion of the concept of identity, that the doctrine is coherent. Identity, he says, is not absolute but relative:

> The identity predicates 'is', 'is the same as', and 'is identical with' are incomplete . . . . Nothing is identical with something absolutely, but only in a certain respect. Nothing is merely self-identical; there is no bare self-identity. Everything is the same such-and-such or so-and-so as something, and if it is not a such-

and-such or so-and-so, it fails to be the same such-and-such or so-and-so. I am the same man as myself, but not the same house as myself.[9]

Thus, Martinich says, we can use the concepts 'person' and 'God' to state coherently the doctrine of the Trinity. Now since identity is relative, such expressions as 'a = B' are incomplete; it must be specified in what way a and B are identical. Thus Martinich adopts the convention that 'a $=_{\phi}$ B' means that a is the same ϕ as B. Thus the central controversial proposition of the doctrine of the Trinity can be written as follows: (f $=_{\phi}$ s & f $=_{\phi}$ s), which means that the Father is the same God as the Son but not the same person as the Son. But the statement, 'The Father is not the same person as the Son but is the same God as the Son' is coherent. Thus the doctrine of the Trinity, Martinich concludes, is coherent and rationally believable.

But while Martinich's article is in some ways a valuable contribution to the doctrine of the Trinity - I will not dispute his thoughts about identity, for example - I believe his main conclusion is too hasty. Clearly, we must know much more about the logic of the terms 'person' and 'God' before we can decide whether or not the statement, 'The Father is not the same person as the Son but is the same God as the Son' is coherent. Surely the statement 'Ronald Reagan is the same <u>person</u> as the president of the United States but is not the same <u>name</u> as "The president of the United States"' is coherent. But the statement 'Ronald Reagan is the same <u>person</u> as the president of the United States but is not the same <u>man</u> as the president of the United States' is not. We know this because we understand the logic of the terms 'name', 'person' (meaning a human person), and 'man' well enough to decide. But we don't understand the logic of the terms 'God' and 'person' (when applied to God) well enough to know whether or not Martinich's claims are correct. Since we are still stuck with the questions 'Three what?' and 'One what?' we have not shown that the doctrine of the Trinity is coherent.

Karl Rahner, in his recent book <u>The Trinity</u>, admits that the doctrine is a mystery and cannot be fully understood by human beings. Nevertheless, he sets out to explain the doctrine and mitigate its contradictory character as best he can by use of the notion of 'relative distinctness'. He states the doctrine in a traditional way -'the one God subsists in three distinct manners of subsisting'[10] - and, like Power and Martinich, does not see himself here as a theological innovator. His aim is to state and defend what he sees as the church's received doctrine.

He first points out that the oneness of the Trinity is what he calls mitigated rather than numerical unity. He says:

When we mean the expression, 'on the <u>one</u> God' literally, this treatise does not speak only of God's essence and its unicity, but of the unity of the three divine persons, of the unity of the Father, the Son, and the Spirit, and not merely of the unicity of the divinity. We speak of the mediated unity, of which the Trinity is the proper consummation, and not of the unmediated unicity of the divine nature. For when we think of this nature as numerically one, we are not yet thinking ipso facto of the ground of God's tri-unity.[11]

But Rahner's main contribution to the doctrine is in his analysis of the threeness of the Trinity. His basic point is that the three persons are not three distinct things per se but are three distinct things only in and through their relations with each other. They are not 'absolute realities' but are 'relative realities', i.e. 'mere and opposed relations'. They are identical to the Godhead but only virtually distinct from each other. He says:

> We must say that the Father, Son, and Spirit are identical with the one godhead and are 'relatively' distinct from one another. These three as distinct are constituted only by their relatedness to one another.[12]

Thus, unlike ordinary persons (i.e. humans), we cannot 'add up' Father, Son and Holy Spirit and get three. For each person subsists directly only as 'relations of opposition'. That is, each person has consciousness of itself as Father, Son or Holy Spirit, but this consciousness is from the one essence or nature, and is common as one to all three persons. Thus we can say, for example, that the Father is 'someone else' from the Son and the Holy Spirit but not 'something else'[13].

Rahner admits that he has not solved the basic logical problem of the Trinity, nor is this his main aim. He only thinks he has shown that the basic problem is not insuperable. But while I have respect for Rahner as a theologian and for the Augustinian and Thomistic tradition he is following here,[14] it does not seem to me that the distinctions he makes are helpful. A reader confused by the doctrine of the Trinity and puzzled by its apparent contradictory nature would, I believe, be all the more confused by Rahner's explanations. I for one simply do not know what 'relative realities' are or how it can be the case that the three persons of the Trinity are only distinct from each other 'in their relations with each other'. Surely there can exist a relation only if there are two items to be related. Thus I simply do not know how to evaluate Rahner's claim that 'when an absolute [in this case the Godhead] is really identical with two opposed relations [e.g. Father and Son] this real identity does not yet imply a formal identity of the two opposed relations'[15]. Rahner calls relations 'the most unreal of realities' but insists that they are 'as absolutely real as other determinations'[16]. But I do not see how this helps. There is nothing in my experience that helps me understand the concepts Rahner is working with; thus they do not help me understand the doctrine of the Trinity.

Perhaps a contemporary philosopher could explicate and criticize Rahner's idea as follows. Suppose there are two beings, A and B, which have all their qualities in common (i.e. there are no substantial, quantitative or qualitative differences between them) except that A   B. If so, we would normally conclude that A and B are two qualitatively identical but numerically non-identical beings which differ at least in their spatial location. For surely if they are both qualitatively identical and have the same spatial location they must be numerically identical as well. But now suppose that A and B are immaterial beings, i.e. that they have no spatial location. If so, an advocate of Rahner's approach might say that the only way A and B can be distinguished from each other, i.e. the only ground we have for denying that A and B are numerically identical, is by their <u>relations</u> to each other.

But the only relationship between A and B stated thus far is that of 'non-numerical identity'. Obviously we cannot use this relationship to distinguish A and B; it is this very relationship which we are trying to find grounds for. And surely any other relationship we might choose - e. g. the Father-Son relationship - will have the effect of denying the claim that A and B are qualitatively identical. If A is the Father of B then B is not the Father of A. Even if we adopt a distinction between, say, existence and subsistence, i.e. even if we say 'A exists as qualitatively identical to B and subsists as B's Father (A is only called "A" in relation to B)', this still appears to follow. It is true that relations aren't substantives, so if Rahner wants to say that relations don't really exist but only subsist, he is perhaps within his rights. But this surely does not help solve the problem at hand.

It appears, then, that the doctirne is still mysterious. The three recent attempts to explain and rationalize the doctrine which I have briefly discussed all fail to do so. I do not dogmatically hold that the doctrine can never be shown to be coherent. I only claim that this has not yet been achieved.

Perhaps it is not surprising that we find mysteries in the Christian doctrine of God. For this understanding is based on the premise that a transcendent being has revealed himself to us. I take the doctrine of divine transcendence to mean not that God cannot be coherently described in human language but that we never fully understand whatever true statements are made about him[17]. Not being ourselves transcendent or infinitely wise, it is obvious that we will not be able to comprehend God with the same skill or insight with which we comprehend rats or pencils or triangles. Perhaps all our thoughts about God are halting, inadequate and partial. Perhaps mysteries will inevitably appear if it is true that a God who in his essence is unknowable to us reveals himself to us. As the Fourth Gospel says, 'No one has ever seen God; the only Son, who is in the bosom of the Father, he has made him known' (John 1: 18). And as Paul says, 'We impart a secret and hidden wisdom of God, which God decreed before the ages' (1 Cor. 2: 7).

Thus we must now turn to the following questions: Is there every any good reason to believe a mystery? Is there good reason for Christians to believe the mystery of the Trinity? In order to answer these questions I must first do something I have postponed till now, namely define the term 'mystery'. Let me do so by contrasting the terms 'mystery' and 'contradiction'[18]. (I do not claim that my analysis of 'mystery' reflects the use of the term in ordinary language or even all uses of the term in theology.)

Let us say that a contradiction is an inconsistent statement of the form 'p and not-p', where there is no suggested or available amplification of the terms in the statement that removes the contradition or shows that it is only apparent (as in my two earlier examples of families and triangles). I take it as given that it is never under any circumstances rational to believe a contradiction. Let me define a mystery, on the other hand, as 'an apparent contradiction which there is good reason to believe'. Religious mysteries are paradoxical religious claims which typically stretch the mind and are difficult to comprehend, but which (it is claimed) there is good reason to believe.

The reason normally provided for believing a mystery is that it is said to have been revealed in some way by God. Thus mysteries are sometimes said to be doctrines which we would never arrive at using our own reasoning ability alone; they must be revealed for us to know them. And since they can be revealed they are capable of being put into language, i.e. they are not gibberish or nonsense. Some Christian mysteries are said to be such that they can be understood once revealed (although the term 'mystery' is being used differently here, this is true of the mystery of the purpose of human life). Others are said to be such that they cannot be fully understood by us, at least in this life (e.g. the mysteries of the incarnation and the Trinity).

An important point in my definition of 'mystery' is the notion of 'apparent contradiction'. To be a mystery as opposed to a contradiction, there must be an amplification of the terms in the statement available that suggests the possibility that the contradiction is only apparent. Perhaps it can even be said that the burden of proof is on the believer here, i.e. that all apparent contradictions ought to be regarded as contradictions unless reasons are supplied for not doing so. (Of course if it can be proven that an apparent contradiction is only apparent, there is ipso facto no mystery either.)

Is there ever any good reason to believe a mystery, then? I will argue that there is, but first I will discuss some arguments raised by Steven Katz in his article, 'The Language and Logic of "Mystery" in

Christology' [19]. We must note that Katz is training his guns against a notion of mystery that I am not defending here, namely, the notion of what might be called total mystery. A mystery, he says, takes the following form: 'Let ϕ be any predicate and M any subject, then "for any ϕ, M is not ϕ"'. This, then, is the sort of mystery that cannot be understood no matter what conceptual system we employ, and where nothing could ever possibly count as a solution to the mystery. Katz correctly points out that 'there are certain minimal conditions of logical and linguistic adequacy and propriety which even the mystery theologian cannot ignore with impunity' [20]. If a doctrine is totally mysterious in the above described way we have no way whatsoever of deciding who is talking appropriately about it and who is not - even the mystery theologian's own language may be inapt.

All this seems quite acceptable and I agree with Katz. However, I am not here defending the notion of total mystery. The doctrine of the Trinity, I claim, is a mystery to us, but it is not mysterious to God, nor, perhaps, will it be mysterious to us forever. Perhaps in the eschaton, to paraphrase St Paul, 'We will understand fully, even as we have been fully understood' (1 Cor. 13: 12). So I am not saying that the mystery of 'three in one' cannot in principle be explained or rationalized or is such that for any ϕ, the Trinity is not ϕ. Perhaps even some future theologian will be able to produce conceptual categories adequate to explain it. All I claim is that it is mysterious to us now.

However, Katz does raise an objection to the use of mystery in theology which is quite relevant to my claims and which I must therefore answer. It is that the use of mystery is - so to speak - unconfinable. That is, once we allow that mysteries can be introduced and believed there is nothing to prevent people from producing any mysterious doctrine they want to produce about anything at all. All kinds of ridiculous and unfalsifiable suggestions can be made. 'We have opened the gates for an endless proliferation of entities, all now invested with ontic equality' [21].

I believe Katz has made an important point here. If mystery talk is to be allowed at all, we need criteria for rational belief in mysteries. That is, we need to be able to decide when belief in a mystery is rational when it is not. Before suggesting some criteria, let me first point out that I am interested in answering the question as posed in this way: are people who believe a mystery (e.g. the Trinity) ever rational in doing so? I am not going to address the quite different question: are people who do not believe a mystery ever rational in changing their minds on the recommendation of someone who does?

I have two criteria to suggest; they are implicit in what has already been said. First, people are rational in believing a mysterious doctrine only if there is good reason to believe that its contradictory character is only apparent. This means both that an amplification of it shows at least that it may be coherent and that its subject matter is something we would expect to be puzzled about (not things like pins or pigeons but things like God). Second, people are rational in believing a mysterious doctrine only if apart from the question of its coherence they have strong reasons to believe it, e.g. they have good reason to believe the doctrine was revealed by God, or the doctrine makes the best available sense of other statements they have good reason to believe.

Of course people will notoriously disagree about whether a given doctrine is revealed by God. As concerns the Trinity, some people hold that the Bible is revelatory and some people do not. Nevertheless, the question whether or not a person, Jones, is rational in believing a mystery may well boil down to questions like: Does God exist? Does God reveal himself to us? Did God in fact reveal what Jones says he revealed? Obviously, such questions will be difficult to answer. So it may well turn out to be difficult to decide whether or not a person who believes a mystery is rational. Nevertheless, I suggest that if both criteria are satisfied, such a person is rational.

Let me now return to the Trinity. Does it satisfy my criteria? Can it be rationally believed? As for the first criterion, I must repeat my earlier admission that we have no apt categories for explaining how God can be three-in-one. We can understand how triangles and familes can be three-in-one, but not how God can be three-in-one. But must we display apt categories? It depends. If we want to prove that propositions (6) and (7) are consistent, that the doctrine of the Trinity is coherent, we must. But while it is never rational to believe a contradiction, we do not have to prove that a doctrine is coherent before it can rationally be believed. The critic may well argue that our inability to provide categories that resolve the mystery of the Trinity shows that

(10) The Father, the Son and the Holy Spirit are one thing and the Father, the Son and the Holy Spirit are separate things

(which is simply the conjunction of (6) and (7) is a contradiction and accordingly ought not be believed. But this is not quite correct. Again, we know that the boundaries of what constitutes a 'thing' are vague and flexible, and we know that Christians (or at least those who follow the line I have been taking) refer to different sorts of 'things' in the two places in (10) where this term appears. They are saying that God may legitimately be described as three-in-one because God is one when considered as a certain sort of thing and three when considered as another sort of thing. I believe this is indeed enough to provide good reason to believe that what we have here is not a contradiction but rather a mystery.

What about the second criterion? It says that people can rationally believe a mystery if the mysterious doctrine makes the best available sense of other statements they have good reason to believe or if they have reason to believe that the doctrine was revealed by God. I believe this criterion is satisfied in the case of the Trinity. Christians have good reason to believe that (1), (2), (3), (4) and (5) are all true. They hold that God has revealed them. Unless they can come up with a better way of understanding God's revelation of himself, they have no choice but to affirm these propositions and thus the doctrine of the Trinity.

What about the part about revelation? Christians claim to have good reason to believe that God is three-in-one because they believe that God has revealed that he is three-in-one. Obviously, I cannot argue this point here. To argue that the Bible and the Christian tradition are correct at this point is far beyond my ability, let alone the limits of this chapter. People will disagree whether Christians have such good reasons, but Christians think they do. And if they do, this is enough for them to be judged rational. I hold, then, as the vast majority of Christians do, that the doctrine of the Trinity is to be believed because it is the best sense we can make of things God has revealed to us.

10 Conclusion

When Pascal, the great French philosopher and mathematician, died, a slip of paper was found sewn into his clothing. It was his <u>Memorial</u> of what he called his 'second conversion', a profound religious experience that occurred on 23 November 1654. Pascal's oft-quoted words are:

> From about 10:30 at night until about 12:30. FIRE. God of Abraham, God of Isaac, God of Jacob, not of the philosophers and of the learned. Certitude, certitude, feeling, joy, peace. God of Jesus Christ . . . Let me never be separated from him [1].

As is well known, Pascal was both a committed Christian and a first-rate philosopher. If Pascal was prepared to make such a forceful distinction between the God of Abraham, Isaac and Jacob, on the one hand, and the God of the philosophers and learned, on the other, we must take the distinction seriously.

Is the distinction relevant to the enterprise of this book? What, for example, is the relationship between the God of Abraham, Issac and Jacob and the God this particular philosopher has been discussing in this book? Are they the same? Or do philosophers distort God's nature in their rational talk about him? Do philosophers inevitably fail to capture the essence of the living God in whom believers trust? This is a poignant and important question. I suspect no Christian who teaches philosophy can help but ask it. We have all had the experience of encountering religious students who are suspicious of philosophy because (usually among other things) the cold, abstract, necessary being discussed there 'is not the God I know'.

This is a murky issue, on which it is not easy to get a firm grip. Two preliminary points must be made before we can intelligibly ask whether Pascal's distinction is apt and how, if apt, it bears on my argument in this book.

First, the issue is complicated by the fact that only a minority of religious people are philosophers or feel any need for philosophy. It is also true that some of the greatest figures in the history of Christian theology, from Tertullian to Karl Barth, believe that philosophy and Christian faith are enemies. Even St Paul seems to argue passionately that secular philosophy is the enemy of the Christian gospel.

> See to it that no one makes a prey of you by philosophy and empty deceit, according to human tradition, according to the elemental spirits of the universe, and not according to Christ. (Col. 2: 8)

For Christ did not send me to baptize but to preach the gospel, and not with eloquent wisdom, lest the cross of Christ be emptied of its power. For the word of the cross is folly to those who are perishing, but to us who are being saved it is the power of God. For it is written, 'I will destroy the wisdom of the wise, and the cleverness of the clever I will thwart'. Where is the wise man? Where is the scribe? Where is the debater of this age? Has not God made foolish the wisdom of the world? For since, in the wisdom of God, the world did not know God through wisdom, it pleased God through the folly of what we preach to save those who believe. For Jews demand signs and Greeks seek wisdom, but we preach Christ crucified, a stumbling block to Jews and folly to Gentiles, but to those who are called, both Jews and Greeks, Christ the power of God and the wisdom of God. For the foolishness of God is wiser than men, and the weakness of God is stronger than men . . . . When I came to you, brethren, I did not come proclaiming the testimony of God in lofty words or wisdom. For I decided to know nothing among you except Jesus Christ and him crucified. And I was with you in weakness and in much fear and trembling; and my speech and my message were not in plausible words of wisdom, but in demonstration of the Spirit and power, that your faith might not rest in the wisdom of men but in the power of God . . . . The unspiritual man does not receive the gifts of the Spirit of God, for they are folly to him, and he is not able to understand them because they are spiritually discerned. (1 Cor. 1: 17-25; 2: 1-5, 14)

But the brief passage from Colossians should not be taken as a condemnation on Paul's part of all philosophy. The speech attributed to him at Athens in Acts 17 shows how Paul could appreciate and even utilize current philosophy. What Paul is criticizing is the fantastic and mythological speculations that were being pushed on the Colossian Christians. He is saying: do not allow yourselves to be deluded by empty, superstitious thought masquerading as philosophy.

And as to the famous Corinthian passage, I agree (1) that Christian faith does not rest on philosophical wisdom but on revealed truth; (2) that the truth that is revealed to the eyes of Christian faith can seem absurd to non-believers; (3) that no rational system of human devising, no matter how eloquently it is expressed, has the power to save human beings; and (4) that the wisdom of God is attained not by reasoning alone but by faith. But again I see no blanket condemnation of the enterprise of philosophy here.

There are, of course, philosophies that are inimical to Christian faith. But philosophy itself, the search for answers to life's deepest and most difficult questions, is neutral. Philosophers are not ideologically neutral, but philosophy is. Some philosophers attack religion and some do not; some propound Christian views of God and some do not. But philosopher per se is neither enemy nor friend to Christian faith. It is true that some Christians ignore philosophy out of lack of interest and some reject philosophy because they think it opposed to Christianity. But neither fact should lead us directly to any conclusion about the relationship between the two Gods Pascal speaks of.

Second, it cannot be denied that God usually plays a different role in philosophy than he does in religion in general or Christianity in particular. The basic difference can be put in this way: in philosophy God is typically the answer to questions that arise out of rational curiosity; in religion God is the answer to questions that arise out of personal need. The philosopher who uses God to answer deep questions about the nature of reality - e.g. Aquinas's use of God to answer questions about the origin of the universe, Kant's use of God to solve troubling problems about morality - is engaged in an activity that is profound and important. Or at least so philosophers (like me) want to believe. But to use God as a metaphysical principle that helps to explain things within some conceptual scheme is far removed from the religious person's use of God to satisfy deep needs, e.g. the need for meaning in life, for freedom from guilt, for hope for the future.

So philosophers and religious people use God differently. Often in philosophy the notion of God that is entertained follows from a prized theistic proof or from the role God plays in a metaphysical system. In religion the notion of God that is entertained follows primarily from religious experience, especially (though not exclusively) experience of events and texts taken to be revelatory. For a religious person God is a matter of passionate concern. He is a living person who created us, sustains us, cares about us, and hears and answers prayers. So perhaps it is understandable that many religious people feel that to discuss God in terms of cold logic or make God a variable in a formal argument is to misunderstand the real point of talk about god, perhaps even to use the same word ('God') to talk about something different. Little wonder believers like Pascal feel that the God of philosophy is a different being from the God they know.

Let us now see if we can formulate a set of properties for the two beings Pascal-like believers see here. I will call them the God of philosophy (GP) and the God of Abraham, Issac and Jacob (GAIJ), respectively. Naturally, the exercise will be somewhat oversimplified. Notoriously, even philosophers who believe in God disagree about God's character, and, as we have seen, so do theologians. Both GP and GAIJ are to a certain extent artificial constructs. Nevertheless, I think it will be helpful to approach matters in this way.

There are perhaps three main differences between the two Gods. (1) GAIJ is personal; he cares about the world, is merciful to human beings, and works to attain his purposes in history. He is a redeemer who works for our salvation, forgives us our sins, and provides meaning and a sense of purpose in life. GP, on the other hand, is impersonal. Like the distant God of the Deists, he is more the indifferent metaphysical lynchpin of the world system than a caring person. Little is typically said about the need to love, worship, serve or obey him. He is more an abstract metaphysical principle than an active saviour; providing human beings with meaning in life is not one of his main concerns. (2) GAIJ is a God whom we know only because he has chosen to reveal himself to us. We know him through his great acts in human history and through the prophets and teachers who have spoken to us on his behalf. If he had not taken the initiative, we would be ignorant of him. GP, on the other hand, is a God who is discovered through the operations of human reason. We know GP because of conclusions we have reached from rational arguments. (3) GAIJ is a God who rules over our lives. We play a role in his plan for human history; he is primarily the object of our obedience and worship. GP, on the other hand, is ruled by us: he plays a role in a metaphysical system we have devised. He is primarily the object of our theorizing.

Two things are evident here. First, GAIJ and GP are two different beings. We can see why a person who worships the one would fail to recognize the other as God. Second, there probably have been philosophers (and perhaps theologians) who had a being more like GP than GAIJ in mind when they discussed 'God'. It cannot be denied that the God spoken of by many of the greatest thinkers in the history of philosophy bears little resemblance to GAIJ. The attributes of GAIJ are just not the same, for example, as Plato's Demiurge, Aristotle's Unmoved Mover, Spinoza's 'God or Nature', or Hegel's Absolute Spirit.

This forces us to sharpen Pascal's distinction. Let us now distinguish between (1) the God of Abraham, Isaac and Jacob (GAIJ); (2) the God or Gods of philosophy (GP), e.g. the God of people like Plato, Aristotle, Spinoza and Hegel; and (3) the God of Christian philosophy (GCP), e.g. the God of Christian philosophers like Anselm, Aquinas, Pascal, Kierkegaard. The key difference is perhaps this: Christian philosophers philosophize about God because they have faith in God, i.e. in GAIJ. Secular philosophers philosophize about God because they lack faith and want to discover what they should believe about God.

Surely the fact that secular philosophers have produced conceptions of God unacceptable to Christians is not an indictment of all philosophical talk about God. Fortunately there have been Christian philosophers, those mentioned above and many others, whose conceptions of God if explained simply would be aceptable to the large majority of Christian believers. Such philosophers were often brilliant and subtle speculative thinkers, but their commitment to the Bible and to the Christian community ensured that it was definitely the God of Abraham, Isaac and Jacob that they wrote about.

I would argue that this is also true of the God described in this book. We can see this in terms of the three differences between GP and GAIJ noted above. (1) The God I believe in and have presented in this book is a personal being who acts in history to redeem his creatures. He is a historical-eschatological God rather than a remote, impersonal force. God is not primarily for me the lynchpin of any metaphysical system; he is a living being. Of course I have used metaphysical arguments to reach conclusions about God, but this by itself does not entail that I have been talking about some other God than GAIJ. Even non-philosophically inclined religious believers, whether they realize it or not, use God as a metaphysical principle. He constitutes for them a way of seeing and interpreting their experience. The question is: is it somehow logically inconsistent or religiously inappropriate to use a living being as a metaphysical principle or the notion of a living being as a variable in a formal argument? Of course not, as long as the properties that make God a personal redeemer are not compromised or ignored.

(2) The God I believe in and have presented in this book is a God that is known not by human speculation about him but by revelation. We know God simply because God has chosen to reveal himself to us. The best efforts of natural as opposed to revealed theology in Western thought have been skimpy and often inconsistent with Christian faith. And for good reason - if we ignore what Christians take to be God's revelation of himself and base our conception of God exclusively on evidence we see or arguments we can generate, some other God beside GAIJ may well emerge. Perhaps Whitehead's finite God or Hume's 'idiot God' or Mill's limited God who has other greater concerns than our happiness will be the best guess we can make.

I suspect Aquinas is correct that there are certain things we can come to know about God by natural reason alone - perhaps he is even correct that the existence of God is one of them. Though God is not know primarily or in the first instance through human reason, nothing prevents God from allowing us to discover certain things about him on our own. But clearly Aquinas is also correct that there are other things we can only know about God through revelation - e.g. that there is but one God.

I would add another - we can only know by revelation that God can know the (undetermined) future. Of course it won't do to use an appeal to revelation to buttress an incoherent claim. The person who says, 'God revealed to me that 2+2=7' is not presenting a good argument for this absurd mathematical claim. But I have never seen an argument which successfully shows the absurdity or incoherence of the notion that some being knows the undetermined future. Many people have correctly pointed out how difficult it is for us to understand how any being could do so. But that is not the same thing.

What Christian philosophers should aim for, in my opinion, is not to use their reasoning ability to decide what God is like but rather to think hard about the implications of the concept of God that has been revealed. This means that there may well be a profound difference between   what   Christian   philosophers   believe   about   God (they may well believe in GAIJ) and what they think they can prove about God (which may be severely limited). But fortunately our inability to prove much about God is not a great tragedy. To the Christian there is no need for theoretical speculation about an unknown God (it would probably lead to wrong results in any case) since God has revealed himself - primarily (so Christians believe) in Jesus Christ. As Pierre Thevenaz says:

> If the God of Jesus Christ reveals himself in a way that he has chosen, through an elect people or through the incarnation of a savior, this does not mean that he has given man a better theosophy or a new theology to put beside so many other conceptions of the divine; on the contrary, it means that he has freed man from every theosophy and every idolatry[2].

Thus, for Christian philosophers, the God who has revealed himself to us is a profound rejection of the God of philosophy.

(3) The God I believe in and have presented in this book is a God on whom we depend and who rules our lives. He is not a being who, as a principle in a humanly-invented philosophical system, depends on us. The Christian holds that the entire universe exists only because of the free choice and mercy of God. In Acts 17 Epimenides's noble saying about God is cited by Paul: 'In him we live and move and have our being' (Acts 17: 28). The truth is that we depend on God for everything, the food we eat, the air we breathe, the people we love, the scenery we admire, the health we enjoy. Without God's sustaining grace, the whole creation itself would lapse into the non-being out of which it came. We like to think we are immortal; we push from our minds the thought of death, but we depend on God most of all for life itself. And this life which usually seems so securely ours is nothing but a thin mist which comes and then fades. Thus St James says (James 4: 13-16):

> Come now, you who say, 'Today or tomorrow we will go into such and such a town and spend a year there and trade and get gain,' whereas you do not know about tomorrow. What is your life? For you are a mist that appears for a little time and then vanishes. Instead you ought to say, 'If the Lord wills, we shall live and we shall do this or that'. As it is, you boast to your arrogance. All such boasting is vain.

Pascal's distinction, then, turns out to be a legitimate distinction, one that should stand as something of a warning to all Christian philosophers. We all need be careful that our speculations are solidly anchored in the Bible and the Christian community. But I see no reason to conclude that the God typically presented by Christian philosophers or the God presented in this book is a different being than the God of Abraham, Isaac and Jacob. I will take Pascal's distinction as a fair warning, but not as a repudiation of the enterprise of this book.

But is the God I have argued for worthy of worship? Well, not if J. N. Findlay is correct in his claim that any proper object of worship must tower over us infinitely and 'must possess its various qualities in some necessary manner'. That is, God cannot be contingently omnipotent, omniscient and perfectly good (as I have suggested he may well be), for this entails that he 'just happens' to have these properties. Findlay says: 'It would be quite unsatisfactory from the religious standpoint, if an object merely happened to be wise, good, powerful and so forth, even to a superlative degree'. It would be sheer idolatry to worship 'anything limited in any thinkable manner'[3].

But we must surely make a distinction here. The expression 'x is contingently φ' might mean merely 'x could still be x if x were not φ' or it might mean 'x would still be x if x were not φ and some being y (where y ≠ x) made x to be φ'. Where the second is meant, I agree with Findlay that if God is contingently omnipotent (i.e. if some other being made God omnipotent) then God is not worthy of worship. But surely there can be beings which contingently possess properties in the first but not the second sense. And this is just what I mean to imply when I say that God may well be, for example, contingently omnipotent - not that some other being made God omnipotent but just that God might still be God if he were, say, slightly less than omnipotent. Now if the expression 'x is contingently φ' is understood in this second way, I see no reason whatsoever to say that no being which possesses any of its attributes contingently can be worthy of worship. There may well be a being who remains worthy of worship (just as there are human beings who remain worthy of praise) so long as he retains his admirable attributes, even though we can coherently imagine him not retaining them.

As a special case of Findlay's general argument, McCloskey argues that a God who is contingently perfectly good is not worthy of worship:

> It would not be proper for people to abase themselves before him, and to yield their wills to his will, for he might choose to will what was evil; yet the yielding of one's will to God's will is a vital part of worship. It can never be fitting to yield our wills completely under such circumstances; nor can it be fitting to adore without reservation or qualification, a being who happens to be virtuous but who may in the future cease to be so.[4]

But what if we are talking about a being who is contingently perfectly good just in the sense that he would still be the very being he is if he sinned but who (in Pike's words) 'cannot bring himself to sin'? That is, what about a being who logically can sin but who is prevented from sinning by a firm resolve not to sin that is an utterly stable aspect of his character? Here McCloskey's argument does not apply: it would be perfectly appropriate to trust such a being fully, to yield one's will to his completely. Perhaps there are possible reservations or qualifications one might have about the goodness of such a being, but since no one could rationally have any actual reservations or qualifications, McCloskey's argument quite apparently fails.

What exactly are the attributes that make a being worthy of worship? This is not easy to say. For me omnipotence and perfect goodness probably constitute separately necessary and jointly sufficient conditions, but others will disagree. However, the point is that whatever properties we agree on as criteria, the criteria will in all probability be satisfied by a being who has them, i.e. by a being for whom these attributes are attributes, whether or not he has them essentially. Now in this book I have not insisted that God is contingently as opposed to essentially omnipotent, omniscient, etc. It is just that I see many problems in, and no compelling arguments for, the claim that God must have these and other properties essentially. But I have insisted that God is omnipotent, omniscient and perfectly good, and this for me is enough to say that he is worthy of worship. Again, since I have not argued that God has these properties essentially, I will also abstain from arguing that God is necessarily worthy of worship.

It is said that on 6 December 1273, while he was celebrating mass, a great change came over Thomas Aquinas. At the age of 49, his Summa Theologica unfinished, he stopped writing. To his faithful secretary and companion Reginald of Piperno, he said, 'Reginald, I can do no more; such things have been revealed to me that all that I have written seems to me as so much straw. Now, I await the end of my life after that of my works' [5]. Aquinas died three months later.

Is there a critique of theology and philosophy here? Perhaps so. I've not experienced the beatific vision, and accordingly I probably won't cease scholarly work. But I confess I see Aquinas's point about straw. Philosophical theology - even when done by a great man like him, let alone by the rest of us - is severely limited in value, especially when compared to eternal things.

In this book I have reached certain conclusions about God that seem to me intellectually and religiously satisfactory. Naturally, they won't be acceptable to everyone else or maybe even to anyone else. But there is a sense in which all Christians, let alone Christian philosophers, must be skeptics about the nature of God. As I said in the Introduction, theology and philosophy are human enterprises. All our talk about God is halting, partial, hopelessly inadequate. This does not mean we should not hold firm beliefs about God or do the best job we can as philosophers and theologians. It simply means that no matter how much skill or effort we bring to the job, God always remains in part a mystery. The gap between God and our ideas about God was, we believe, salvifically narrowed by God's revelatory initiative, but not closed.

Like Aquinas, all Christians can see that human talk about God ultimately comes to an end. Its best efforts are like straw. All that we say about God becomes inept when we see God.

Notes and References

INTRODUCTION

1. For my own view of the Bible, see The Debate About the Bible: Inerrancy Versus Infallibility (Philadelphia: Westminster Press, 1977).
2. See Alvin Plantinga, The Nature of Necessity (Oxford University Press, 1974) pp. 44-87 for a clear and helpful discussion of essential predication.
3. J.N. Findlay, 'Can God's Existence Be Disproved?', Alvin Plantinga (ed.), The Ontological Argument (Garden City, New York: Anchor Books, 1964) pp. 117-18.

CHAPTER 1: TIME

1. Anselm, St Anselm: Basic Writings (LaSalle, Illinois: Open Court Publishing Company, 1958) p. 25.
2. Boethius, The Theological Treatises and the Consolation of Philosophy (Loeb Classical Library, London: William Heinemann, 1918) pp. 403-5; cf. also pp. 21-3, 401-5.
3. The Summa Theologica of St Thomas Aquinas (London: Burns, Oates and Washbourne, 1920) Pt. I, Q. X, Arts. 2 and 4.
4. These points are taken from Nelson Pike's God and Timelessness (New York: Schocken Books, 1970) p. 7. Pike's work is an outstanding study of this subject and has influenced me at several points.
5. Ibid., pp. 97-118, 125-8; Richard Swinburne, The Coherence of Theism (Oxford University Press, 1977) pp. 221-2.
6. Thomas Aquinas, Summa Contra Gentiles, trans A.C. Pegis (Notre Dame, Indiana: University of Notre Dame Press, 1975) II, 35.
7. This has been argued by Nicholas Woltersdorff in his 'God Everlasting'. See God and the Good, ed. Clifton J. Orlebeke and Lewis B. Smedes (Grand Rapids, Michigan: William B. Eerdmans, 1975) pp. 181-203.
8. See Pike, God and Timelessness pp. 128-9; Swinburne, The Coherence of Theism pp. 220-1.
9. See Swinburne, The Coherence of Theism pp. 220-1.
10. William Kneale, 'Time and Eternity in Theology', Proceedings of the Aristotelian Society, vol. 61 (1961) p. 98.
11. 'Eternity', The Journal of Philosophy vol. 78, no. 8 (August 1981) pp. 429-58.

12.   Ibid., p. 445.
13.   Ibid., p. 439.
14.   Ibid., p. 443.
15.   Ibid., p. 445.
16.   Ibid., p. 447. The quotation is from Kenny's essay 'Divine Foreknowledge and Human Freedom' in his Aquinas: A Collection of Critical Essays (Garden City, New York: Doubleday-Anchor, 1969) pp. 255-70.
17.   A good discussion of such solutions is found in C.W.K. Mundle's article on 'Time, Consciousness of' in vol. VIII of the Encyclopedia of Philosophy, ed. Paul Edwards (New York: Macmillan Publishing Company, 1967).
18.   'Eternity', pp. 449-50.
19.   Ibid., p. 450.
20.   Ibid., p. 451.
21.   Augustine, The Confessions of St Augustine, trans. E.B. Pusey (New York: Thomas Nelson, n.d.) pp. 282-4.
22.   See Pike, God and Timelessness pp. 181-3.

CHAPTER 2: OMNISCIENCE

1.   See Edmund Gettier, 'Is Justified True Belief Knowledge?', Analysis, 22 (1963) pp. 121-3.
2.   Nelson Pike, God and Timelessness (New York: Schocken Books, 1970) pp. 89-95.
3.   Despite his argument in Chapter 5 of God and Timelessness that a timeless being can know temporal facts (facts whose description requires the mention of temporal relations or temporal position or extension), Pike seems to admit the truth of premises which seem to entail that no timeless being can be omniscient. On page 89 he seems to admit that an omniscient being must know on 12 May that it is 12 May and that any being that knows on 12 May that it is 12 May has temporal location. He agrees with Robert Coburn whose argument (stated by Pike) is 'a necessary condition of knowing that today is the twelfth of May is that one have temporal location - more specifically, that one exist on the twelfth of May'. But since no timeless being has temporal location (Pike, p. 7), no timeless being can know on 12 May that it is 12 May. Thus no timeless being can be omniscient. (Perhaps, then, Pike wants to deny the premise that an omniscient being must know on 12 May that it is 12 May, i.e. the premise that an omniscient being must know temporal facts. But this denial does not seem prima facie plausible, leaving me unsure what Pike would say here.)
4.   I owe this point to Alvin Plantinga.
5.   Paul Helm, 'Timelessness and Foreknowledge', Mind, vol. 84, no. 336 (Oct. 1975) p. 513.
6.   Brian Davies, 'Kenny on God', Philosophy, vol. 57, no. 219 (Jan.

1982) p. 110.
7.   Hector-Neri Castaneda, 'Omniscience and Indexical Reference', Baruch Brody, Readings in the Philosophy of Religion (Englewood Cliffs, New Jersey: Prentice-Hall, 1974) p. 381.
8.   Richard Swinburne, The Coherence of Theism (Oxford University Press, 1977) p. 165.
9.   Swinburne omits the phrase 'I know' here, but it is surely needed to make the argument work.
10. See A.N. Prior, 'The Formalities of Omniscience', Brody, Readings p. 416 and 'Thank Goodness That's Over', Philosophy, vol. 34, no. 128 (Jan. 1959) p. 17.
11. Anthony Kenny, The God of the Philosophers (Oxford: Clarendon Press, 1979) p. 47.
12. Castaneda, 'Omniscience and Indexical Reference' pp. 381-2.
13. I am indebted for part of this analysis of omniscience to A.N. Prior's pioneering article, 'The Formalities of Omniscience', Brody, Readings pp. 413-27.
13. 'Is Omniscience Possible', Australasian Journal of Philosophy, vol. 41 (May 1963) p. 92.
15. Ibid., p. 93.
16. Ibid.
17. John Lachs, 'Professor Prior on Omniscience', Philosophy, vol. 38 (Oct. 1963) p. 362.
18. Ibid., p. 364.
19. See A.N. Prior, 'Rejoinder to Professor Lachs on Omniscience', Philosophy, vol. 38 (Oct. 1963) p. 365.

CHAPTER 3: IMMUTABILITY

1.   Plato, The Republic of Plato, trans. F.M. Cornford (New York: Oxford University Press, 1945) II, 381 B.
2.   Aristotle, Metaphysics, trans. R. Hope (Ann Arbor, Michigan: University of Michigan Press, 1960) XII, 9 1074b.
3.   P.T. Geach, Logic Matters (Oxford: Basil Blackwell, 1972) p. 322; cf. also Providence and Evil (Cambridge University Press, 1977) pp. 42-3.
4.   Keith Ward, The Concept of God (Glasgow: William Collins, 1977) pp. 153, 155.
5.   Geach, Providence and Evil, p. 6.
6.   A helpful discussion of this is T.P. Smith's 'On the Applicability of a Criterion of Change', Ratio, vol. 15, no. 2 (Dec. 1972) pp. 325-33.
7.   Norman Kretzmann, 'Omniscience and Immutability', William Rowe and William Wainwright (eds), Philosophy of Religion (New York: Harcourt, Brace, Jovanovich, 1973). pp. 60-70.
8.   Geach, Providence and Evil, p. 41.
9.   See Lawrence B. Lombard, 'Relational Change and Relational Changes', Philosophical Studies, vol. 34, no. 1 (July 1978) pp. 75,

78, for a presentation and defence of this criterion.

10. Thomas Aquinas, Summa Contra Gentiles, trans. A. Pegis (Notre Dame, Indiana: University of Notre Dame Press, 1975) I, 55, 6-9.

11. Nor is God's omniscience endangered by this sort of mutability. It is still true that at each moment in time God knows all the true propositions and disbelieves all the false ones. At each moment he knows all the propositions that can logically be known.

12. W. Norris Clarke, S.J., 'A New Look at the Immutability of God', Robert J. Roth, S.J. (ed), God: Knowable and Unknowable (New York: Fordham University Press, 1973) p. 58.

13. Ibid., p. 48.

14. Ibid., p. 51.

15. Ibid., p. 54.

16. We do not have to do this, of course. Instead of saying that the world is the set of all created things we could say that it is the set of all existing things. In this case God would be part of the world and would be the creator not of the world but of all the created things in the world. It seems to me a matter of theological and philosophical indifference which definition of the term 'the world' we use.

CHAPTER 4: FOREKNOWLEDGE

1. I am indebted to Alvin Plantinga for this procedure. See God, Freedom, and Evil (New York: Harper and Row, 1974) p. 25.

2. That is, '(1) Gbp; (2) $\sim \Diamond$ (Gbp & $\sim$ p); (3) $\therefore \sim \Diamond \sim$ p' is invalid.

3. That is, '(1) Gbp; (2) Gbp $\rightarrow \Diamond \sim \Diamond$ p; (3) $\therefore \sim \Diamond \sim$ p' is valid by modus ponens.

4. Nelson Pike, 'Divine Omniscience and Voluntary Action', Philosophy of Religion, ed. Steven Cahn (New York: Harper and Row, 1970) pp. 68-88.

5. Plantinga, God, Freedom, and Evil, pp. 69-73.

6. Nelson Pike, 'Divine Foreknowledge, Human Freedom, and Possible Worlds', The Philosophical Review, vol. LXXXVI, no. 2 (April 1977).

7. Ibid., p. 216.

8. It should also be noted that whatever forcefulness this argument possesses has nothing whatever to do with essential omniscience or even with omniscience. In fact, all one must do is omit the words 'that God knew' in premises (32), (35), (37) and (39), and one produces an equally forceful argument for fatalism. But this argument too is unsound, as Pike will be quite prepared to admit. For it is his claim that determinism is produced only by foreknowledge of an essentially omniscient being. Foreknowledge by a contingently omniscient being or by a non-omniscient being does not produce determinism, nor (I am

sure he would say) does an argument for non-theologica fatalism.

9.   Pike, 'Divine Omniscience and Voluntary Action', p. 77. (Bu Pike admits that he does not really understand what th doctrine means.)
10. <u>Summa Theologica</u> (New York: Benzinger Brothers, 1947) I, 14 9, emphasis added.
11. Ibid., I, 14, 8.
12. Richard Taylor, 'Deliberation and Foreknowledge', Bernar Berofsky (ed.), <u>Free Will and Determinism</u> (New York: Harpe and Row, 1966) pp. 277-93.
13. See Joseph Runzo's paper, 'Omniscience and Freedom for Evil <u>International Journal for Philosophy of Religion</u> vol. 12, no. (1981), for an alternative analysis of the crystal ball analogy.

CHAPTER 5: OMNIPOTENCE

1.   Antony Flew, <u>God and Philosophy</u> (New York: Delta Books 1966) p. 47.
2.   Ibid., p. 48.
3.   Ibid., p. 44.
4.   See Linwood Urban and Douglas N. Walton, <u>The Power of Go</u> (New York: Oxford University Press, 1978) pp. 84-5.
5.   Ibid., p. 85.
6.   Douglas Walton, 'The Omnipotence Paradox', ibid., p. 157.
7.   Ibid., p. 159.
8.   C. Wade Savage, 'The Paradox of the Stone', ibid., p. 140.
9.   George Mavrodes, 'Some Puzzles Concerning Omnipotence' ibid., pp. 131-4.
10. Savage, ibid., pp. 138-43.
11. Richard Swinburne, <u>The Coherence of Theism</u> (Oxfor University Press, 1977) pp. 152-8.
12. See Alvin Plantinga, <u>God and Other Minds</u> (Ithaca, New York Cornell University Press, 1967) pp. 168-73; Bernard Mayo, 'Mr Keene on Omnipotence', <u>Mind</u>, vol. 70, no. 278 (April 1961) pp 249-50.
13. Mavrodes, 'Some Puzzles Concerning Omnipotence', p. 132.
14. Savage, 'The Paradox of the Stone', p. 139.
15. Including Mavrodes, in the penultimate paragraph of his paper See 'Some Puzzles Concerning Omnipotence', pp. 133-4. Se also G.B. Keene, 'A Simpler Solution to the Paradox o Omnipotence', <u>Mind</u>, vol. 69, no. 273 (Jan. 1960) pp. 74-5.
16. Savage, 'The Paradox of the Stone', p. 141.
17. See J.L. Cowan, 'The Paradox of Omnipotence Revisited' <u>Canadian Journal of Philosophy</u>, vol. III, no. 3 (March 1974) p 440: 'The real thing a being who is able to lift anything is no able to do is . . . to create something it cannot lift <u>instead o</u> being able to lift anything'. See also Swinburne, <u>The Coherenc</u>

of Theism pp. 154-5.
18. J.L. Cowan, 'The Paradox of Omnipotence', Urban and Walton, The Power of God p. 149.
19. Swinburne, The Coherence of Theism pp. 157-8. It should be pointed out that Swinburne's basic approach to the paradox was first suggested by Alvin Plantinga. See God and Other Minds p. 169.
20. As long as the phrase 'make a stone he subsequently cannot lift' is understood to be an act which is successfully performed if a stone is created which the creator cannot lift on a finite number of attempts or for a finite period of time, there is no reason why a formerly omnipotent being who does such a thing cannot later regain his omnipotence by lifting the stone. This will only be ruled out if the phrase 'make a stone he subsequently cannot lift' is understood to be an act which is successfully performed only if the stone, once created, can never be lifted by its creator.
21. P.T. Geach, Providence and Evil (Cambridge University Press, 1977) p. 3.
22. Swinburne, The Coherence of Theism p. 150.
23. This general point has been made by Jonathan Harrison, 'Geach on God's Alleged Ability to do Evil', Philosophy, vol. 51, no. 196 (April 1976) p. 215. The 'power to do' approach does lead to absurdities on some views of omnipotence. For example, if an omnipotent being can do anything logically possible, and if 'Socrates sits' is logically possible, then an omnipotent being can do Socrates sits. (See James F. Ross, Philosophical Theology (Indianapolis: Bobbs-Merrill, 1969) p. 200.) But this problem will not arise on the view of omnipotence I will embrace.
24. There is another difficulty here too, something of an infinite regress. If God can violate the laws of logic in L (by creating, say, a married bachelor), can he violate the laws of logic in L'? If he can do so in terms of a third system of logic L", can he violate the laws of logic in this system? Where does all this end?
25. Plantinga, God and Other Minds p. 169.
26. Thomas Aquinas, Summa Theologica (New York: Benzinger Brothers, 1947) I, 25, 3.
27. As Swinburne does. See The Coherence of Theism p. 151.
28. See Swinburne, ibid., p. 150; Urban and Walton, The Power of God p. 13.
29. It seems to be a peculiar temption of contemporary philosophers to use the notion of essential prediction to generate hypothetical entities which a moment's reflection will show cannot possibly exist. Perhaps I succumbed to this temptation earlier when I spoke of a table that is essentially unmade by an omnipotent being. (Certainly the point made

there still stands, however.) A classic case is found in a recent article in which the author seriously discusses a rock which is essentially unable to do anything at all.

30. James F. Ross (Philosophical Theology p. 207) points out a related difficulty: if logical fatalism (the doctrine that all true statements are necessarily true and all false statements are necessarily false) is true, everyone is omnipotent on (D), i.e. whenever 'B does x' is false for any being and for any action, it is also incoherent. But logical fatalism, in my opinion, is not only false but necessarily false.

31. It is hard to see the exact relationship, but the argument presented here seems essentially similar to that of Richard LaCroix in 'The Impossibility of Defining "Omnipotence"' (Philosophical Studies vol. 32, no. 2 (Aug. 1977)) and the reply I will give to it presupposes some points made by George Mavrodes in his 'Defining Omnipotence'.

32. Though much of my thinking in this chapter has been influenced by Swinburne's clear work on omnipotence, I believe there is a problem with his penultimate definition of omnipotence (see The Coherence of Theism p. 152). He tries to solve the 'randomness' and 'freedom' problems by adding to his definition the stipulation that any state of affairs an omnipotent being P is able to bring about is one 'the description of which does not entail that P did not bring it about'. The problem is that this definition, failing as it does to distinguish between does not and cannot, may well lead (via the argument to which I have been replying) to the conclusion that everybody is omnipotent.

33. In this section I have been assisted at points by an unpublished paper by Michael Sean Quinn entitled 'Omnipotence' and by a doctoral dissertation by Rebecca D. Pentz entitled A Defense of the Formal Adequacy of St Thomas Aquinas' Analysis of Omnipotence (University of California at Irvine, 1980).

CHAPTER 6: BENEVOLENCE

1. Anselm, The Basic Writings of St Anselm (LaSalle, Illinois: Open Court Publishing Company, 1962) pp. 12-13.
2. Thomas Aquinas, Summa Theologica (New York: Benzinger Brothers, 1947) I, 25, 3 (see also I, 19, 9).
3. Ibid., I, 25, 1.
4. Thomas Aquinas, Summa Contra Gentiles, trans. A. Pegis (Notre Dame, Indiana: University of Notre Dame Press, 1975) I, 95, 3.
5. Richard Swinburne, The Coherence of Theism (Oxford University Press, 1977) p. 202; cf. also pp. 146, 148, 204, 209.
6. Stephen C. Tornay (ed.), Ockham: Studies and Selctions (LaSalle, Illinois: Open Court Publishing Company, 1938) p. 180.
7. Soren Kierkegaard, Fear and Trembling (Garden City, New

York: Doubleday Anchor Books, 1954) pp. 64-77.

8. Here I am essentially following John Stuart Mill. See An Examination of Sir William Hamilton's Philosophy (London: Longmans, Green, Reader and Dyer, 1867) pp. 122-5.
9. P.T. Geach, Providence and Evil (Cambridge University Press, 1977) p. 79; cf. pp. 80-81.
10. Ibid., p. 127.
11. Jonathan Harrison, 'Geach on God's Alleged Ability to do Evil', Philosophy, vol. 51, no. 196 (April 1976) p. 213.
12. Nelson Pike, 'Omnipotence and God's Ability to Sin', Baruch Brody (ed.), Readings in the Philosophy of Religion (Englewood Cliffs, New Jersey: Prentice-Hall, 1974) pp. 362-3. This is a helpful article that has influenced my thinking on the subject.
13. Providence and Evil, p. 19.
14. Ibid., p. 15.
15. Ibid., p. 20.

CHAPTER 7: EVIL

1. Free will defenders sometimes argue that free will in itself is such a great moral good that it will outweigh any possible bad consequences that might follow from it. But this claim seems both false and unnecessary to the FWD. What if in the end no free moral agent chooses to love and obey God? I hardly think God's policy can fairly be called wise if this were to happen, even if free will, as claimed, is in itself a great moral good.
2. Alvin Plantinga has so argued. See God, Freedom, and Evil (New York: Harper and Row, 1974) p. 61.
3. Ibid., p. 25.
4. Steven Boer, 'The Irrelevance of the Free Will Defense', Analysis, vol. 38, no. 2 (March 1978) p. 111.
5. John Hick argues along these lines. See Evil and the God of Love (New York: Harper and Row, 1966) pp. 68-9.
6. J.L. Mackie, 'Evil and Omnipotence', Nelson Pike (ed.), God and Evil (Englewood Cliffs, New Jersey: Prentice-Hall, 1964) p. 56.
7. See Plantinga, God, Freedom, and Evil, pp. 34-44 on this.
8. Ibid., p. 58.
9. I am indebted to my friend and colleague John Roth for making remarks that led me to see that the EPE is distinct from the LPE.
10. I should point out here that a 'universe' is not the same thing as a Leibnizian 'possible world', and so my claim that there is only one universe is not falsified by our ability to imagine various possible worlds. There is only one actual universe, and all possible worlds are conceived of and talked about in it. Imagined possible worlds are only possible (not actual) states of the actual world. Inductive arguments can only be based on past actual states of affairs, not possible ones. Thus this argument

might or might not count as a good inductive argument: 'I have
seen thousands of tigers and they all had stripes; therefore it is
probable that the next tiger I will see will have stripes'. But this
one will certainly not count as a good inductive argument: 'The
next tiger I see will probably have no stripes, because I can
imagine possible worlds that contain nothing but stripeless
tigers'.

11.   Hume has Philo make this sort of statement. See Dialogues
      Concerning Natural Religion (New York: Hafner, 1959) p. 73.
12.   Plantinga has recently shown that it is highly doubtful that
      skeptics can achieve their aim here. See 'The Probabalistic
      Argument From Evil', Philosophical Studies, vol. 35, no. 1 (Jan.
      1979).
13.   God, Freedom, and Evil, p. 62.
14.   To the question why God would create Satan with the facility
      freely to cause natural evil, free will defenders can give the
      same answer that they give in the case of moral evil: for some
      reason (that is now hard to see) God's decision to do so is wise.
      It will turn out better in the end that God allow Satan the
      degree of free will he has given him than follow any other
      course he could have followed.
15.   God, Freedom, and Evil, pp. 48-53.
16.   Evil and the God of Love, pp. 377-81.

CHAPTER 8: INCARNATION

1.   Henry Bettenson (ed.), Documents of the Christian Church (New
     York: Oxford University Press, 1960) pp. 72-3.
2.   Thomas Aquinas, Summa Contra Gentiles (Notre Dame, Indiana:
     Notre Dame University Press, 1975) Book IV: 195.
3.   William Temple, Christus Veritas (London: Macmillan and
     Company, 1924) p. 139.
4.   John Hick (ed.), The Myth of God Incarnate (Philadelphia:
     Westminster Press, 1977) p. 178.
5.   See Richard Swinburne, The Coherence of Theism (Oxford
     University Press, 1977) pp., 38-9, for a discussion of this
     matter.
6.   The latter line is taken by Brian Hebblethwaite in 'Incarnation -
     The Essence of Christianity?', Theology, 80 (March 1977) p. 86.
7.   Philosophers have disagreed about the proper analysis of what it
     is to be something. Often this notion has been analysed in terms
     of fairly abstruse metaphysical concepts, e.g. substance (x is
     God if x has divine substance), essence (x is a chair if x has the
     essence of a chair), or, in the case of human beings, mind or
     soul (x is a human being if x has a human soul). Despite the use I
     will make of the notion of an essential property, I have no wish
     to become involved in such debates, and I propose my analysis
     as a simple way of avoiding them.   For surely whatever

metaphysical theory is correct, its claims will be accounted for in my very general notion of <u>having certain properties</u>. For example, if it is true that nothing is a human being unless it has a human soul, then <u>having a human soul</u> is certainly a property and thus is included in my theory.

8.   See P.T. Geach, <u>Providence and Evil</u> (Cambridge University Press, 1977) pp. 24-8. See also R.T. Herbert's facinating proposal in <u>Paradox and Identity in Theology</u> (Ithaca: Cornell University Press, 1979) pp. 79-101.

9.   Some may find problematical the notion of God 'giving up' a property. But if the problems connected with theological predication are solved, as I noted I am pretending, i.e. if we know what it is for God to <u>have</u> a property, then it is not difficult to see what it would be for him to <u>give up</u> a property. Roughly, 'God gives up property p' means 'God has p at one time and of his own free choice does not have p at a later time'.

10. John Calvin, <u>The Institutes of the Christian Religion</u>, ed. John T. McNeill (London: SCM Press, 1960) pp. 464-5.

11. <u>Incarnation and Myth: The Debate Continued</u>, ed. Michael Goulder (Grand Rapids, Michigan: William B. Eerdmans, 1979) p. 62.

12. An analogy: suppose we define an 'android' as a robot that is behaviourally indistinguishable from a human being. If so, it would follow that no observation of a given android's behaviour could count as evidence for the claim that it is an android. But does this mean there could be no evidence of <u>any</u> sort for the claim? Of course not. For one thing, the android's manufacturer could enlighten us.

13. In the traditional doctrine of the 'communication of properties', however, we can still legitimately speak of the man Jesus forgiving sins and the Second Person of the Trinity dying.

14. Don Cuppitt, 'The Christ of Christendom', in Hick, <u>The Myth of God Incarnate</u> p. 137.

15. See Claude Welch (ed.), <u>God and Man in Mid-Nineteenth Century German Theology</u> (New York: Oxford University Press, 1965) and Frank Weston, <u>The One Christ</u> (London: Longmans Green, 1907).

16. See Temple, <u>Christus Veritas</u>, pp. 143ff. and D.M. Baille, <u>God Was in Christ</u> (New York: Charles Scribner's Sons, 1948) pp. 94-8.

17. <u>Incarnation and Myth</u> p. 43. In the same book Cuppitt offers two far more substantive criticisms of kenosis: (1) that it breaks with monotheism, leads to anthropomorphism, and is destructive of belief in God (pp. 44-5); and (2) that it leads to an incoherent 'triple consciousness in the incarnate Lord' (p. 45). However, I will not attempt to reply to these objections because in my view Brian Hebblethwaite has already successfully done so in his contribution to <u>Incarnation and Myth</u>

(see pp. 61, 89-90).
18. Ibid., pp. 7-8.

CHAPTER 9: TRINITY

1. Saint Augustine, On Christian Doctrine, trans. D.W. Robertson, Jr (Indianapolis, Indiana: Bobbs-Merrill, 1958) p. 10.
2. Keith Ward, The Concept of God (Glasgow: William Collins, 1977) p. 106.
3. Some biblical scholars doubt that these are the ipsissima verba of Jesus. Whether or not this is true, the text still shows an early Christian commitment to theses which led to the doctrine of the Trinity.
4. See On the Trinity, trans. A.W. Haddan (Grand Rapids, Michigan: William B. Eerdmans, 1956) pp. 92, 109, 112.
5. For example, the term 'person' does not mean the same thing to us that it did to people like Athanasius, Augustine and Aquinas. To us the term means something like 'self-consciousness', 'personality' or 'locus of knowledge and will'. But if we say that God is three persons in any of these senses we are in danger of tri-theism. The doctrine of the Trinity is not meant to include the idea that there are three divine self-consciousness, knowers or will.
6. William L. Power, 'Symbolic Logic and the Doctrine of the Trinity', The Illif Review, vol. XXXII, no. 1 (Winter 1975) p. 39.
7. Ibid., p. 40.
8. Having accused Power of failing to avoid modalism, I should in fairness explain my attitude toward this heresy. I believe modalism should be avoided in favour of the biblically and theologically more acceptable view that the three persons of the Godhead are three distinct and metaphysically real things. However, it is my opinion (implicitly shared, I dare say, by the consensus of orthodox thinkers in the history of doctrine) that modalism is perhaps the least egregious of the trinitarian heresies.
9. 'Identity and Trinity', The Journal of Religion, vol. 58, no. 2 (April 1978) p. 175.
10. Karl Rahner, The Trinity, trans Joseph Donceel (New York: Sanbury Press, 1974) p. 12.
11. Ibid., pp. 45-6.
12. Ibid., p. 72; cf. p. 70.
13. See ibid., pp. 75, 104-5, 113-4.
14. Augustine speaks of the persons of the Trinity as relations in On The Trinity, pp. 93, 101, 111. For Aquinas, see Summa Theologica (New York: Benzinger Brothers, 1947) I, 28, 3-4; I, 29, 4; and I, 30, 1-2.
15. Rahner, The Trinity p. 72.
16. Ibid., p. 103.

17. See Donald Hudson's excellent discussion of transcendence in 'The Concept of Divine Transcendence', Religious Studies, vol. 15, no. 2 (June 1979) pp. 197-210.

18. This despite Charles Hartshorne's sardonic but incisive comment: 'A theological paradox, it appears, is what a contradiction becomes when it is about God rather than something else, or indulged in by a theologian or a church rather than an unbeliever or a heretic.' The Divine Relativity (New Haven: Yale University Press, 1948) p. 1.

19. Steven Katz, 'The Language and Logic of "Mystery" in Christology', S.W. Sykes and J.P. Clayton (eds), Christ, Faith and History (Cambridge University Press, 1972) pp. 239-61.

20. Ibid., p. 239.

21. Ibid., p. 252.

CHAPTER 10: CONCLUSION

1. Cited in 'Pascal, Blaise', by Richard Popkin in The Encyclopedia of Philosophy ed. Paul Edwards (New York: Macmillan, 1967) vol. VI, p. 52.

2. Pierre Thevenaz, 'God of the Philosophers and God of the Christians', Studies in Religion, vol. 5, no. 4 (1975/1976) p. 338.

3. J.N. Findlay, 'Can God's Existence Be Disproved?', New Essays in Philosophical Theology (New York: Macmillan Company, 1955) pp. 51-3.

4. H.J. McCloskey, 'Would Any Being Merit Worship?', Southern Journal of Philosophy, vol. 2, no. 4 (Winter 1964).

5. Quoted in Jacques Maritan, St Thomas Aquinas (New York: Meridian Books, 1958) p. 54.

Bibliography

Anselm, St Anselm: Basic Writings (LaSalle, Illinois: Open Court Publishing Company, 1958).

Thomas Aquinas, Summa Contra Gentiles, trans. A.C. Pegis (Notre Dame, Indiana: University of Notre Dame Press, 1975).

Thomas Aquinas, Summa Theologica (New York: Benzinger Brothers, 1947).

Augustine, On Christian Doctrine, trans. D.W. Robertson, Jr (Indianapolis, Indiana: Bobbs-Merrill, 1958).

Augustine, On the Trinity, trans. A.W. Haddan (Grand Rapids, Michigan: William B. Eerdmans, 1956).

Augustine, The Confessions of St Augustine, trans. E.B. Pusey (New York: Thomas Nelson, n.d.).

Steven Boer, 'The Irrelevance of the Free Will Defense', Analysis, vol. 38, no. 2 (Mar. 1978).

Boethius, The Theological Treatises and the Consolation of Philosophy, Loeb Classical Library (London: William Heinemann, 1918).

Hector-Neri Castaneda, 'Omniscience and Indexical Reference', Readings in the Philosophy of Religion, ed. Baruch Brody (Englewood Cliffs, New Jersey: Prentice-Hall, 1974).

W. Norris Clarke, S.J., 'A New Look at the Immutability of God', God: Knowable and Unknowable, ed. Robert J. Roth, S.J. (New York: Fordham University Press, 1973).

J.L. Cowan, 'The Paradox of Omnipotence', The Power of God, ed. Linwood Urban and Douglas Walton (New York: Oxford University Press, 1978).

J.L. Cowan, 'The Paradox of Omnipotence Revisited', Canadian Journal of Philosophy, vol. III, no. 3 (Mar. 1974).

Don Cuppitt, 'The Christ of Christendom', The Myth of God Incarnate, ed. John Hick (Philadelphia: Westminster Press, 1977).

J.N. Findlay, 'Can God's Existence Be Disproved', The Ontological Argument, ed. Alvin Plantinga (Garden City, New York: Anchor Books, 1964).

Antony Flew, God and Philosophy (New York: Delta Books, 1966).

P.T. Geach, Logic Matters (Oxford: Basil Blackwell, 1972).

P.T. Geach, Providence and Evil (Cambridge University Press, 1977).

Michael Goulder (ed.), Incarnation and Myth: The Debate Continued (Grand Rapids, Michigan: William B. Eerdmans, 1979).

Jonathan Harrison, 'Geach on God's Alleged Ability to do Evil', Philosophy, vol. 51, no. 196 (Apr. 1976).

Brian Hebblethwaite, 'Incarnation - The Essence of Christianity?', Theology, vol. 80 (Mar. 1977).

R.T. Herbert, Paradox and Identity in Theology (Ithaca, New York: Cornell University Press, 1979).

John Hick, Evil and the God of Love (New York: Harper and Row, 1966).

John Hick (ed.), The Myth of God Incarnate (Philadelphia: Westminster Press, 1977).

Donald Hudson, 'The Concept of Divine Transcendence', Religious Studies, vol. 15, no. 2 (Jun. 1979).

Steven Katz, 'The Language and Logic of "Mystery" in Christology', Christ, Faith, and History, ed. S.W. Sykes and J.P. Clayton (Cambridge University Press, 1972).

G.B. Keene, 'A Simpler Solution to the Paradox of Omnipotence', Mind, vol. 69, no. 273 (Jan. 1960).

Anthony Kenny, The God of the Philosophers (Oxford: Clarendon Press, 1979).

William Kneale, 'Time and Eternity in Theology', Proceedings of the Aristotelian Society, vol. 61 (1961).

Norman Kretzmann, 'Omniscience and Immutability', Philosophy of Religion, ed. William Rowe and William Wainwright (New York: Harcourt, Brace, Jovanovich, 1973).

John Lachs, 'Professor Prior on Omniscience', Philosophy, vol. 38 (Oct. 1963).

Richard La Croix, 'The Impossibility of Defining "Omnipotence"', Philosophical Studies, vol. 32, no. 2 (Aug. 1977).

Lawrence B. Lombard, 'Relational Change and Relational Changes', Philosophical Studies, vol. 34, no. 1 (Jul. 1978).

J.L. Mackie, 'Evil and Omnipotence', God and Evil, ed. Nelson Pike (Englewood Cliffs, New Jersey: Prentice-Hall, 1964).

A.P. Martinich, 'Identity and Trinity', The Journal of Religion, vol. 58, no. 2 (Apr. 1978).

George Mavrodes, 'Some Puzzles Concerning Omnipotence', The Power of God, ed. Linwood Urban and Douglas Walton (New York: Oxford University Press, 1978).

Bernard Mayo, 'Mr. Keene on Omnipotence', Mind, vol. 70, no. 278 (Apr. 1961).

H.J. McCloskey, 'Would Any Being Merit Worship?', Southern Journal of Philosophy, vol. 2, no. 4 (Winter 1964).

John Stuart Mill, An Examination of Sir William Hamilton's Philosophy (London: Longmans, Green, Reader and Dyer, 1867).

Nelson Pike, 'Divine Foreknowledge, Human Freedom, and Possible Worlds', The Philosophical Review, vol. LXXXVI, no. 2 (Apr. 1977).

Nelson Pike, 'Divine Omniscience and Voluntary Action', Philosophy of Religion, ed. Steven Cahn (New York: Harper and Row, 1970).

Nelson Pike, God and Timelessness (New York: Schocken Books, 1970).

Nelson Pike, 'Omnipotence and God's Ability to Sin', Readings in the
    Philosophy of Religion, ed. Baruch Brody (Englewood Cliffs, New
    Jersey: Prentice-Hall, 1974).
Alvin Plantinga, God and Other Minds (Ithaca, New York: Cornell
    University Press, 1967).
Alvin Plantinga, God, Freedom, and Evil (New York: Harper and Row,
    1974).
Alvin Plantinga, The Nature of Necessity (Oxford University Press,
    1974).
Alvin Plantinga, 'The Probabalistic Argument From Evil',
    Philosophical Studies, vol. 35, no. 1 (Jan. 1979).
William L. Power, 'Symbolic Logic and the Doctrine of the Trinity',
    The Illif Review, vol. XXXII, no. 1 (Winter 1975).
A. N. Prior, 'Rejoinder to Professor Lachs on Omniscience',
    Philosophy, vol. 38 (Oct. 1963).
A. N. Prior, 'Thank Goodness That's Over', Philosophy, vol. 34, no.
    128 (Jan. 1959).
A. N. Prior, 'The Formalities of Omniscience', Readings in the
    Philosophy of Religion, ed. Baruch Brody (Englewood Cliffs, New
    Jersey: Prentice-Hall, 1974).
Roland Puccetti, 'Is Omniscience Possible?', Australasian Journal of
    Philosophy, vol. 41 (May 1963).
Karl Rahner, The Trinity, trans. Joseph Donceel (New York: Sanbury
    Press, 1974).
James F. Ross, Philosophical Theology (Indianapolis: Bobbs-Merrill,
    1969).
Joseph Runzo, 'Omniscience and Freedom For Evil', International
    Journal for Philosophy of Religion, vol. 12, no. 3 (1981).
C. Wade Savage, 'The Paradox of the Stone', The Power of God, ed.
    Linwood Urban and Douglas Walton (New York: Oxford University
    Press, 1978).
T.P. Smith, 'On the Applicability of a Criterion of Change', Ratio,
    vol. 15, no. 2 (Dec. 1972).
Eleanore Stump and Norman Kretzmann, 'Eternity', The Journal of
    Philosophy, vol. 78, no. 8 (Aug. 1981).
Richard Swinburne, The Coherence of Theism (Oxford University
    Press, 1977).
Richard Taylor, 'Deliberation and Foreknowledge', Free Will and
    Determinism, ed. Bernard Berofsky (New York: Harper and Row,
    1966).
Pierre Thevenaz, 'God of the Philosophers and God of the Christians',
    Studies in Religion, vol. 5, no. 4 (1975/1976).
Stephen C. Tornay (ed.), Ockham: Studies and Selections (LaSalle,
    Illinois: Open Court Publishing Company, 1938).
Linwood Urban and Douglas Walton (eds.), The Power of God (New
    York: Oxford University Press, 1978).

Douglas Walton, 'The Omnipotence Paradox', The Power of God, ed. Linwood Urban and Douglas Walton (New York: Oxford University Press, 1978).

Keith Ward, The Concept of God (Glasgow: William Collins, 1977).

Claude Welch (ed.), God and Man in Mid-Nineteenth Century German Theology (New York: Oxford University Press, 1965).

Frank Weston, The One Christ (London: Longmans Green, 1907).

Nicholas Woltersdorff, 'God Everlasting', God and the Good, ed. Clifton J. Orlebeke and Lewis B. Smedes (Grand Rapids, Michigan: William B. Eerdmans, 1975).

Index